North America's GREATEST Waterfowling Lodges & Outfitters

Willow Creek
GUIDES

North America's
GREATEST
Waterfowling
Lodges &
Outfitters

100 Prime Destinations in the
United States and Canada

BY CHUCK PETRIE

Printed in the United States of America

Illustrations by R. L. Gretter
Cover Photograph by Dale C. Spartas

Library of Congress Cataloging-in-Publication Data

Petrie, Chuck
    North America's greatest waterfowling lodges and outfitters : 100 prime
destinations in the United States & Canada / by Chuck Petrie.
        p. cm. -- (Willow Creek guides)
    ISBN 1-57223-312-5 (softcover : alk. paper)
    1. Waterfowl shooting--United States--Guidebooks. 2. Hunting lodges--
United States--Guidebooks. 3. United States--Guidebooks. 4. Waterfowl
shooting--Canada--Guidebooks. 5. Hunting lodges--Canada--Guidebooks.
6. Canada--Guidebooks. I. Title. II. Series.
SK315 .P48 2000
799.2'44'029673--dc21   00-011102

WILLOW CREEK PRESS
PO Box 147
Minocqua, WI 54548

To Keyni, Baxter, and Gunnar

C o n t

e n t s

Contents

Introduction

SOMEONE ONCE asked an author how long it had taken him to write his most recent book. The scribe answered, "All my life." I don't know whether this actually happened, or who the writer was, but here's the gist of it: The actual writing process doesn't take much time relative to the years of living the experiences that go into writing the work.

In writing this book, living the experiences has been an adventure as well as a privilege. I've been a waterfowl hunter for more than 40 years, and, like you, I've paid my dues in quiet blinds under empty skies many times. But I've also seen some of the finest waterfowl hunting available on this continent. In many instances, that hunting has taken place with the outfitters and guides described on the following pages. I have not hunted with all the outfitters portrayed in this book, but of many of those I have not, I have trusted friends who have and who have recommended their services. In other instances, I have hunted with guides who operate in the same areas as other outfitters listed here, and I personally know the type and quality of waterfowl hunting potentially available to visiting hunters. (Nonetheless, I strongly encourage anyone using this as a reference book to read the following chapter, titled "Selecting a Waterfowl Hunting Guide.")

Of course, personal recommendations and accounts of one's own experiences with an outfitter are peculiar animals. I may show up in an outfitter's camp the day you are leaving and end up having a mediocre hunt where you reported having an excellent one. Waterfowl are migratory birds, after all, and where they appear in abundance one week they may be difficult to find the next. Where waters were calm and fields are dry today, you may find maelstroms and quagmires tomorrow. Such things are not under the outfitter's control. Also, an "excellent" hunt to one person may be a "mediocre" hunt to another. Rating new adventures is subjective and depends a great deal upon a hunter's personality and experiences.

Also, rating a hunting experience with an outfitter or guide should take into consideration more than the number of birds you put in the bag. During your time with a guide, try to get to know him (or her) for more than what he is or does as your temporary duck caller and bird finder. You'll meet some very interesting people in this occupation, men and women with varied backgrounds and other skills that may at least enthrall and possibly amaze you. They can also be good teachers, not only of waterfowling skills and lore but of interesting facts about the history, flora, fauna, and folklore of the localities in which they live. Some may become lifelong friends.

Selecting a Waterfowl Hunting Guide

IT MAY BE YOUR MUCH-ANTICIPATED TRIP of a lifetime, or it could be an annual getaway with a couple of your best hunting buddies. In any event, the foray may require hiring the services of a waterfowl guide—be your adventure only a few hours away from home, an out-of-state junket, or one that takes you all the way to some remote prairie in Canada—and will require an investment of your time, money, and expectations. You'll want to make sure, then, that the outfitter with whom you cast your lot is experienced, qualified, and willing to and capable of making your hunt all you expect it to be. That's what you'll want. That's what you'll expect. But for many waterfowlers, guided hunts unfortunately turn out to be disasters, at worst, or barely satisfactory at best.

Many of these disappointed nimrods can only blame themselves for not taking the time to select the right guide or for not thoroughly researching the guide's services. The fact is, making a hunt for hire a successful and rewarding one will be greatly determined by how discriminating you are in your search for an outfitter capable of producing what you want and expect. Not researching a guide and his services prior to hiring one is a bit like playing the slots—you can pour in a lot of money, but you're just as likely to come up with three lemons as a jackpot. Finding out as much as you can about an outfitter before you hire one is more like playing poker—pay a small ante and you can look at the hand you're dealt, then fold, hold, or raise. You won't win every pot, but your chances at a winning hand aren't left entirely to chance, and if you play your cards right, you'll come out way ahead of the game.

As an outdoor writer with 23 years of experience with guided hunts in Europe, South America, Mexico, and across Canada and the U.S., sometimes traveling on a half-dozen junkets a year, when it comes to outfitters' services, I've seen the good, the bad, and the ugly. It's been a learn-as-you-go education, and while I still experience the occasional mediocre hunt, most of my trips today are fun and rewarding. That's because I high-grade my opportunities and research the outfitters with whom I hunt. The following is a list of questions I'll have had answered before I book a hunt and pack my bags.

I'll use the terms "outfitter" and "guide" interchangeably. Generally, an outfitter may be a guide himself, but may also have additional guides who work for him. Some outfitters, however, may only manage lodge services and book your reservations, leaving field duties to guides he employs. The term guide applies to one-man guiding services, although they may call themselves outfitters, or to those peoples who work for an outfitter.

What Background Information Is Available on the Guide?

First, I like to know how many years the guide's service has been in existence. As a rule of thumb, I avoid outfitters who have been in business for less than three years. Experience breeds efficiency, and any start-up business has kinks in its operation to iron out. I'd rather not be there for the ironing process.

Second, what percentage of the guide's business comes from repeat clients? Hunters returning to the same guide service year after year are a good gauge of how successful the operation is and how satisfied the clients are with it. Some outfitters see as much as 80 percent or more repeat business each year. This is an excellent indication of how well hunters rate an operation, and it also means the outfitter may have limited openings for new or additional guests, so you may have to book your hunt as early as possible.

References? Any reliable outfitter will supply you with a list of his clients who have agreed to act as references for his services. Keep in mind, though, that this is a group of folks who have been hand picked by the outfitter and have had mostly favorable experiences with him or her, and may have hunted with the guide on only a single trip. The most reliable references will come from clients who have hunted with an outfitter for several seasons.

Is the guide licensed and insured? If he operates a boat as part of his business on the Great Lakes, U.S. coastal waters, or other federally regulated waters, does he have a captain's license, which is required by the U.S. Coast Guard? The state or province where you will be hunting will no doubt require your guide to be licensed, but that doesn't mean, in many instances, that the guide has had to pass any kind of competency requirements to become licensed. Nor do governmental agencies require a guide to carry liability insurance to cover his clients, should he be responsible for accidents involving them. Only outlaw guides operate without required licenses, and only irresponsible ones operate without insurance. Make sure your outfitter carries the appropriate and required licenses as well as insurance. Preferably, he'll also be a member of a guides' or outfitters' association that restricts its membership according to some form of competency requirements.

How much does the outfitter invest in marketing his services? Generally, I avoid those who only place small advertisements in classified sections of sporting magazines. The more serious outfitters are about their businesses, and the more successful they are, the more they will invest in marketing their services. Most established outfitters advertise their businesses with full-page or fractional ads in

3

magazines, will supply you with a comprehensive color brochure, and have an established Web site. Some provide potential customers with newsletters and videos that portray hunts (usually biased toward very successful ones) and provide footage of the outfitter's lodging and other accommodations.

How Much? And What's Included?

The old adage "if you have to ask how much it costs, you can't afford it" doesn't cut it here. You'll want to know exactly what you are paying for, and what the final tally will be. Guided hunts can range from full-service outfitting businesses that provide transportation, guide services, trained retrievers, lodging and meals, bird cleaning and packaging, and even complementary cigars and liquor, to half-day-trip operations where you meet your guide at a restaurant for breakfast (on your dime) and follow him in your own vehicle to the hunting site. You can pay up to $750 a day for the former services and as little as $75 a day for the latter (excluding gratuities). Whatever you can afford and makes you happy, I guess, but I wouldn't want to shell out $750 for a day of guided hunting and then find out I'm supposed to meet my guide at the local greasy spoon for biscuits and gravy. If you get my drift.

Here's what you need to know beforehand.

What is the outfitter's daily rate? Does he have package rates? Group rates? What's included? Most but not all guides have a daily rate. They provide this to accommodate hunters who may live close to their hunting areas and who can sometimes only get away for a day or two of hunting. Other guides have multiple-day package rates, usually based on three or more days of hunting and which may or may not include lodging and meals. Still others offer comprehensive package rates that include guiding services, lodging, meals, licenses, shells, airport transportation, and other amenities such as bird cleaning. If you'll be making your trip with friends, check into the outfitter's group rates. Some will discount from their single-party rates if you guarantee a booking of three or more hunters on the same trip.

Almost any guide who has been in business long enough and wants to stay that way will require that you pay a deposit, usually at the time you book your hunt. This can amount to as much as 50 percent of the total daily, package, or group charges that cover the booking you've reserved. Usually, the deposit is nonrefundable, but some outfitters will refund some or all of your deposit if you cancel within a specified period before your arrival date and they can fill your slot with another client. If they can fill your booking, they may apply your deposit toward your visit on another date. Be sure to check your outfitter's refund policy on deposits in the event you have to cancel your trip.

If you've doled out a sizable deposit, you may want to check into trip insurance (call CSA Travel Protection, 800-348-9505). A trip insurance package will cover your deposit should you have to cancel your planned outing, but only for medical reasons or a death in your immediate family. The package will also cover emergency medical evacuation costs and medical expenses, rental car damage, baggage loss, and expenses you incur for travel delays. This is especially important to consider when traveling outside the U.S., where your personal health insurance and Medicare do not cover health care costs. You may, however, be able to get a short-term rider on your personal health insurance policy to cover medical costs outside the U.S. Check with your insurance agent.

Does the outfitter provide lodging as part of his package rate? What type of accommodations? Here again, you can expect a great deal of variance from one operation to the next, and to pay for the quality of lodging and meals accordingly. Some outfitters don't provide lodging or meals at all, and you will have to search out your own. Otherwise, you may have a private room and personal bath in a modern lodge with a Jacuzzi, hot tub, and open bar. You may be put up in a bed-and-breakfast, a cabin, a tent, or a motel room.

Not all guides can afford their own lodges, as seasonal as their occupation is, but that doesn't necessarily reflect the quality of the hunts they can provide. In the Canadian prairies, especially, expect to be housed, more often than not, in a local motel and to take your meals at restaurants. Prairie country guides sometimes make arrangements with motel and restaurant owners to provide services to hunting clients at a discount, which may or may not be reflected in the package rate.

Meals. These will only be important when you're hungry. When you spend a hard day hunting in the fresh air, however, you'll probably be hungry most of the time. Again, expect a great deal of variation in both quality and quantity. You may be eating a la carte in a restaurant or be served a five-star meal prepared by a chef in a fancy lodge. More often than not, the gustatory truth will lie somewhere in between. Some guides' packages don't include breakfast (and lunch can be a sandwich and an orange); others don't include the evening meal. If you have special dietary requirements, you should also find out, if meals are included in your package, whether those can be accommodated. (Speaking of special dietary requirements, don't forget liquor. Some lodges and outfitters provide it, with or without charge, others don't. You may have to BYO. Check before you reach your destination; "dry" counties remain in many parts of the U.S., and complete restrictions on alcohol sales are in effect in some communities in Canada.)

Be sure to ask your guide what his rate includes for hunting. Many guides, regardless of what they charge you, only provide half-day hunts from early morning until noon. After you've filled your day's waterfowl limit, or after lunch, whichever comes first, you may find yourself twiddling your thumbs, with nothing to do. Other guides provide day-long hunting opportunities: morning hunts for waterfowl, afternoon hunts for upland game, for instance, or morning goose hunting and afternoon duck hunting. Sometimes the afternoon hunts (or guided fishing) are included in the basic package rate, other times there is an additional charge.

Also, ask if bird cleaning and packaging are included as part of your guide's services. If not, can those chores be accommodated for an additional fee? If you are flying to your destination, will he pick you up and drop you off at the airport? Will you have to rent a car and provide your own airport and ground transportation to and from hunting sites?

You should also not be afraid to ask about gratuities. Some operations, believe it or not, do not accept them. Most do, however, and suggest something in the range of 10 to 20 percent or more of the daily rate or of your total bill. This should be up to your discretion, though, depending upon the quality of service you receive. When tipping, don't forget lodge staff, including the cook, and especially the guide or guides you hunt with. Some lodge operators do not pay their guides, who rely solely on gratuities for their income.

What, Where, and How?

This information is as important as the rates you'll be charged for lodging and guiding services. The first thing you may want to ask is what is the best time to book your hunt to coincide with peak migrations. In some areas, although the waterfowl season may be a couple of months long, there will only be a period of a few weeks that the bird populations can be expected to reach maximum numbers, or the species you are seeking can be expected to migrate through the area. Your outfitter can give you a pretty good indication of when that will be, but don't expect miracles—these are migratory birds, after all, and migrations are weather dependent.

What type of land will you be hunting: Private? Leased? Public? Some outfitters own or lease land that is reserved exclusively for hunting by their clients. If so, find out how many acres are under the outfitter's control and how many blinds he has established. Good outfitters will not shoot the same areas from the same blinds day after day, but will rotate their hunt sites to rest the birds and not burn out their best fields, potholes, or timber holes. If you will be hunting public areas, ask about the gunning pressure there. Don't be afraid to book a guided hunt on sites open to public access. Some of these areas offer great waterfowl hunting, regardless. And in some jurisdictions—the province of Alberta, for example—it is illegal to lease private land for hunting purposes, yet there is so much agricultural land available to hunt that competition from other waterfowlers is not a problem.

Ask the outfitter how large of a group you'll be hunting with. If you arrange a group hunt with three or four friends, you'll probably end up hunting together with your own guide. But if you arrive by yourself, the outfitter will most likely place you with a group of strangers. This can be anywhere from one additional hunter to as many as eight or more. If you don't like gang-bang shooting from pit blinds or timber holes, being placed with a large group is something you'll want to avoid. Hunting by yourself with just a guide might be something you can arrange, but expect to pay an extra charge, which may be considerable, for that type of individual service.

Who will call the birds and call the shots? Most often, the guides will expect to do this themselves. Some are adamant about it, and will tell you that's the only way you can hunt with them. If you are a competent caller, they may let you join in. Too often, though, their clients aren't good callers or can't read the birds' reaction to calling, and the only thing they end up blowing is an opportunity. Besides, most guides like to show off their own skills and, after all, that's what you're paying them for.

Do the guides shoot? Get this established right off the bat. A guide shooting and expecting you or your party to accept his birds as part of your bag limit is totally unacceptable, and illegal. Some guides shoot only toward their own bag limits, but if you have objections to your guide hunting with you, let him or your outfitter know that that's unacceptable, too. Some clients prefer their guide only carry a shotgun with him for chasing down and shooting crippled birds. Your call.

Ask your outfitter before you book a hunt package how physically demanding his hunts can be. This is especially important if you are physically challenged in any way. Some guides transport you by boat, ATV, or Suburban directly to and from the blind you'll be shooting from, drop you off, and set out the decoys themselves. All you have to do is shoot. Other guides may expect you to help pack in decoys over a long march through a muddy field. Or, at least, help deploy the decoys (and some field sets for geese may employ up to 1,000 or more rags, full-body, or shell decoys).

Finally, and this can be a stickler, can you bring your own retriever? If so, what type of facilities does the outfitter have to accommodate dogs? Some lodges, for example, have first-class kennel runs, but won't allow your dog inside the lodge. If your dog is used to sleeping at the foot of your bed, this can be a problem. Some outfitters do not have facilities for guests' dogs at all, or discourage or prohibit guests from bringing their retrievers with them. If you will only go hunting if your dog comes along, shop for accommodating outfitters accordingly.

Sounds like a lot of information you'll need before you book a hunt, and it is. Good outfitters are used to responding to these questions, though, and should be willing to give forthright answers to all of them. Remember that it's your money—and you don't want to prove P.T. Barnum correct.

Licenses, Seasons, Bag Limits

THE TYPES OF LICENSES AND PERMITS you'll need to hunt waterfowl—and the corresponding prices thereof—vary from state to state and province to province. In many instances, your outfitter may be able to arrange to have your licenses and permits available for you when you arrive for your hunt. Other times you'll have to procure them yourself. Certain hunting opportunities, such as swan hunts in North Carolina, are restricted by special permit only, and that permit must be obtained directly from state authorities well before the season begins. In other instances, such as most nonresident waterfowl hunting opportunities in South Dakota, only a limited number of licenses are issued, and then only to hunters who apply for and are selected in a special license lottery drawing in early summer. Waterfowl season dates, and bag and possession limits also vary throughout the U.S. and Canada.

To learn more about licenses, permits, season dates, and other such regulations, pertinent information can be obtained directly from state or provincial fish and game departments. Call for toll-free directory information or contact the appropriate agencies at the Web sites listed on the next page.

LICENSING INFORMATION WEB SITES

UNITED STATES

Alabama
www.dcnr.state.al.us

Alaska
www.state.ak.us/local/akpages/FISH.G AME/ADFD-HOME.HTM

Arizona
www.gf.state.az.us

Arkansas
www.agfc.state.ar.us

California
www dfg.ca.gov

Colorado
www.dnr.state.co.us

Connecticut
www.dep.state.ct.us/burnatr/wdhome. htm

Delaware
www.dnrec.state.de.us/fw/huntinl.htm

Florida
www.state.fl.us/gfc

Georgia
www.dnr.state.ga.us

Hawaii
www.hawaii.gov/dlnr

Idaho
www2.state.id.us/fishgame

Illinois
http://dnr.state.il.us

Indiana
www.state.in.us/dnr

Iowa
www.state.ia.us/government/dnr

Kansas
www.kdwp.state.ks.us

Kentucky
www.state.ky.us/agencies/fw/kdfwr.htm

Lousiana
www.wlf.state.la.us

Maine
www.state.me.us/ifw

Maryland
www.dnr.state.md.us

Massachusetts
www.state.ma.us/dfwele

Michigan
www dnr.state.mi.us

Minnesota
www.dnr.state.mn.us

Mississippi
www.mdwfp.com

Missouri
www.conservation.state.mo.us

Montana
www.fwp.mt.gov

Nebraska
www.ngpc.state.ne.us

Nevada
www.state.nv.us/cnr/nvwildlife

New Hampshire
www.wildlife.state.nh.us

New Jersey
www.state.nj.us/dep/fgw

New Mexico
www.gmfsh.state.nm.us

New York
www.dec.state.ny.us/website/outdoors

North Carolina
www.state.nc.us/Wildlife

North Dakota
www.state.nd.us/gnf

Ohio
www.dnr.state.oh.us

Oklahoma
www.state.ok.us/~odwc

Oregon
www.dfw.state.or.us

Pennsylvania
www.dcnr.state.pa.us

Rhode Island
www.state.ri.us/dem

South Carolina
www.water.dnr.state.sc.us

South Dakota
www.state.sd.us/state/executive/gfp

Tennessee
www.state.tn.us/twra

Texas
www.tpwd.state.tx.us

Utah
www.nr.state.ut.us

Vermont
www.anr.state.vt.us

Virginia
www.dgif.state.va.us

Washington
www.wa.gov/wdfw

West Virginia
www.wvwildlife.com

Wisconsin
www.dnr.state.wi.us

Wyoming
http://gf.state.wy.us

CANADA

Alberta
http://www.gov.ab.ca/env/

British Columbia
www.env.gov.bc.ca

Manitoba
http://www.gov.mb.ca/natres/

New Brunswick
http://www.gov.nb.ca/dnre/

Newfoundland and Labrador
http://www.gov.nf.ca/

Northwest Territories
http://www.gov.nt.ca/RWED/wf/

Nova Scotia
http://www.gov.ns.ca/natr/

Ontario
http://www.mnr.gov.on.ca/MNR/

Prince Edward Island
http://www.gov.pe.ca/

Quebec
http://www.mef.gouv.qc.ca/en/

Saskatchewan
http://www.gov.sk.ca/serm/WWW/FISHWILD/INTRO.HTM

Yukon Territories
http://www.touryukon.com

Flying with your Retriever

SPORTSMEN FLYING TO WINGSHOOTING destinations in the U.S. and Canada might consider having their retrievers accompany them to share what are often-remembered, exceptional hunting experiences.

Most airlines transport dogs—reservations are often required—in pressurized, temperature-controlled baggage compartments on the same flight with their owners. However, federal regulations on how and when your dog can be transported are imposed on all commercial air carriers, whose individual animal transportation policies are not consistent.

First, to be transported, the dog must be contained in an approved kennel, preferably a hard plastic crate with a metal door, such as a Vari-Kennel. Crates come in standard sizes; most Labs will fit nicely inside a size 300 (intermediate) or 400 (large), but very large dogs that require a size 500 (extra large) cannot be accommodated on some aircraft. On commuter lines operated in conjunction with major airlines, most smaller aircraft cannot carry even size 300 or 400 kennels.

The crate should include two empty dishes for food and water accessible from the outside, and should contain material that will absorb urine, saliva, and spilled drinking water.

Some airlines have kennels available for purchase or rent at certain airports, but buying a crate at an airport is usually more costly than purchasing one at a sporting goods store or through a catalog. A good reason to buy your own crate before flying is to allow your dog time to get used to going inside the kennel and to being lifted and carried about while contained in it. Excitable or nervous dogs especially need an extended acclimation period before they are transported in a crate.

Sedating a nervous dog prior to flying is an option, but Wisconsin veterinarian Marty Smith advises avoiding medication unless necessary. Only then, and through prescription from a qualified vet, should the animal receive Acepromazine an hour or two prior to flight time. Smith also notes that airlines or animal health officials may require a dog health certificate issued within 10 to 30 days of the flight and carried with you when flying with your dog. The certificate must describe the dog and its vaccination history, and must be signed by a veterinarian. Finally, Canadian customs officials require you to show a certificate of proof that your dog was vaccinated for rabies within 36 months of entering that country.

Another factor to consider is most airlines will not transport dogs during weather extremes. If in doubt, call the airline early on your day of departure. They will advise you if temperatures at any point in your itinerary are too warm or cold to allow pet transportation.

The cost of flying your dog to a hunting destination has recently increased. Most carriers once charged approximately $75 to fly your pooch one way within the U.S. or from the U.S. to Canada. However, the recent passage of the Safe Air Travel for Animals Act, passed by Congress to control the rising number of complaints of animal deaths during air transit, has changed that. The act requires more airline employee training in animal handling and mandates stricter industry safeguards for pet transportation. As a result, some air carriers have increased their one-way animal transportation rates by as much as 300 percent and have added a per pound fuel service charge. Be aware, too, that airlines will only insure the loss of your dog to the same liability limit covering the loss of a suitcase, about $1,200. Additional coverage is available for a nominal fee.

Prepare for Take-Off

- The days before you fly, give your dog plenty of exercise.

- Be sure your retriever is wearing a collar (no choke collars) containing complete information: your name, address, and phone number.

- Arrive at the airport well ahead of departure, so you have time to walk the dog and allow it to void itself and become accustomed to the airport environment.

- When picking up the dog at your destination or claiming it between flights, be very careful when opening the kennel door. Dogs not use to flying often bolt and run as soon as the crated door is opened after a flight.

Run for the Border

N O, I DON'T MEAN TACO BELL. Canada, eh? The land of mountains, forests, wheat fields, and hockey pucks. Also the land where waterfowl hunting seasons begin as early as September 1, where bag limits are more generous than those imposed in the U.S., and where hunting opportunities on both public and private lands (relative to what's available here in the states) abound.

These facts aren't lost on a large number of Yankee hunters who head north every fall to their favorite Canadian waterfowling and wingshooting locales. However, whether you're a veteran traveler to the provinces or making your first trip across the border to hunt there, there are rules you need to follow before Canadian customs officials will let you into the country. (And once you're there, there are some new waterfowl hunting restrictions that have become effective over the last couple of seasons.) Failure to adhere to these rules may result in you or your dog being denied entry into Canada, fines or tariffs for bringing certain goods into the country, the confiscation of prohibited firearms you might be carrying, or a host of other unpleasantries. The following is a heads-up on how to avoid becoming an undesirable alien, and, worse yet, ruining a long-anticipated (and no doubt well-deserved) hunting trip.

Dogs

Whether you are flying commercial or private aircraft or driving into Canada, you must accompany your dog when you enter the country. At your point of entry (and possibly elsewhere once you enter the country) you must be able to produce for Canadian customs officials a valid certificate issued by a licensed American or Canadian veterinarian clearly identifying the dog and certifying that it has been vaccinated against rabies during the previous 36 months. This is a change from a few years back, when three-year rabies vaccines became available in the U.S., but Canada still demanded, at that time, that dogs be vaccinated during the previous 12 months. Also, be sure to bring your dog's signed rabies certificate; simply showing a rabies tag on its collar may result in the animal being denied entry into Canada.

If you are flying commercial airlines into Canada, you should also obtain from your veterinarian a health certificate certifying that your dog is current with other vaccinations such as parvoviris, distemper, leptospirosis, and kennel cough. Certain airlines require this certificate be made available when you are flying with your dog, and it's a good idea to have the certificate with you in the event Canadian provincial or municipal authorities request one. (Some U.S. states also require—but rarely enforce—that you carry a health certificate for your pet when crossing state lines.)

When flying commercial aircraft, you'll also have to transport your dog in an airline-approved animal crate (available through some airlines, but best purchased at pet stores or through catalogs). Be sure the crate is the correct size for the animal to avoid its being pitched around in too large a crate or cramped in one too small for it. Most airlines require that you supply food and water for the dog while it is in transit. This is best accomplished with the purchase of accessory food and water dishes that clamp directly onto the crate's grated door (supposedly to avoid spillage, but it doesn't work that way with most baggage handlers; and, by the way, your dog will by flying in the baggage hold).

Of course, before you even consider booking a flight for yourself and your dog, be sure to check with the airlines regarding costs and their policies on transporting animals. Some carriers won't fly pets during certain times of the year, including September, because of warm temperatures; others have moratoriums later in the fall and early winter because of the possibility of extreme cold weather (commercial aircraft baggage holds are not climate controlled).

People / Motor Vehicles

Okay, Ol' Spot passes muster and gets into Canada. But what about you? And what about your 13-year-old son? He's making his first duck hunting trip to Canada with you. You are such a great guy, you even allowed your boy to bring his best buddy, also a juvenile, along on the trip.

You and each of the kids will need to verify your citizenship. A passport is the ideal identification to have when crossing the border, but one is not required (nor is a visa, unless you are not a citizen of the U.S. or Canada). You will, however, have to produce, if requested, an original or certified copy of your birth certificate, as well as a picture identification card, such as a driver's license. Each child with you must provide similar identification. Your son's pal should also be carrying a letter of permission from his parents or a legal guardian, stating that they know you are bringing the child into Canada and are doing so with their permission. Further, if you are divorced and share legal custody of your son with an ex-spouse, you should carry legal documents establishing that status. (Additionally, by law, those people admissible to Canada must not have a criminal record, including any convictions for driving while intoxicated.)

If you are driving your vehicle into Canada, your U.S. driver's license will be required and valid there. You must carry with you proof of ownership of the vehicle, as well as proof of automobile liability insurance. (Check with your insurer regarding coverage for your vehicle while in Canada, and also check into the applicability of your health insurance coverage. You may need short-term insurance riders for one or both while out of the country.)

Two additional minor points regarding motor vehicles and driving: (1) The possession and use of radar detection devices is illegal in most Canadian provinces and territories. If you have one of these gadgets, disassemble it and put it in your luggage. Operating radar devices are subject to confiscation by Canadian police. (2) Speed limits are posted in kilometers per hour. When you see a sign declaring a speed limit of 100, don't go NASCAR nuts. Multiply the posted speed limit by .62 to convert to miles per hour (in this case, 62mph).

Guns, Goods, and Other Personal Items

Most of the things you bring into Canada—including items such as your personal baggage, fishing tackle, hunting gear, boats and motors, cameras, and so on—have no import restrictions. Canada does have strict laws on bringing firearms across the border, however, and on the possession and use of certain prohibited firearms. Sporting rifles and shotguns to be used while hunting in Canada are not restricted, subject to minimum barrel lengths on rifles and shotguns (not applicable to the majority of sporting arms used for waterfowl or upland bird hunting). Fully automatic weapons and handguns are absolutely restricted from importation, possession, or use, as are Mace and pepper-type sprays.

Much has been mentioned about new, egregious restrictions on firearms and their use under Canada's new federal Firearms Act. Most of the new restrictions apply only to Canadian citizens and, as of this writing, do not apply to American hunters bringing shotguns with them into Canada. Before you visit Canada, however, things may change. The new law, when its importation restrictions go into effect, will require Americans to register their shotguns with customs officials at the respective point of entry into the country and pay a $50 registration fee per gun. Renting a Canadian outfitter's or guide's gun won't let you off the hook—you'll still have to pay a $50 fee and register the gun as a "rental" firearm. Before venturing to Canada this fall, then, check with your nearest Canadian consulate (listed in telephone books in most larger cities, or try the Web telephone search engine www.swithcboard.com) regarding the new gun-import restrictions.

Whether the new registration rule is in effect or not, you'll have to declare to Canadian customs officials that you are bringing a firearm into the country, and your intended use for it. While it isn't legally necessary to do so for entry into Canada (but highly recommended before transporting guns and other expensive gear into other foreign countries), you may want to stop at a U.S. Customs office with your gear (for verification) and fill out a registration form listing the serial numbers and descriptions of your guns, cameras, computers, and other expensive items you may transport cross-border. Once certified by U.S. Customs, there will then be no question regarding the origin (and thus avoid any potential tariff, import questions, or duties) of your equipment when you bring it back to the U.S.

Alcohol, Tobacco, and Prescription Medications

You may transport into Canada, duty free, a restricted amount of alcohol and tobacco. Depending on the legal drinking age of the province or territory where you cross into Canada (19 in most provinces, 18 in Alberta, Manitoba, and Quebec), you may bring into the country, if you are of age, per person, the following: Alcohol: 1.14 liters (40 ounces of liquor or wine); or 24 12-ounce containers of beer or ale. Any alcohol in excess of these amounts (including that extra thermos full of premixed manhattans) will be subject to duty, provincial fees and taxes (which involves a lot of time-consuming paperwork and will irritate the hell out of a customs agent—trust me on this) or, possibly, a fine. You're better off just buying any additional hooch you may want while in Canada.

Tobacco carries a high "sin tax" in some provinces, so you are only allowed to import into Canada, duty free, 200 cigarettes, 50 cigars, or seven ounces of loose tobacco.

When taking prescription drugs into Canada, make sure they are clearly identified and carried in their original packaging with a label that specifies both what they are and that they are being used under prescription. If you are diabetic and use syringes, carry some evidence of your medical need for them, a copy of your prescription, and a contact number for your doctor.

New Nontoxic Shot Regulation

Effective September 1, 1999, the possession or use of shot other than nontoxic shot for the purpose of hunting migratory game birds (ducks, geese, brant, cranes, rails, gallinules, and snipe) was prohibited throughout Canada. Lead shot is still permitted for hunting woodcock, mourning doves, and band-tailed pigeons, except within National Wildlife Areas, where possession of lead shot is prohibited for all hunting including upland game and small mammals.

In Canada, approved nontoxic shot loads include bismuth-tin shot and steel shot, which have gained final nontoxicity approval from the Canadian Wildlife Service; tin, tungsten-iron, tungsten-matrix and tungsten-polymer shot, which have gained conditional approval, are also legal to use in Canada.

You are permitted to bring into Canada, duty free, a maximum of 200 shotgun shells. If you are transporting those shells by commercial aircraft, be sure to pack them in a piece of baggage other than the airline-approved gun case in which you transport your shotgun. Also, some airlines do not allow you to carry partial boxes of ammunition; they now insist that only full boxes of shotshells be transported in your luggage.

Coming Home

Well, it was a successful waterfowling junket, and now you're on your way home. But if you are bringing migratory birds back to the states with you, you still have to deal with customs agents (this time U.S. Customs agents) when you cross the border. When crossing into the U.S., you will have to declare with customs the number of each species of migratory bird you are transporting. Be sure the birds have at least one fully feathered, attached wing on each of them for identification, as required by law. You'll be required to fill out a declaration form delineating not only the number of each species you are transporting, but also your name, home address, and provincial hunting license number. Most often, you can transport back into the U.S. a possession limit of two daily bag limits from the province in which you hunted. Any whole birds you bring back for taxidermy purposes count against your possession limit.

When filling out the declaration form, do it accurately, and do not, to save time, put all the birds claimed by your hunting party on one form (or you'll be contacted by a U.S. Fish and Wildlife Special Agent in the not-too-distant future). Each hunter must claim his game individually on a single form.

* * *

This is all probably more than you wanted to know about hunting trips north of the border, and chances are you'll be waved through Canadian customs after a few perfunctory questions from agents. But you may also become one of the random tourists who will have all your gear searched for contraband (and if you're crossing by motor vehicle, this means you completely unload the Suburban, the trailer full of gear, the duck boat, decoy bags, personal luggage . . . you get the point). And even if you are "clean" but have forgotten a document necessary for crossing the border, you can still ruin a trip. Be diligent.

CANADA REGULATIONS

For more information on Canadian migratory bird hunting regulations, contact these regional Canadian Wildlife Service offices:

Newfoundland and Labrador
Lewisporte 709-535-0601
St. John's 709-772-5585

P.E.I. and New Brunswick
Sackville 506-364-5032

Nova Scotia
Dartmouth 902-426-1188

Quebec
Ste-Foy 418-648-7225

Ontario
Geulph 519-826-2100

Manitoba
Winnipeg 204-983-5263

Saskatchewan and N.W. Terr.
Saskatoon 306-975-4919

Alberta
Edmunton 403-951-8749

British Columbia
Delta 604-940-4710

Yukon
Whitehorse 867-667-3406

For additional information on Canadian customs regulations, contact Canada Customs and Revenue Agency at the Web site: http://www.re.gc.ga

UNITED STATES REGULATIONS

For additional information on U.S. Fish and Wildlife Service regulations, contact the agency at the Web site: www.fws.gov
See the lists on page 9.

ATLANTIC FLYWAY

MAINE, MASSACHUSETTS, MARYLAND,
VIRGINIA, NORTH CAROLINA

AMERICA'S COASTAL WATERS FROM the rugged Atlantic shores of Maine to Chesapeake Bay and south to the Carolinas are steeped in waterfowling history. For centuries, people here eked a living from the ocean and its bays, harvesting seafood and market hunting for ducks, geese, and shorebirds. Hunters crafted their own decoys, shot from sink boxes and punt boats, and enjoyed hunting during "the golden age of waterfowling."

The days of commercial hunting are thankfully a thing of the past. But the enthusiasm for waterfowl hunting remains as strong as ever in these climes. For example, the Easton, Maryland, annual waterfowl festival, held each November, is one of the biggest gatherings of duck and goose hunters on the East Coast. The U.S. champion goose caller is crowned here each year, and thousands of folks assemble not only to see that contest but to attend waterfowl art exhibitions, retriever training demonstrations, to trade and buy old and new hand-crafted decoys, and enjoy just about every phase of the waterfowler's lifestyle.

The hunting is still spectacular, too. The northern part of the flyway is especially noted for its preponderance of black ducks, mallards, a variety of diving ducks, and sea ducks. Greater snow geese winter here as far north as the Delmarva (Delaware-Maryland-Virginia) Peninsula, as do Atlantic Canada geese. While North Carolina holds scaup, redheads, and canvasbacks in its huge coastal bays, it also attracts good numbers of pintails, mallards, green-winged teal, snow geese, and even boasts a huntable population of tundra swans. And, as you are about to read, there are waterfowl hunting guides and lodges awaiting to accommodate you should you make a trip to this historic region.

Coastal Maine Outfitters

W a l d o ,   M a i n e

VITAL STATISTICS:

SPECIES:
Common eider; oldsquaw; whitewing, surf, and black scoters; black ducks; bufflehead; goldeneye; red-breasted and American mergansers

Season: Sea ducks, October 1 through January 20; puddle ducks and mergansers, October 1 through October 16 and November 8 through December 18 (split season)

Hunting Sites: Atlantic Ocean coastal waters of Penobscot Bay, Isle au Haut Bay, and Jerico Bay

Accommodations:
Restored 19th century farmhouse; four semi-private bedrooms with semi-private baths; large living room with fireplace, bar

MEALS: Three full meals per day including five-star evening dining on lobster, prime rib, steak, lamb, area seafoods

RATES: Three-day packages, sea duck only: $325 per person/day; puddle and sea duck combination: $375 per person/day

MAXIMUM NUMBER OF HUNTERS: 8

GRATUITIES: Suggested $100 per hunter for three-day hunt

PREFERRED PAYMENT: Cash or check

Getting There: The lodge is located on Route 131 and is five miles inland from Belfast, which is on the northwest corner of Penobscot Bay

NEAREST COMMERCIAL AIRPORT:
Bangor International Airport (airport pickup and return included in lodging rates)

Dogs and Facilities: Hunters' dogs welcome. Six insulated indoor kennels with fenced, concrete runs

Guides: Two guides with trained dogs service eight hunters

Other Services: Bird cleaning

Other Activities: Ruffed grouse and woodcock hunting over pointers and flushing dogs

S EA DUCK HUNTING on the rocky, windswept coast of Maine is a sport rich in tradition. Yankee gunners, however, have had a monopoly on this type of hunting for almost two centuries. Well, not quite two centuries, because for the last 20 years, Joe Lucey has been making the experience available to anyone willing to give this unique style of waterfowling a try.

Lucey's hunting guests get a taste of rural Maine the moment they check into his lodge, a farmhouse originally built in 1840. The lodge has been extensively restored but maintains its early American charm in its antiques, hand-hewn beams, and hardwood floors. Modern amenities include a hot tub attached to the living room, a bar, and a full-service game- and gun-cleaning room in the attached barn.

There are no typical routines when it comes to sea duck hunting; tides, wind speed and direction, and other weather variables all influence where and when a daily hunt takes place. On high tides, if you want to pursue puddle ducks, Lucey's guides will set you up in nearby shoreline coves; on low tides, hunters are taken offshore to hunt on rock ledges near mussel beds where eiders and other sea ducks come to feed.

But, come on, you're here for the sea duck hunting, and if there is a "typical" sea duck hunt day, it will go something like this: After a sumptuous breakfast between 6:30 and 7:00, you drive to a dock where either a 45-foot crew boat or the 36-foot passenger vessel *Quicksilver* will be waiting for you to board. You load your gear aboard and set out on either of these U.S. Coast Guard-certified vessels, heading for rocky offshore ledges—wind direction, intensity, and tides dictating which ones you will hunt. There are many ledges to choose from.

Upon arrival at the designated hunting spot, the mother ship drops anchor and two licensed guides will launch a pair of 18-foot dories equipped with outboard motors. One dory motors to the downwind side of the ledge to start setting decoys, the other transports the hunters, dogs, and gear to the rock outcrop that will serve as a duck blind—there is no cover, you sit motionless in camouflaged clothing—for the next couple of hours. One guide, equipped with a radio to reach the mother ship and the guide in the tender dory, will come on shore to direct hunting operations; the other guide in the tender dory will stand by some distance away to dispatch and pick up cripples missed by the dogs.

CONTACT:
Joseph Lucey Jr.
Coastal Maine Outfitters
1007 Waldo Station Rd.
Waldo, ME 04915
Ph: 207-722-3218
Web: www.maineguides.com/
members/coastal

And when the eiders and scoters do come, they will come in flocks, decoying fast and hard. Better be prepared with nothing less than a 12-gauge, preferably a 3-inch or 3½-inch, and with shot sizes from No. 1 to steel BB. These are big birds. Dispatching them cleanly takes a lot of punch.

If the sea duck hunting isn't enough of a treat, you'll also enjoy the breathtaking scenery and other wildlife of the rugged coast of Maine, including offshore fishing villages that are usually only accessible to summertime yachtsmen.

A view of the rocky ledges of coastal Maine from the wheelhouse of the 36-foot vessel Quicksilver, operated by Coastal Maine Outfitters. The ledges are where shooters are deposited to hunt sea ducks over decoys.

Guides in dories towed behind the mother ship Quicksilver set decoys along a rocky ledge in Jerico Bay.

Eggemoggin Lodge

B r o o k l i n ,   M a i n e

VITAL STATISTICS:

SPECIES: common eider, scoter (three species), oldsquaw, mergansers, bufflehead, goldeneye, black duck

Season: October 1 to January 20

Hunting Sites: Maine coastal waters: Jericho, Blue Hill, and Penobscot bays

Accommodations: beautiful ocean-side lodge with 11 guest rooms, great room, fully stocked bar, recreation room with cable TV, pool table, ping pong

MEALS: breakfast, lunch, and dinner (specializing in local seafood) provided by lodge chef

RATES: $300 to $350 per hunter/day, includes guided hunt, lodging and meals

MAXIMUM NUMBER OF HUNTERS: 15

GRATUITIES: $30 to $50 per guide/day

PREFERRED PAYMENT: cash, check, MasterCard, Visa

Getting There: 60 miles south of Bangor on Eggemoggin Reach

NEAREST COMMERCIAL AIRPORT: Bangor International Airport, Bangor, ME

Dogs and Facilities: well mannered dogs may stay in guests' rooms

Guides: four to six hunters per guide

Other Services: birds cleaned and packaged for travel

Other Activities: sporting clays; sight-seeing

CONTACT:
Susan LeMoine or Richard Duffy
Eggemoggin Lodge
HC 64 Box 380
Brooklin, ME 04616
Ph: 888-559-5057
Fax: 207-359-5057
Email:
info@mainecoastexperience.com
Web:
www.mainecoastexperience.com/duck-hunting/index.htm

EGGEMOGGIN LODGE in Brooklin, Maine, offers first-class accommodations for sea duck hunters. The lodge has spacious rooms, some with ocean views, and private baths. Rooms are available with single king-size beds or two queen-size beds, so you can have a private room or share with a friend. The patio and great room overlook Eggemoggin Reach, and the view is breathtaking. You're surrounded by the beauty of coastal living here, and you'll be comforted to know that each morning all you have to do is sit down to a prepared breakfast, then get your gear and walk down to the pier to the awaiting guide and boat.

But we're getting too far ahead of ourselves. The first afternoon you arrive at the lodge you'll be shown to your room. Unpack. Rest a while. Then head for the great room, where you'll be issued your hunting licenses and duck stamps before enjoying a cocktail or two before a crackling fireplace. Dinner will be prepared by the chef and ready shortly. Local seafood, including Maine lobster, is a staple here. After dinner, you'll meet with your guide to discuss the details of the following day's hunt, especially what you should wear. Neoprene waders and warm, waterproof, camouflage clothing are a must. The temperatures range from 20 degrees to 40 degrees during the first part of the season, then drop between the teens and 30s later on.

About 4:30, your morning begins with the sounds and smells of the Atlantic Ocean and that of a hot breakfast. The morning meal is followed by a trip to the lodge's 36-foot cruiser, which is waiting at dockside. The big boat allows for comfortable hunting under most conditions. Once aboard, you'll travel to rock ledges, which are islands in Penobscot, Jericho, and Blue Hill bays. Along the way, you'll have the opportunity to witness a spectacular sunrise.

All the lodge guides are registered Maine hunting guides and also fully licensed U.S. Coast Guard captains, so you'll be in reliable company. Once they arrive at the area they intend to hunt that morning, the guides will deploy from six to eight dozen decoys and then transport you and your hunting party by duck boat to the ledge from which you'll be hunting. No blinds here. Don't need one. Just scrunch down in the rocks and don't move. Make sure you have two or three boxes of nontoxic shot with you. That's what most hunters go through on an average day as eider, scoters, and other sea ducks start bombing the decoys during the early morning hours. Maine has a seven-bird daily limit, which hunters usually meet by mid-morning or early afternoon. Of course, you're not required to shoot that many; it's just as much fun to shoot a few and watch dozens of others come in to the decoys.

Getting hungry? Don't worry, the lodge chef has prepared lunch, which is provided on the cruiser before heading back to the lodge. You'll need those vittles to keep you going before a nap, a wet shower, and returning to the lodge for a dry martini. Dinner tonight, by the way, will be Lobster Newburg.

Eiders Down, Inc. Coastal Guide Service

Gouldsboro, Maine

VITAL STATISTICS:

SPECIES: eider; oldsquaw; black, common, and white-winged scoter; black duck

Season: early October through late January

Hunting Sites: Maine coastal islands and ledges

Accommodations: private lodge with private rooms and baths

MEALS: local seafood and other entrees at lodge, prepared by executive chef

RATES: single, three-, and six-day packages; $325 per hunter/day, includes guided hunt, meals, accommodations

MAXIMUM NUMBER OF HUNTERS: eight

GRATUITIES: hunters' discretion

PREFERRED PAYMENT: cash or check

Getting There: Gouldsboro is situated at the head of Frenchman's Bay and 50 miles from Bangor International Airport

NEAREST COMMERCIAL AIRPORT: Trenton (24 miles)

Dogs and Facilities: guests' dogs are kenneled in a heated garage

Guides: two guides service up to eight hunters

Other Services: bird cleaning and shipping at additional charge

Other Activities: sightseeing; island cookouts

CONTACT:

Bill Pidgeon
Eiders Down Inc.
Box 133P Bar Island
Millbridge, ME 04658
Ph: 207-546-7167
Web: www.maineguides.com/members/eiders-down

I F YOU'VE ALWAYS wanted to visit coastal Maine and its quaint seaside villages and spectacular scenery, why not do it and get in some duck hunting, too? If you do, you'll want to strongly consider booking with Eiders Down Coastal Guide Service. The owner and chief guide, Bill Pidgeon, will put you up in a beautiful bed-and-breakfast, Sunset House, overlooking Frenchman's Bay, and the views from the rooms are spectacular. To top off any sightseeing you want to accomplish, Acadia National Park and Mount Desert Island are right next door.

Pidgeon's guide service caters to small parties and offers quality hunting experiences. A retired Maine game warden, Pidgeon knows the coastal waters here as well as anyone and is well versed in the area's natural history and culture. When not guiding, he spends his time lobster fishing in the same areas he will take you hunting for sea ducks.

Hunting success here always depends on a number of factors, including weather, moon phase, and migration movements, but, as Pidgeon says, "Planning, preparation, and hard work are trademarks of success. The old saying that 10 percent of the hunters kill 90 percent of all game has a lot of truth to it, but we also believe that you do not measure the quality of an outdoor experience by the number of birds you kill."

But you will kill birds, and most of that hunting takes place on offshore islands and ledges. Pidgeon and another guide will transport you there in a 30-foot diesel-powered lobster boat, the *Sea Pidgeon*. When you arrive at the appointed island or ledge, you transfer to one of two 18-foot Lund Alaskans that are towed behind the mother ship. These big aluminum boats are seaworthy and powered by new 40-hp outboards. One boat is used to set decoys, the other to ferry hunters from *Sea Pidgeon* to shooting locations on shore.

By the time you are ready to start shooting, don't be surprised if eiders and scoters are already landing in the decoys. Eiders nest in this area and are plentiful, and as early as October and November, more eiders as well as migratory oldsquaws and scoters start to congregate in Maine's coastal bays. Be prepared to meet these tough birds with plenty of firepower: 12-gauge 3-inch or 3½-inch shells loaded with nontoxic shot in sizes up to No. 1 or No. 2.

If you haven't limited out early, Pidgeon might start a fire and prepare a shore lunch for you and your party. It will be a delicious treat, and part of a unique duck hunting experience. So are the meals at Sunset House. It is, during the summer tourist season, a bed-and-breakfast. But you'll enjoy an unbelievable evening meal as well as breakfast as part of your hunt package with Eiders Down. Carl Johnson, who along with his wife, Kathy, owns Sunset House, is on hiatus at this time of year as the executive chef for three major resorts in Bay Harbor. He'll be on hand to prepare delicious meals for you and your hunting partners, including, if you so desire, his masterfully prepared eider duck.

A yellow Lab poses with a couple of his retrieves for the day: a scoter and a drake oldsquaw.

Penobscot Bay Oufitters

S e a r s p o r t ,   M a i n e

VITAL STATISTICS:

SPECIES: eider, oldsquaw, scoter, black duck, mallard, bufflehead, goldeneye, hooded merganser, Canada goose

Season: sea ducks: October 1 through January 20 puddle ducks: first week in October for 14 days geese: November 10 through December 18

Hunting Sites: islands and ledges of Penobscot and Blue Hill bays for sea ducks; marshes and salt marshes for puddle ducks; private grainfields for geese

Accommodations: lodging in four-bedroom (two hunters per room) turn-of-the-century farmhouse with queen beds and wood floors; other lodging available in nearby hotels

MEALS: classic Maine seafood dishes such as lobster and scallops

RATES: $325/day

MAXIMUM NUMBER OF HUNTERS: eight per day

GRATUITIES: $25-$75/day

PREFERRED PAYMENT: cash, check, or money order

Getting There: 25 miles south of Bangor at the head of Penobscot Bay

NEAREST COMMERCIAL AIRPORT: Bangor, Maine

Dogs and Facilities: kennels are available, trained dogs welcome

Guides: yes

Other Services: airport pickup; bird processing and storage

Other Activities: grouse, woodcock, and deer hunting

CONTACT:

Todd Jackson
Penobscot Bay Outfitters
118 Nickerson Road
Searsport, ME 04974
Ph: 888-SEA-DUCK; 207-338-1883
Email: penbayeiderhunt@acadia.net

CLASSIC SEA DUCK HUNTING is something every waterfowler should experience at least once, no matter how far they live from the sea. And when it comes to sea duck hunting, few places can match the midcoast of Maine. Just visiting this beautiful part of the country is worth the trip. The fact that you're there at a time when the area is rarely seen, when frigid air and rough seas have sent most tourists scurrying home, makes it all the better.

Penobscot Bay Outfitters offers classic sea duck hunting for the uninitiated as well as for old salts. This is rugged, cold-weather hunting, so insulated wet-weather clothing and warm gloves, in olive drab or brown camo, are a must. Hip boots or chest waders are also recommended.

Just as the cold air and sea have a way of chilling you to the bone, sea duck hunting has a way of getting into your blood, especially in this part of Maine, where eiders, oldsquaws, and scoters nest and migrate in the tens of thousands. After the cold pre-dawn boat ride to a spot among the islands and ledges of Penobscot and Blue Hill bays, things can really heat up fast as the ducks wing in out of mist and darkness and buzz your spread. And with liberal limits of seven sea ducks per hunter, you and your party should have plenty of shooting before noon rolls around and it's time to head back to the lodge.

You'll be hunting from one of two boats that hold up to four hunters and a guide, which eliminates the need for ocean transfers to slippery rocks and slopes. All guides are Coast Guard licensed and registered, and the boats are equipped with the latest in radios, GPS, and safety equipment.

For sea duck hunting, a 12- or 10-gauge shotgun with modified chokes is recommended. Shotguns must be plugged to hold no more than three shells, and ammunition must be nontoxic shot in sizes 1, 2, or 3. A cleaning kit is also recommended to keep the salt water from corroding the gun.

Penobscot Bay Outfitters offers puddle duck hunts in the afternoon in the area's marshes and salt marshes. Species include black ducks, mallards, goldeneyes, buffleheads, ringnecks, and pintails. For the upland hunter, ruffed grouse and woodcock hunts are also available in the afternoon.

A total package includes airport pickup, lodging, meals, morning and afternoon hunts, and bird processing and storage. Meals feature fresh Maine seafood such as lobster and scallops. The lodge also has a bar with a pool table and a place to clean guns and clothes.

High Sea's Guide Service

Plymouth, Massachusetts

If you're fond of sand dunes and salty air . . . you're sure to fall in love with old Cape Cod.

VITAL STATISTICS:

SPECIES: eider, oldsquaw, scoters, other divers and puddlers
Season: early October through mid-January
Hunting Sites: Atlantic Ocean, bays and tidal rivers of Cape Cod
Accommodations: hotels with ocean view; full restaurants, bars, room service; all rooms double occupancy
MEALS: hotel restaurants
RATES: based on per boat fee: $150 for one or two hunters; plus various package fees
MAXIMUM NUMBER OF HUNTERS: four
GRATUITIES: $25 minimum
PREFERRED PAYMENT: cash or check
Getting There: Plymouth, five miles north of Cape Cod Canal
NEAREST COMMERCIAL AIRPORT: T.F. Green International Airport, Providence, RI
Dogs and Facilities: no accommodations for hunters' dogs
Guides: one guide for every two hunters; guides have trained dogs
Other Services: licensing; bird cleaning; firearms
Other Activities: historic and scenic sightseeing; biking; golf; shopping
CONTACT:
Christopher Whitten
47 Ellisville Drive
Plymouth, MA 02360
Ph: 508-224-5254
Email: hseasduck@aol.com

SO GOES A LYRIC, or at least part of one, of an old classic. And, if you're fond of shooting fast, incoming ducks from a layout boat, you're sure to fall in love with old Cape Cod's tidal rivers and bays when you hunt with High Sea's Guide Service.

Captains Chris Whitten and Keith Baker have something different to offer when it comes to sea duck hunting. Instead of Maine-style hunting from offshore islands and rock ledges, Whitten and Baker hunt from layout boats in open water. Sea ducks—eider, oldsquaw, and scoter—are the main fare here, but large numbers of diving ducks also mass in Cape Cod waters in fall, and brant are also common migrants here.

A typical day's hunt starts at 5:30 or 6 with a boat ride onto the coastal waters of Cape Cod. The boat is a seaworthy, dependable 17-foot TDB (The Duck Boat), which carries the hunters and guides, and tows anywhere from one to three layout boats to the shooting grounds. Once on location, the layouts are deployed—the number of which depends on the number of hunters on board—and surrounded with decoys. After each layout boat is boarded by a shooter, the TDB chase boat departs a reasonable distance and waits to pick up birds shot by the hunters in the layout boats.

Layout boat shooting is a goose of a different color. You lay down in the low-profile floating blind, shotgun laying beside you but with its muzzle safely pointed above your toes (and the hull), your head tilted forward and your eyes scanning the horizon for ducks. Invariably, it's cold. But when the ducks start coming, they come in low and fast. Quick, sit up and shoot! Sea ducks decoy very well. As a result, many targets will be within 10 yards of your muzzle when you pull the trigger. Of course, if shooting out of a layout boat is too uncomfortable or out of the question, your guides will set you up to hunt out of the TDB, which, due to its construction, makes an excellent boat blind.

By the time you return to the dock at about noon, you'll be ready for lunch and a hot shower, not necessarily in that order. A great place to get both, though, is the Inn at Onset Bay (one of several hotels offering discounts to High Sea's clients). Actually a huge, restored oceanfront Victorian home, the inn offers all the amenities of a full-service hotel.

Fair Winds Gun Club

Chestertown, Maryland

VITAL STATISTICS:

SPECIES: wood duck, teal, pintail, mallard, blacks, scaup, canvasback, sea duck, snow goose, Canada goose

Season: October through January

Hunting Sites: 3,000 acres of agricultural fields, freshwater impoundments, flooded timber, and Chesapeake Bay shoreline for the exclusive use of clientele.

Accommodations: private lodge with four bedrooms

Meals: famous grilled "poppers" hors d'oeuvres and Chesapeake Bay oysters.

Rates: $600/day for blind, max. four hunters; $250/day lodging covers first four hunters

Maximum Number of Hunters: 12, four per guide

Gratuities: $60-$100

Preferred Payment: cash/check; no credit cards

Getting There: near Chestertown on Maryland's Eastern Shore

Nearest Commercial Airport: Easton, MD, or Wilmington, DE, both 40 minutes

Dogs and Facilities: dogs welcome

Guides: one guide per four hunters

Other Services: bird processing and packaging

Other Activities: dove and upland bird hunting; sporting clays; horseback riding; freshwater and saltwater fishing; crabbing

CONTACT:

Clint Evans
Fair Winds Gun Club
5886 Quacker Neck Road
Chestertown, MD 21620
Ph: 410-778-5363
Email: rce@dmv.com
Web: www.huntguide.com

THOUGH DUCK populations and bag limits have been on the rise in the Chesapeake Bay area in recent years, good outfitters are always hard to come by. Still, your chances of success are enhanced greatly with the services of a skillful guide who can tilt the odds of taking these wary and unpredictable birds in your favor.

The Fair Winds Gun Club, on Maryland's Eastern Shore near Chestertown, is such an outfit. While some operations are licensing themselves as Regulated Shooting Areas and releasing pen-raised mallards to replace or supplement wild birds, Fair Winds, owned and operated by veteran guide Clint Evans, puts hunters in touch with the real thing: wild ducks and geese that offer the greatest challenge, and therefore the greatest reward.

The club's 3000 acres of farmland, freshwater impoundments, flooded timber, and Chesapeake Bay shoreline feature a wide variety of hunting situations for wood ducks, teal, pintails, mallards, black ducks, scaup, canvasbacks, sea ducks, and snow geese. There's even the promise of a Canada goose season for 2000-2001 and beyond, as the moratorium on hunting Canadas seems likely to be lifted.

If puddle ducks are what you're after, you'll hunt flooded impoundments planted with corn, sorghum, and millet, where ice and cold weather are only a bonus, as the ponds and impoundments are equipped with bubblers to keep the water open. Flooded timber hunting will give you a chance to test your wingshooting skills on fast-flying teal and wood ducks, as well as black ducks and mallards later in the season.

If sea ducks are your game, late December through January is the time for classic diver hunting in deep-water blinds on Chesapeake Bay and the Chester River, where scaup and canvasbacks offer exciting gunning. For snow geese, you'll head off to the fields where the birds fed the day before, or out to the roost ponds where the geese spent the night and will return to drink mid-morning. The snow goose season lasts from October to March 10, and Evans and his team of expert guides are specialists in helping hunters bag these elusive birds.

You can sharpen or test your wingshooting skills in the afternoon with a round of sporting clays or dove shooting, or relax by the fireplace, enjoying the view of the Chester River, while indulging in Chesapeake Bay oysters and the lodge's famous grilled "poppers." The area also offers great freshwater and saltwater fishing, as well as crabbing. Miles of lightly traveled roads make it perfect for bicycling and horseback riding.

Chestertown, a historic village along the banks of the Chester River, dates back to 1706, when it served as a thriving mid-Atlantic port of entry for the colonial settling of Maryland. As such, the town is a treasure trove of historic homes and shops, most of which are perfectly preserved. Chief among these are the grand estates built along the river by wealthy, eighteenth- and nineteenth-century merchants.

Pintail Point

Q u e e n s t o w n ,   M a r y l a n d

VITAL STATISTICS:

SPECIES: mallard, teal, pintail, canvasback, black duck, wigeon, Canada goose

Season: October through January

Hunting Sites: 500 acres marshland, flooded impoundments, Honga River and Great Marsh Creek

Accommodations: Orvis-endorsed lodging in two bed-and-breakfasts

Meals: breakfast provided

Rates: call for prices

Maximum Number of Hunters: 15

Gratuities: $100

Preferred Payment: cash, checks, major credit cards

Getting There: Maryland's Eastern Shore, an hour east of Annapolis

Nearest Commercial Airport: Baltimore, MD

Dogs and Facilities: dogs welcome, climate-controlled kennels

Guides: one guide with dog for up to three hunters

Other Services: gun rental; ammo sales; bird cleaning and shipping at additional charge

Other Activities: deer hunting; dove hunting; preserve hunting for quail, Huns, chukars, pheasants; sporting clays; saltwater fishing

CONTACT:

Pintail Point
511 Pintail Point Lane
Queenstown, MD 21658
Ph: 410-872-7029
Email: info@pintailpoint.com
Web: www.pintailpoint.com

WHILE specializing in waterfowling, Pintail Point lodge, on Maryland's Eastern Shore, offers a variety of hunting opportunities that will please even nimrods with the most catholic of tastes. Situated on 500 acres of marshland just outside of Cambridge, Maryland, on the Honga River, this Orvis-endorsed lodge can put you on to wild mallards, teal, pintails, canvasbacks, black ducks, wigeon, and Canada geese in flooded impoundments or along three and a half miles of scenic shoreline on the Wye River.

Pintail Point also offers sea duck hunting from aboard its charter boat, and many hunters take advantage of its fall cast-and-blast special—sea duck hunting in the morning and rock fishing in the afternoon—to satisfy their passions for both shooting and angling.

The hunting, however, doesn't stop with ducks and geese. You can hunt deer from the many comfortable and sturdy deer stands located on the property. You can also hunt wild doves on fields of bright sunflowers and buckwheat, or stroll through acres and acres of upland cover, kicking up released pheasants, chukar, and Hungarian partridge.

The many services offered by Pintail Point make it the perfect getaway for all hunting parties, even couples and families. The lodge features two bed-and-breakfasts—Manor House, a luxurious English Tudor-style home, circa 1936, on the Wye River, and Irish Town, a turn-of-the-century farmhouse that offers all the comforts of home, and then some. Pintail Point also features a variety of other services, including a private kennel for dog boarding, gun rental and ammunition sales, as well as bird cleaning and shipping.

In the off-season, the lodge offers month-long dog training sessions for retrievers and other bird dogs. They even offer dogs for sale, from young pups to "started" dogs. And of course there are sporting clays and fly-fishing lessons. How's that for a full-service lodge!

Maryland's Eastern Shore also features a variety of fun for the whole family. From the quaint seaside villages with historical homes and shops beautifully preserved to the many wild birds living among the reeds and rushes of the tidal shore, the area is a visitor's delight. Add the numerous restaurants serving up fresh, catch-of-the-day seafood, as well as golf courses, miles of bicycling paths and horse riding trails and you have a vacation paradise.

Schrader's Hunting

Millington, Maryland

VITAL STATISTICS:

SPECIES: mallard, pintail, canvasback, wood duck, black duck, snow goose, Canada goose, various sea ducks

Season: October through January, with snow goose hunting through March

Hunting Sites: 40,000 acres of marsh, flooded timber, farm ponds, and agricultural fields

Accommodations: guests are lodged at two bed-and-breakfasts near Chestertown

Meals: a variety of home-cooked meals

Rates: $150 per person/day, with a minimum of 4 hunters; lodging is $35 per person per night

Maximum Number of Hunters: 25 per day

Gratuities: $20 per person/day

Preferred Payment: cash or check

Getting There: Maryland's Eastern Shore, an hour east of Annapolis

Nearest Commercial Airport: Baltimore, MD

Dogs and Facilities: hunters' dogs welcome; outside kennel runs

Guides: one guide per four to six hunters

Other Services: bird cleaning facilities in area

Other Activities: deer hunting; preserve hunting; fishing; sporting clays

CONTACT:

Shrader's Hunting
900 Red Lion Branch Road
Millington, MD 21651
Ph: 410-778-1895
Fax: 410-778-9542
Email: letsgohunting@shradershunting.com
Web: www.shradershunting.com

MANY OUTFITS boast about the number of hunting opportunities they offer, or about the number of acres they have at their disposal. But few can match Shrader's Hunting in scope or size. If you like hunting snow geese and wild ducks—no problem. Deer hunting and upland birds? They have it covered. How about doves or sea ducks? Look no further. They'll even throw in released "flighted" mallards, if that's your game.

Indeed, there's plenty to do at Shrader's Hunting, and plenty of room in which to do it. With over 40,000 acres of prime hunting property on Maryland's Eastern Shore, on Chesapeake Bay, at your disposal, the possibilities are, well, virtually limitless.

Snow geese are a specialty here—that's a good way to start off your season and a great way to end it, too, since the snow goose hunting runs from October through March. A guide will take you out before dawn to a scouted field, where you'll hunker down in a pit or A-frame among a variety of decoys, including silhouettes, shells, hand-painted full-bodied decoys, and stuffers.

Or, if you'd like a different angle on this fascinating sport, try lying out on the ground among the decoys. There you'll get an up-close look at these beautiful birds, as well as unpredictable shots. The whole thing is reminiscent of a bygone era, when hunter and hunted shared a closer intimacy.

You can also hunt wild ducks on 10,000 acres of prime waterfowl property, including freshwater marsh, flooded timber, flooded farm fields, and farm ponds. And, of course, there are sea ducks out on Chesapeake Bay. These birds come in from every angle, often in groups, offering fast-paced and challenging shooting. If you've never tried it, you're in for a real treat.

In the afternoon, you can choose to hunt upland birds—preserve pheasants, chukar, quail—over setters and pointers, or you can further satiate your appetite for waterfowling with a released mallard hunt. These "flighted" mallard hunts are set up in natural surroundings, under natural conditions, and the birds come very close to the flight patterns of wild ducks. Moreover, these mallards are mature, full-feathered birds—great for the table or the trophy room.

For one of wingshooting's finest challenges, try dove hunting in a number of locations that feature the right combination of food, gravel, water, and roosting areas to ensure a great hunt. Each plot is large enough to prevent overcrowding, providing good shooting for everyone.

If you'd like a chance at a trophy buck, Shrader's offers a wide range of hunting terrain, including swampland, deep woods, marshes, and open fields. All of these are in areas that are heavily populated with white-tailed deer, and all have everything that deer need: food, cover, water, and the security of light hunting pressure. On some tracts, called Managed Trophy Areas, deer taken must have a minimum antler spread of 16 inches. These areas are closely managed to produce trophy bucks and can be hunted with bow and arrow, shotgun, or muzzleloader.

Chincoteague Hunting and Fishing Center

Chincoteague, Virginia

VITAL STATISTICS:

SPECIES: bufflehead, brant, greater snow goose, black duck, oldsquaw, scaup, pintail, gadwall, wigeon, shoveler, goldeneye, scoter, eider, greater blue goose, redhead, canvasback, merganser, teal, and Canada goose (limited season)

Season: ducks: November 17 to January 20
snow geese: November through February

Hunting Sites: approximately 30 miles of saltmarsh and bays on the seaside, which border the Assateague National Wildlife Refuge, and approximately a 10-mile radius on the Chesapeake Bay around the Saxis Wildlife Refuge

Accommodations: local motels, or cabins with kitchen, living room, and two bedrooms

MEALS: fine restaurants in the area featuring Eastern Shore cooking

RATES: $119/day, plus lodging at $39 to $79 per day

MAXIMUM NUMBER OF HUNTERS: 30

GRATUITIES: hunters' discretion

PREFERRED PAYMENT: cash or credit card

Getting There: on the Del-Mar-VA peninsula's lower eastern shore, approximately 50 miles south of Ocean City, MD

NEAREST COMMERCIAL AIRPORT: Baltimore, MD, with connections to Salisbury

Dogs and Facilities: dogs allowed

Guides: one guide accompanies maximum of three hunters per blind

Other Services: bird cleaning

Other Activities: saltwater fishing

THE LOWER PORTION of the Del-Mar-Va peninsula—from Ocean City, Maryland, to the entrance of the Chesapeake Bay—is the wintering ground of one of the largest and most diverse populations of waterfowl on the Eastern Flyway, including one of the largest concentrations of greater snow geese in the country. It is here, along the unpopulated Barrier Islands that shield the mainland from the fury of the Atlantic Ocean, and on Chincoteague Bay, that Capt. Pete Wallace has set up a waterfowling outfitting service that will gladden the heart of any hunter.

The variety of ducks you may encounter in a typical day's hunt is dizzying—divers, puddlers, brant, geese, and seaducks all in the same day. And make no mistake about it, this is hunting, not just idle shooting. In a typical day you may move three to four times to hunt a variety of species. The local guides Capt. Wallace uses are all U.S. Coast Guard-licensed captains, using 18- to 21-foot skiffs or scows to transport you to and from the blinds. They know the ins and outs of the oyster beds and mud flats like no one else (during the summer season they are commercial fishermen), so you are in good hands at all times. Depending on conditions, your guide will select either one of the more than 100 marsh blinds that overlook ponds or creeks, a pole blind constructed in the open bays, a portable blind, or grassboats and floating blinds. There is always a fresh location near birds and no more than three hunters are assigned to any one blind, all from the same party.

Typical decoy spreads on the seaside consist of three to five decoys in the ponds and a dozen or so in the open water. Most of the birds are wintering here and travel in small flocks, pairs and singles, with the exception of brant and snow geese. Brant will often travel in flocks of one hundred or more birds and snows will literally fill the morning sky as far as you can see in the early season. As the season progresses, the snow geese flights become less predictable with smaller flocks of 10 to 50 birds flying all day. The best and most consistent snow goose hunting typically occurs in January and February. The most consistent duck shooting is on the Eastern Shore. But no matter what the conditions, there are usually ducks to shoot at. Even on bluebird days when shooting puddle ducks can be tough, there are divers, seaducks, and brant. Brant are one of the most predictable quarry; they move

CONTACT:
Capt. Pete Wallace
Chincoteague Hunting and Fishing
Center
P.O. Box 404
Chincoteague, VA 23336
Ph: 888-231-4868
Fax: 757-336-6863
Web: www.esva.net/~pwallace/

with the tide and no matter what the weather, there is always a change of tide. Seaducks are attracted to the commercial boats clamming, crabbing, and oystering. As these boats dredge the bottom, they churn up food for old-squaws, scoters, buffleheads, and mergansers. Even an occasional eider stops by for an easy meal.

If you're looking for a wide variety of ducks, huge concentrations of snow geese, or the challenge of hunting fast-moving birds in their wintering grounds, this classic Eastern Shore hunting is sure to please and certain to be remembered for many seasons to come.

Pungo Acres

Pantego, North Carolina

VITAL STATISTICS:

SPECIES: tundra swan, snow goose, Canada goose, mallard, pintail, wood duck, canvasback

Season: October through January, with season splits; swan-November 12 to January 31

Hunting Sites: Pamlico River, Lake Phelps, Pungo Lake, leased agricultural fields for geese and swans

Accommodations: Pungo Acres Hunting Retreat farmhouse lodge or motels in nearby Plymouth, NC

MEALS: lunch provided with hunt; other meals at nearby commercial establishments

RATES: daily and two-day special packages, rates depend on species hunted; call for additional rate information

MAXIMUM NUMBER OF HUNTERS: 10

GRATUITIES: $25 to $50

PREFERRED PAYMENT: cash, check, or credit card

Getting There: located 60 miles southeast of Greenville, NC

NEAREST COMMERCIAL AIRPORT: Greenville, NC

Dogs and Facilities: no accommodations for guests' dogs

Guides: one guide for two to four hunters

Other Services: bird cleaning and packaging

Other Activities: fishing for bream, largemouth bass, stripers; bird-watching

CONTACT:
Edwin "Booger" Harris
Pungo Acres
PO Box 55
Pantego, NC 27860
Ph: 252-935-5415
Email: pungoacres@pantegonc.com
Web: www.pungoacres.com

NO, IT MAY NOT appeal to every hunter, and it may be only a once-in-a-lifetime ambition, but it is a part of North America's waterfowl hunting heritage, especially in the Carolinas. Shooting a swan, that is. A true "big game" trophy for a bird hunter, the tundra swan can range from 18 to 28 pounds and has a wing span up to 7½ feet. Only four states have a swan season, and North Carolina, which winters from 90,000 to 120,000 of the magnificent birds, is one of them.

Swan hunting is restricted here. The state issues only 6,000 permits each year, and the permits have to be applied for, by the hunter, in the first week of October (for information, write: North Carolina Res. Comm., ATT: Swan Permits, 512 North Salisbury St., Raleigh, NC 27604).

Once the coveted permit is obtained, you'll want to contact Edwin "Booger" Harris, a second-generation guide in eastern North Carolina who operates Pungo Acres Hunting Retreat and guide service. Harris guides for fishing, deer and bear hunting, as well as for waterfowl. One of his specialties is swan hunts, and his clients enjoy an 85 percent success rates.

Harris offers both one- and two-day packages for waterfowl hunts that can include snow goose, swan, and duck hunting. Diving duck hunting is conducted out of blinds on the Pamlico River, while swan, puddle duck, and goose hunting take place in fields surrounding the Pungo National Wildlife Refuge.

In the few western states that allow swan hunting (also by special permit), most of the birds are bagged incidental to pursuing other types of waterfowl. That is, shooting the stray swan that passes over a decoy-studded pothole where hunters have set up for ducks or geese. Not so in North Carolina. Here it's a field hunt inside a blind, hunting over swan decoys, and with guides calling by mouth or using goose calls modified to sound like a swan's vocalizations.

Greater snow geese, thousands of which also winter in this area and along the North Carolina coast, will also decoy to the swan spreads. Pintails and mallards may visit the decoys, too, but if you're here to fill a swan tag, you'll want to be prepared with enough gun to get the job done properly. That means a 10- or a 12-guage loaded with anything from a minimum of 3-inch to 3½-inch shotshells stuffed with steel BBB's or T's, or the largest non-steel, nontoxic shot you can find in bismuth or tungsten-type shot. Shotgun chokes should be either modified or improved cylinder, because the shooting will often be closer than you'd think, often as close as 20 to 25 yards. At that range, an incoming tundra swan looks like it's lumbering toward you and is as big as a Greyhound bus, and you'll think you can hit it with a slingshot. But, believe me, the birds are moving faster than they appear to be, and with their long neck, it's easy not to lead them enough. Concentrate on the bird's bill, give yourself the right forward allowance (lead), and don't forget to keep swinging the muzzle after the shot. It's very embarrassing to miss a couple of shots at these flying leviathans, even at close range. I speak from experience.

A tundra swan is a once-in-a-lifetime trophy.
North Carolina is one of the few states where these
stately birds are hunted over swan decoy spreads.

Williams Farms

Fairfield, North Carolina

VITAL STATISTICS:

SPECIES: mallard, pintail, wigeon, black duck, wood duck, tundra swan (with required permit)

Season: split season; November, and again in December through January 20

Hunting Sites: 9,000 acres of flooded impoundments (cornfields) near Lake Mattamuskeet

Accommodations: local motels

MEALS: local restaurants

RATES: $150 per hunter/day; three-hunter per blind minimum

MAXIMUM NUMBER OF HUNTERS: 15

GRATUITIES: $50 to $100

PREFERRED PAYMENT: cash or check

Getting There: in northeast North Carolina on the north shore of Lake Mattamuskeet

NEAREST COMMERCIAL AIRPORT: Raleigh-Durham or Greenville, NC

Dogs and Facilities: hunters encouraged to bring dogs if desired, but no accommodations

Guides: one guide per maximum of four hunters; some guides provide dogs

Other Services: none

Other Activities: sightseeing; bird-watching

CONTACT:

Joseph B. Williams
Williams Farms
1966 Newlands Rd.
Fairfield, NC 27826
Ph: 252-926-5221

THE WHOLE North Carolina coastal area is steeped in waterfowling legend and lore. For more than two centuries the watermen here have scratched out a living crabbing, clamming, oystering, netting, or trapping any commercially significant creature their home waters provided. Years back, some of these men also gunned waterfowl from battery boxes and used live decoys to lure Canada geese and ducks within effective shooting range. The geese and ducks the market hunters harvested were shipped to buyers for use in restaurants in New York and other East Coast cities.

When commercial hunting was outlawed, many of these watermen became guides for the sport hunters whom, having learned of the area's incredible waterfowl hunting, flocked to Ocracoke Island and the waters of Pamlico, Albemarle, Currituck, and Core sounds. And to Lake Mattamuskeet.

Today, the legends and the waterfowling live on. Hyde County, North Carolina, is a small, rural county in which, it is said, all roads lead to one place: Lake Mattamuskeet. The lake is North Carolina's largest natural lake and, since 1934, has been managed as a national wildlife refuge, including 50,000 acres of water, marsh, timber, and croplands. Eighteen miles long and six to seven miles wide, the lake's basin averages only three feet deep, making it a prime feeding area for waterfowl. Much of the lake contains submergent vegetation, including dense beds of wild celery and pondweed, which are preferred foods of canvasback, scaup, and tundra swans. Water management and vegetation control on the shallow lake produces impressive stands of emergent vegetation such as wild millet, panic grasses, and spikerushes, which feed large numbers of puddle ducks, including some 25,000 pintails and another 25,000 green-winged teal that winter on the lake.

For six generations, Williams Farms has been located on the north shore of Lake Mattamuskeet, where its corn and wheat fields have been an inviting haven to a vast number of ducks, geese, and tundra swans. Joey Williams has become, in the tradition of area watermen, one of the most well known waterfowl guides of the Mattamuskeet area.

Williams maintains flooded cornfields as hunting areas for his duck hunting clients. His guests hunt tundra swan over winter wheat fields, 1,000 acres of which he leases specifically for that purpose.

While he doesn't provide lodging or meals, Williams can provide names, rates, and phone numbers of small motels only a few minutes away from his hunting operation. The night before you hunt, you'll meet Williams or one of his guides at your motel or at a local restaurant to discuss logistics for the next morning. "We meet at about 5:30 on the morning of your hunt," says Williams, "then head out to the blinds. We hunt until mid-morning, then come in for breakfast at a local restaurant. We're usually back in the blinds by 2:00 and stay until you shoot a limit or shooting time is up."

Sounds simple enough, but when you get up for that first morning hunt, anticipate a great day, and don't forget to whistle the tune "Nothing could be finer than to be in Carolina in the morning" all the way to the duck blind.

The Mattamuskeet National Wildlife Refuge hosts tens of thousands of tundra swans, snow geese, and pintails, as well as other species of ducks every winter.

MISSISSIPPI FLYWAY

MINNESOTA, WISCONSIN, IOWA, ILLINOIS, OHIO, INDIANA,
TENNESSEE, ARKANSAS, MISSISSIPPI, LOUISIANA

HUNT FAST, HUNT HARD. Often, at least in the more northern part of this flyway, ice-up can send the birds south before the waterfowl season closes. Wisconsin, Minnesota, and Michigan offer mixed-bag hunting for divers and dabblers. Northern wild rice lakes attract mallards, ring-necked ducks, and scaup. Marshes lure the same ducks, and big lakes are notorious staging areas for huge concentrations of bluebills, redheads, and canvasback, as is the Upper Mississippi River between Minnesota and Wisconsin.

States farther to the central portion of this flyway don't see migrant ducks as early as the states to the north, but the weather is at least a little kinder a little longer, too. That doesn't mean it won't get cold south of the northern tier of states. It does. And when it does, the birds fly to a variety of wetlands, including marshes, lakes, and river habitats, that offer hunting for dabblers, primarily, as well as geese. Read on and discover who can lead you to these waterfowl hotspots.

Lots of ducks. That's what I like about the South. This is the small end of the funnel, where migrating waterfowl from parts of the Central Flyway and the Mississippi Flyway concentrate to spend the winter months. Arkansas is the mallard capital of the continent, wintering more of the birds than any other state, and is world famous for its flooded timber hunting. Nearby Tennessee is another hot mallard location and, like Arkansas, also winters dabblers such as pintail, wigeon, and teal. Louisiana is the end of the line for most migrant waterfowl, and a hunt on one of the state's coastal marshes can produce a fascinating mixed bag of diving and dabbling ducks, as well as snow geese and white-fronted geese.

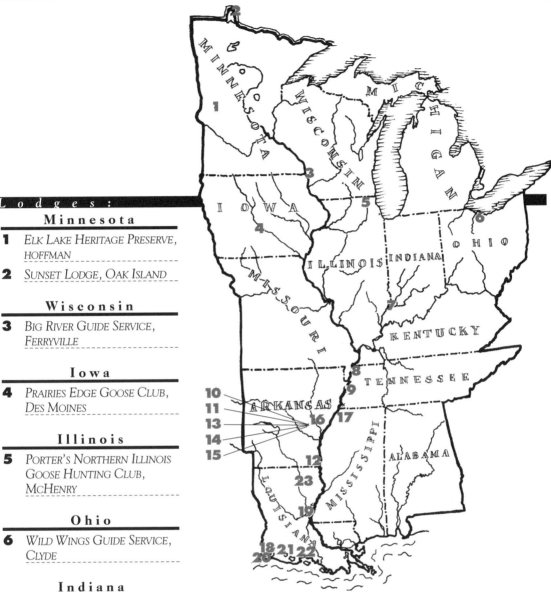

Lodges:

Minnesota

1 ELK LAKE HERITAGE PRESERVE, HOFFMAN

2 SUNSET LODGE, OAK ISLAND

Wisconsin

3 BIG RIVER GUIDE SERVICE, FERRYVILLE

Iowa

4 PRAIRIES EDGE GOOSE CLUB, DES MOINES

Illinois

5 PORTER'S NORTHERN ILLINOIS GOOSE HUNTING CLUB, MCHENRY

Ohio

6 WILD WINGS GUIDE SERVICE, CLYDE

Indiana

7 MCCORMICK FARMS, VINCENNES

Tennessee

8 HAMILTON'S RESORT, HORNBEAK

9 HATCHIE RIVER OUTFITTERS, TIPTON COUNTY

Arkansas

10 BANDED DUCK HUNT CLUB, STUTTGART

11 BLACK DOG HUNTING CLUB, STUTTGART

12 GRAND LAKE LODGE, EUDORA

13 KENNETH MCCOLLUM DUCK CLUB, STUTTGART

14 PINTAIL PENINSULA, STUTTGART

15 WILD WINGS HUNTING CLUB, STUTTGART

16 WILDLIFE FARMS, CASSCO

Mississippi

17 BEARTAIL OUTFITTERS, COLDWATER

Louisiana

18 CALCASIEU CHARTER SERVICE, LAKE CHARLES

19 GILES ISLAND HUNTING CLUB, FERRIDAY

20 GROSSE SAVANNE LODGE, LAKE CHARLES

21 HACKBERRY ROD AND GUN CLUB, HACKBERRY

22 LOUISIANA FLYWAY LODGE, KAPLAN

23 PIN OAK MALLARDS LODGE, RAYVILLE

Elk Lake Heritage Preserve

H o f f m a n ,   M i n n e s o t a

VITAL STATISTICS:

SPECIES: mallard, teal, wood duck, divers, Canada goose

Season: ducks: October through November;
geese: September through December

Hunting Sites: 400 leased acres plus freshwater marshes of 150 to 200 acres

Accommodations: two private lodges; main lodge sleeps eight, log cabin lodge sleeps six to eight; both with lounge areas, dining rooms.

MEALS: meal preparation provided or guests may prepare their own meals in lodge kitchens.

RATES: vary according to package selected, call for information.

MAXIMUM NUMBER OF HUNTERS: lodges accommodate 15 to 20 people

GRATUITIES: 10% to 15%

PREFERRED PAYMENT: cash, check, credit card

Getting There: west-central Minnesota, 20 miles west of Alexandria

NEAREST COMMERCIAL AIRPORT: Alexandria, MN

Dogs and Facilities: guests' dogs welcome; four outside kennel runs

Guides: one guide and retriever for two to four hunters

Other Services: bird cleaning and freezing; pro shop; conference room

Other Activities: upland hunting for released pheasants and chukar; walleye fishing; 50-round sporting clays course; flurry shoot; golf courses in close proximity

CONTACT:

Ed Loeffler
Elk Lake Heritage Preserve
Box 422
Hoffman, MN 56339
Ph: 320-986-2200
Fax: 320-986-2200
Email: elhp@elklakepreserve.com
Web: www.elklakepreserve.com

A T ED LOEFFLER'S Elk Lake Heritage Preserve, flexibility is the name of the game, both in the activities you can take part in and in the rates you pay. The preserve offers everything from annual memberships and package plans to day-rate hunting and fishing.

Waterfowl hunting here takes place on private marshes in strategically placed duck blinds. An early September goose season and another in December are in effect to help reduce the local population of giant Canadas. During October and November, migratory Canadas visit the area, as do mallards, teal, woodies, scaup, ring-necked ducks, canvasback, and other diving ducks. Visiting waterfowlers can arrange for a multiple-day stay, including lodging, meals, and guide and retriever services or, if they wish, may bring their own dogs and rent a blind for a daily rate.

But waterfowling isn't the only game in town. You can include lots of other activities here and include them in a package plan or pay as you go. Care to try your hand at sporting clays? The preserve's 50-round sporting clays range meanders through a wooded area adjacent to Torstenson Lake. The range offers a great opportunity for those who would like to sharpen their shooting skills for feathered game. After a round of clays, you can walk the preserve's rolling grasslands, woodlands, and wetlands in quest of released pheasants and chukar. You can request that birds be planted for you, or you can shoot scratch birds—those already in the cover and left over from previous hunts—at a less expensive rate. If you don't bring your own dog, Loeffler will provide a guide and a trained bird dog to go with you.

Want to wet a line? The preserve encompasses two 70-acre bodies of water, Torstenson and Church lakes, that are stocked with plenty of good-sized walleyes. Catches of these great-eating fish include stringers of two- to four-pounders, but there is a 21-inch maximum size limit, unless you want to pay a trophy fee for a wallhanger. You can also fish catch-and-release if you please, and 50-fish days are not uncommon on these productive little lakes. Boats, motors, and bait are available on site, and you can rent these or have the price included in a guided fishing package.

If you plan on staying a night or two, Loeffler offers you accommodations in one of two lodges on the site. The main lodge sleeps from eight to 10 people comfortably. It includes an all-purpose kitchen, large dining room, a lounge area with a television and VCR, and two bathrooms, each with a shower. The log lodge building sleeps from six to eight and includes a loft, fireplace, kitchen, spacious dining room, and a lounge area with a television and VCR. Both lodges are located on one of the preserve's private fishing lakes. At either lodge building, you can provide your own groceries and do your own cooking. Otherwise, Loeffler will provide a cook and vittles.

[M I S S I S S I P P I   F L Y W A Y]

Sunset Lodge

O a k   I s l a n d ,   M i n n e s o t a

LAKE OF THE WOODS is a massive body of water straddling portions of Minnesota, Manitoba, and Ontario. In fall, when the island-studded lake's trees turn to shades of gold, yellow, and red, you'll find some of the most breath-taking scenery in the north country. You'll also find some excellent duck hunting on the lake, which is a staging area for migrating divers. Island sloughs and bays with wild rice beds also hold good numbers of teal and mallards early in the season.

Sunset Lodge is located on Oak Island, on the north side of the lake but still within Minnesota's boundary waters. Still, the lodge is only 200 yards from the Ontario border, so visiting, properly-licensed hunters can begin waterfowling here as early as mid-September on the Ontario side of the lake, hunt the Minnesota side after the state's early October duck opener, or, with licenses for both Ontario and Minnesota, hunt either side of the border.

Lodge manager Bill Caputa accommodates hunters who don't want a guided hunt by providing boats, motors, and decoys. But this lake is huge, easy to get lost in, and studded with submerged gravel reefs that eat lower units of outboard motors for breakfast. Although guides are not required, hiring one is a good idea for hunters traveling during the pre-dawn hours on the lake (and a good deal less expensive than replacing a mangled lower unit).

The majority of the hunting for divers here is done from shore on points and isolated rock piles not too distant from the lodge. Early in the season, mallards and teal can also be found in sloughs and wild rice bays on the Canadian side. Caputa says that duck hunting is best in October. Lesser scaup (bluebill) and bufflehead show up early in the month (October 1-10) and provide great action during relatively mild weather conditions. Greater scaup, goldeneye, redhead, and canvasback arrive a bit later (October 15-30), after colder weather sets in.

A hunting day at Sunset Lodge begins with a pre-dawn rise for coffee and rolls. Then it's off to whatever hunting spot you or your guide has chosen for the morning. Most of the morning flights will be over by mid-morning, at which time you can return to the lodge for a more traditional breakfast. Caputa says most groups, however, opt to pack a lunch with them and stay on the lake to fish during midday. This is probably the best time of year to jig for the lake's abundant walleye, smallmouth bass, perch, and crappie. Muskie are lurking the reefs during fall, too, fattening up on bait fish for the winter, and casting surface plugs is a technique that can put a 30-pounder on the end of your line.

During the last few hours of daylight, it's back to the rock point to catch up on the bluebill bag again, or perhaps visit a slough for mallards. Don't worry about being late for dinner. It's served until 9 each evening.

Large numbers of canvasbacks, as well as lesser scaup and ring-necked ducks, flock to wilderness waters in northern Minnesota every fall, providing waterfowlers great sport and fast shooting.

[M I S S I S S I P P I   F L Y W A Y]

Big River Guide Service

F e r r y v i l l e ,   W i s c o n s i n

VITAL STATISTICS:

SPECIES: canvasback, redhead, mallard

Season: mid-October to late November

Hunting Sites: Pool 9 on the Mississippi River National Fish and Wildlife Refuge

Accommodations: local hotels, motels

Meals: breakfast provided; other meals at local restaurants

Rates: $120 per hunter/day

Maximum Number of Hunters: 11

Gratuities: 10-20%

Preferred Payment: check, cash

Getting There: forty miles south of LaCrosse, WI

Nearest Commercial Airport: LaCrosse, WI

Dogs and Facilities: no accommodations for hunters' dogs

Guides: one guide with dog for up to four hunters

Other Services: none

Other Activities: bird-watching; sightseeing

CONTACT:

Tony Toye
Big River Guide Service
43605 CTH E
Boscobel, WI 53805
Ph/Fax: 608-375-7447
Email: toyedecoys@tds.net

S O, YOU'VE ALWAYS wanted to bag a canvasback but you've never even seen one, much less had a shot at one? Well, Pool 9 of the Upper Mississippi River in Wisconsin is about as sure a thing as you'll find for a canvasback hunt in the U.S. From mid-October through November, migratory cans stage on this wide spot in the river in almost unbelievable numbers, and it's not uncommon to see thousands in a single day. Aerial observations by waterfowl biologists making duck counts in fall here once described a raft of cans a half mile wide and five miles long.

Cans aren't the only ducks on the river in the fall, of course. Mallards, wigeon and teal, and diving ducks, including redhead and bluebills are common. Which is good, because even though there is a largesse of canvasback, in recent years the bag limit for the species has been one per day.

Tony Toye's Big River Guide Service is the sole waterfowl outfitter operating on Pool 9. He doesn't own a lodge, but he can point you in the right direction for local accommodations. And he'll take you on a memorable hunt on big water between the scenic river bluffs of Wisconsin and Minnesota. According to Tony, the best time to enjoy that hunt if you're looking for a trophy canvasback is between the third week of October until the second week of November. If mallards are your game, the best hunting is in November, and the later the better.

A day with Tony starts with a meeting at a local boat landing in the little town of Ferryville. There you and your partners will board one of his large (18- to 20-foot) duck boats equipped with a heater, stove, and individual seats. The boat itself is grassed over and serves as a blind. You'll shove off well before dawn because there are plenty of decoys—150 floaters and four or five dozen silhouttes—to set up before the shooting starts. The massive spread helps because these are public waters where lots of other hunters spread out and set up, and Tony's decoy layouts give the ducks a more attractive look than spreads the birds will see elsewhere. So bring along chest waders, because you and your partners, unless you have a physical limitation, will be helping deploy and pick up the blocks.

If all that work makes you hungry by midmorning, don't worry. Sometime during a lull in the action, Tony will be at the boat's stove, preparing a hot breakfast of bacon and eggs for everyone on board. While you're chowing down, you might well have an opportunity to witness a bald eagle at breakfast, too. Pool 9 is a major wintering area for eagles from all over the north country. The grand birds perch in trees along the picturesque (hint: bring a camera) Mississippi River bluffs when they're not soaring over the river in search of fish and other critters to feed on.

Your hunt will last until 1. Then it's time to pick up and head back to the dock. By then, I assume, Tony will already have told you about his guided spring hunts for snow geese in Missouri.

Pool #9 of the Upper Mississippi River between Minnesota and Wisconsin is a major staging area for tens of thousands of canvasbacks and other ducks in October and November.

Prairies Edge Goose Club, LC

D e s   M o i n e s ,   I o w a

VITAL STATISTICS:

SPECIES: Canada goose, snow goose

Season: September through March, depending on location and species

Hunting Sites: leased properties in Minnesota, Iowa, Missouri

Accommodations: local motels

MEALS: local restaurants

RATES: $115 per hunter/half day (Iowa and Missouri hunts); $110-$125 per hunter/half day (Minnesota); $145 per hunter/half day (spring snow geese)

MAXIMUM NUMBER OF HUNTERS: six (Minnesota early metro hunt); six to eight (central Iowa); six (northern Missouri); eight (Iowa spring snow goose hunt)

GRATUITIES: 10%

PREFERRED PAYMENT: cash, check, credit card

Getting There: varies, see text

NEAREST COMMERCIAL AIRPORT: varies, see text

Dogs and Facilities: only guides' dogs permitted

Guides: one guide and Labrador retriever provided per hunter group

Other Services: assistance with bird cleaning

Other Activities: none

CONTACT:
Shawn Eldredge
Prairies Edge Goose Club, LC
308 S.W. Park Ave.
Des Moines, IA 50315
Ph: 515-243-1441
Fax: 515-283-0641
Email goosgru@aol.com
Web: www.gooseguru.com

IT'S NOT REALLY a club per se, more of a mobile guide service. Though headquartered in Iowa, Prairies Edge Goose Club (PEGH) doesn't stay in one place. It follows the geese and the goose hunting opportunities through three states of the Mississippi Flyway, and at each of these multistate destinations it leases fields for the exclusive hunting of its clients.

Goose guru Shawn Eldredge heads up PEGH and has been waterfowling for 23 years, including 10 years as a professional guide. He starts his season in Minnesota, where early season (September) Canada goose hunts are designed to help reduce populations of large, nonmigratory Canadas that have set up shop in city parks. Of course, those birds don't get enough to eat in the parks, so they make daily feeding forays into farmers' fields surrounding the metro areas, where the farmers aren't that happy to accommodate their voracious appetites. Eldredge scouts out those fields and arranges for his clients to be in them as soon as the season opens.

Following the metro goose operations, Eldredge retreats to Des Moines, where he first started PEGH. Des Moines is a good place to start a professional guiding business for goose hunters, because thousands of Canada geese migrate through the state, and often stay there throughout the winter. Eldredge and his guides have leased fields within an 80-mile radius of Des Moines, enough properties that they can rotate fields and pick and choose which ones to hunt, depending on wind direction, field conditions, and bird use during Iowa's 80-plus day Canada goose season.

After the Iowa season, Eldredge and his guides move to northern Missouri to hunt on their leases around the Kansas City metro area. Here, not only giant Canadas but snow geese (both white and blue color phases) are the targets of opportunity.

With today's spring snow goose seasons there's no rest for the wicked or for goose guides. So, in February and March it's back to Iowa, this time the southwest part of the state, and Eldredge and his guides are at it again.

Of course, PEGH being as mobile as it is, Eldredge does not have an established lodge. He will, however, provide you with a list of motels you can stay at near any of his hunt locations. Once you're there, the m.o. for the morning hunt will be the same, regardless of the venue. He'll call you the evening before the hunt and after he or his guides have scouted the territory to see which fields they'll hunt in the morning. He'll meet you the next morning at a prearranged location to take you to the field, where he's already been earlier to set up decoys and portable blinds. About all you have to do is crawl into the blind (which, if it's cold outside, will be heated).

From then on, for the hunters at least, it's easy street. Eldredge and his guides will set out goose kites, flag and call distant birds into gun range, and call the shot. When you drop geese, the guides' Labs will retrieve them for you. If you want to know just how close those birds might be before the shooting starts, ask Eldredge to send you one of his PEGH videos and see for yourself.

Goose hunters take aim at snow geese inspecting their rag spread. The whole flock may not come down within shotgun range, but a few low, interested birds are all that's necessary as each flock passes overhead.

Porter's Northern Illinois Goose Hunting Club

M c H e n r y ,   I l l i n o i s

VITAL STATISTICS:

SPECIES: Canada goose, mallard, scaup, redhead, canvasback, ring-neck, goldeneye

Season: ducks: October through December

geese: September through January

Hunting Sites: geese: private agricultural fields; mallard: private ponds; diving ducks: Lake Michigan

Accommodations: lodging not provided; local motels available

Meals: available at local restaurants

Rates: goose hunting: $125 per hunter/day; mallard hunt: $125 per hunter/day; Lake Michigan diver duck hunt: $150 per hunter/day

Maximum Number of Hunters: goose hunt: 20 hunters per day; call for information on duck hunts

Gratuities: hunters' discretion

Preferred Payment: cash, check, or credit card

Getting There: McHenry, IL, one hour from Chicago

Nearest Commercial Airport: Chicago O'Hare

Dogs and Facilities: well trained dogs welcome; dogs stay with hunters in motel

Guides: four hunters per guide; dogs provided as necessary

Other Services: bird cleaning available (extra charge)

Other Activities: duck and goose hunting only

CONTACT:

Matt Porter
Porter's Northern Illinois Goose Hunting Club
703 Porten
McHenry, IL 60050
Ph: 847-639-8590
Fax: 847-639-7065
Email: huntporters@cs.com
Web: huntporters.com

MOST WATERFOWL hunters in the Upper Midwest are familiar with southern Illinois' goose hunting opportunities. Traditional goose hangouts there include Rend Lake and the Crab Orchard and Horseshoe Lake national wildlife refuges. Commercial goose camps in that country are numerous. What many hunters don't know is that goose and duck hunting can be just as good or better in northern Illinois, merely an hour's drive from Chicago.

Matt Porter figured it out eight years ago when he formed Porter's Northern Illinois Goose Hunting Club. With a couple of hundred thousand nonmigratory giant Canada geese roaming the countryside and many more Canadas migrating through the area in fall and winter, he figured that starting a commercial goose hunting operation would be a can't-miss proposition.

He was right. "The goose hunting at Porter's is so good," Porter claims, "that we guarantee your success. If you don't get an opportunity to shoot geese, we'll have you back as our guest. We're not in the habit of giving things away for free, so we're pretty darn sure that you're going to get your geese. We don't do any pass-shooting or sky busting, either. When we put you up to shoot, the geese are right in your face.

"We hunt 20 different fields spread out across three counties," says Porter. "We have 33 pits and two portable blinds for hunting those fields, but we don't hunt the same ones every day. We hunt the sites on a rotating basis, which allows us to rest the fields between hunts, so they don't get burned out, and so the birds don't become shy of gunning pressure. We have enough pits to hunt 80 hunters a day, but to keep our success rate high and in order to rotate the fields, we only take a maximum of 20 per day. Also, we use only the best decoys and set them out every morning and pick them up at the end of the hunt, so the geese don't get used to seeing decoys in the same spots every day."

On a typical day, hunters meet their guides at 5 a.m. at Porter's clubhouse in Wauconda, Illinois, where they enjoy a cup of coffee and meet their guide for the day. From there, the hunters follow the guides out to the field that they will be hunting. When the hunters arrive at the pit blind, which is dug into the ground, it will be pumped and heated as necessary. Once the decoys are set, the guide will do the calling, the rest is up to the hunters. "We hunt from a half hour before sunrise until 1 p.m." says Porter, "but we are usually at the restaurant eating breakfast well before then."

Porter also offers mallard hunts on a private pond, but his most exciting duck hunts are for divers on Lake Michigan. His clients hunt from a guide-manned blind boat surrounded by 10 dozen diver decoys. Another guide in a chase boat helps deploy and pick up decoys, and is the downed-duck retriever. The shooting, according to Porter, can be fast and furious when divers are migrating through the area. Only one of these hunts, accommodating a maximum of five hunters, is available per day, so call ahead and book early.

Wild Wings Guide Service

Clyde, Ohio

VITAL STATISTICS:

SPECIES: mallard, black duck, blue-bill, canvasback, redhead, goldeneye

Season: October to December

Hunting Sites: Lake Erie's Sandusky and Maumee bays and tributaries; private marshes

Accommodations: private three-bedroom condo, semi-private rooms (lodging not included in hunt rate)

Meals: guides serve breakfast in blind; other meals at local restaurants

Rates: one day for two hunters: $350; three hunters $375; four hunters $500; add $25 per hunter/day for lodging

Maximum Number of Hunters: four hunters per boat blind; up to 16 hunters per day

Gratuities: $20 to $50 per day

Preferred Payment: cash or check

Getting There: in north-central Ohio on the south shore of Lake Erie, 35 miles east of Toledo

Nearest Commercial Airport: Toledo, OH (35 miles); Cleveland, OH (55 miles)

Dogs and Facilities: due to the special nature of the hunt, guests not encouraged to bring dogs

Guides: one guide with dog per four hunters

Other Services: bird cleaning and packaging

Other Activities: released pheasant, quail, chukar shooting (extra charge); sporting clays (extra charge)

CONTACT:

Captain Kenneth S. Lewis
Wild Wings Guide Service
279 E. Cherry St.
Clyde, OH 43410
Ph: 800-392-5292 or 419-547-6961
Email: captken@wild-wings.org
Web: www.wild-wings.org/hunts

CAPTAIN KEN LEWIS is a bit of a rounder. Not *that* kind of a rounder. What I mean is that he gets all around Lake Erie during the fall, starting his hunts in Canada in September, then moving to Michigan waters (Maumee Bay), and later to Ohio's part of the lake, then to the Ohio River in December and January, and he finishes up the season with Mississippi Delta waterfowl hunts.

Lewis specializes in big water hunts. While his hunts on Canada's famed Mitchell's Bay focus on canvasback and bluebills, his Lake Erie hunts are for puddlers as well as divers. He also offers a limited number of private marsh hunts, early season teal hunts, and late season (February) goose hunts. But let's focus on Lake Erie, where he offers boat blind and layout boat hunts starting October 16 and running until December 21.

Captain Ken and his guides hunt from big boats, which are necessary for big water. The shooting day begins early. He meets his clients at 4:30, taking them with him to a boat ramp to launch his 24-foot duck boat. (Because the ducks utilize different areas as weather dictates and the season progresses, hunting sites change daily, and thus the need for mobility.) This is a big, stable craft capable of holding a guide, four hunters, a retriever, and five dozen decoys, while maintaining plenty of freeboard. It also carries a heavy-duty heater for those frosty, windy mornings when ducks fly best.

Once the boat is launched, it's load up and head out into the lake. Don't worry about the dark and navigation—Ken is a U.S. Coast Guard licensed skipper and knows these waters like his own living room. The departure at the dock is usually timed so you arrive at the hunt site 45 minutes before legal shooting time. This allows guide and guest a proper interval to set out 60 decoys in an appealing pattern, to prepare the waterproof boat blind, and position the boat.

OK, you're ready. But there's still time till first light. Now what? Twiddle your thumbs? Or . . . hey, what's that heavenly smell wafting through the blind? Could it be . . . ? Yes, it is. Potatoes O'Brien. And eggs. And sausage. Grab a hot cup of coffee off the stove while the guide finishes up a Wild Wings Guide Service tradition: hot breakfast cooked and served in the boat.

Properly fortified with carbohydrates, caffeine, and cholesterol, you're now ready to face whatever nature throws your way. If you've set up near shoreline cover, nature will probably throw mallards and black ducks your way. In other locations, depending on the timing of the migration, you may have opportunities to shoot puddlers and divers over the same decoy spread on the same day.

But if you're a died-in-the-wool diver hunter and want to focus on those birds exclusively, Wild Wings also offers layout boat shooting in open water. These special hunts over decoys require at least two hunters, but Ken and his crew can handle up to a party of four. The shooting is fast and exciting. Whole flocks of bluebills can buzz the blocks as you struggle to sit up and shoot from a low-profile layout craft that extends only inches above the water. Not for the faint of heart, perhaps, but a unique hunting experience you shouldn't miss, either.

A backwater marsh shoot for mallards is just one of several types of waterfowl hunting offered by Wild Wings Guide Service.

[M I S S I S S I P P I   F L Y W A Y]

McCormick Farms, Inc.

Vincennes, Indiana

VITAL STATISTICS:

SPECIES: mallard, black duck, pintail, Canada goose
Season: ducks: November 20 to January 11;
geese: December 4 to January 24
Hunting Sites: natural marshes and flooded fields in the Wabash and White river bottoms
Accommodations: local motels
MEALS: local restaurants
RATES: $75 per hunter/day
MAXIMUM NUMBER OF HUNTERS: eight
GRATUITIES: optional
PREFERRED PAYMENT: cash or check
Getting There: in southwestern Indiana, near Vincennes
NEAREST COMMERCIAL AIRPORT: Evansville, IN
Dogs and Facilities: guides have trained retrievers and request guests not bring their own dogs
Guides: two to four hunters per guide
Other Services: none
Other Activities: none
CONTACT:
Ray McCormick
McCormick Farms Inc.
6751 S. McCormick Rd.
Vincennes, IN 47591
Ph: 812-886-6436
Email: mccfarms@wvc.net
Web: www.wvc.net/~mccfarms

Ray McCormick is a Hoosier farmer who knows a good thing when he sees it. Four years ago, he saw the opportunity to do some additional harvesting on his property. Harvesting ducks and geese, that is. His land is located in southern Indiana's Knox County, in the heart of the White and Wabash river bottoms.

Ray's is a day-trip guiding service. He has no lodging and doesn't provide meals for his clients. Those accommodations are available at nearby motels and restaurants. You merely meet Ray and his guides at a two-story log cabin on the morning of your hunt, and they'll take over from there. The guides will transport you to your blind, do the calling, and work their own dogs on retrieves.

What kind of a blind you'll be hunting from depends on what you're after—ducks or geese—on any particular day. Ray hunts from heated pit blinds and above-ground blinds, depending on the location: flooded agricultural fields, flooded timber, or marshes.

One of Ray's hotspots is overlooked by the log cabin where you meet in the morning. Here he owns 1,000 acres below the East and West Fork of the White River. This is one of the most celebrated waterfowl areas in Indiana. It consists of hundreds of acres of natural marshes that are protected from hunting and serve as a waterfowl refuge. His pit blinds are adjacent to the refuge area, in fields of flooded corn and weeds.

Another good location he hunts is an 84-acre flooded field that's only a half mile from a 3,000-acre lake at the confluence of the White, Patoka, and Wabash rivers. The lake is a warm-water-discharge reservoir for the Gibson electric generating station, and holds the largest concentration of mallards in the state of Indiana.

Across the Wabash, in Illinois, Ray is working on developing new hunting spots. He has recently purchased 600 acres in Laurence County, 10 miles from the Indiana-Illinois state line. This new acreage will, come duck season, comprise flooded fields and pin oak timber. Also in Illinois, across the Wabash from Gibson Generating Station, he's working on developing an additional 600 acres of agricultural fields. Once his pumping equipment and pit blinds are in place here, Ray says, it will be one of the finest mallard holes in southeastern Illinois.

The goose hunting on McCormick Farms, like the duck hunting, takes place on properties scattered throughout Knox County. These are privately owned parcels exclusively hunted by Ray's clients. Currently, Indiana's daily bag limit on Canada geese is two. According to Ray, the area's best goose hunting occurs during the last two week of the Indiana South Zone Goose season, which runs from early December until January 24. The duck season here ends on January 11, so if you are looking for a duck and goose combination encounter, be sure to book accordingly.

Pothole hunters wait for another flight of mallards to descend on their marshland blind in Indiana farm country. Ducks as well as geese will be greeted with equal enthusiasm by this eager pair of waterfowlers.

[**M I S S I S S I P P I   F L Y W A Y**]

Hamilton's Resort

H o r n b e a k ,   T e n n e s s e e

TUCKED AWAY in Tennessee's northwest corner, a stone's throw from the Mississippi River and a few miles south as the crow flies from the Kentucky border, lies Reelfoot Lake. Fourteen miles long and seven miles wide, Reelfoot is an historical and cultural focus for Mississippi Flyway duck gunners, much as Mattamuskeet Lake roots hunters to Eastern waterfowling traditions.

It was at Reelfoot in the late 1880s that Victor Glodo crafted what is considered the first modern-style duck call. It is here, too, that seasoned duck guides hunt from blind sites formerly occupied by "my daddy, his daddy before him, and my great-granddaddy before all the rest of 'em."

During the 1800s and early 1900s, Reelfoot saw a flourishing commercial hunting economy. The lake's proximity to railways, unlike other great waterfowling venues in the South, and the nearby markets of St. Louis and Chicago allowed market gunners to make shipments to city meat markets and restaurants almost overnight. The area also became a favorite spot for hunters from throughout the Midwest and mid-South.

The commercial hunting of waterfowl here went the way of the buggy whip, but sport hunting traditions live on. The shallow lake has an Everglades-like atmosphere: expanses of open water here, there a maze of backwater passages flanked by cypress and tupelo gum trees and leading to backwater bays and sloughs. Most of the northern third of the lake lies within the Reelfoot Lake National Wildlife Refuge (where no hunting is allowed). The southern two-thirds is open to public hunting, where some 250 privately owned "grandfathered" blinds and an additional 40 state-controlled blinds (available each year under a permit draw system) are located.

The grandfathered blinds are owned by individual hunters and the area's legion of waterfowl guides. These are permanent blinds that have, in the case of most guides, been in their families for generations. The way it works here, the guides are affiliated with resorts bordering the lake, and the resorts, in turn, offer lodging and guided hunt packages to their guests. Your assigned guide on one particular day may be different from the one you are assigned the next day, then, depending on bookings and prior requests. But even if you are assigned a different guide each day, you'll find these folks knowledgeable, excellent duck and goose callers, and, invariably, great storytellers.

Then there's the blinds! Reelfoot Lake blinds are legends unto themselves. Some are two-story affairs. Almost all of them are roomy, heated, and contain stoves for cooking (breakfast and/or lunch, depending on the pace of the day). They may be floating affairs located in open water or staked to the bottom in a back bay. All of them will be surrounded by up to hundreds of decoys (when you get there, by the way, so there's no putting them out and picking them up).

Hamilton's is one of Reelfoot's longtime resorts, having been in business over 60 years. In addition to coordinating your waterfowl hunt and providing lodging, resort personnel can also arrange for an afternoon of fishing for the lake's burgeoning populations of crappie, bream, bass, and catfish. After all, as long as you're there, you may as well try it all.

Tennessee's Reelfoot Lake is a traditional stopover for migrating ducks and geese. Part of the lake is open water, another part a maze of cypress swamp that is reminiscent of the Florida Everglades.

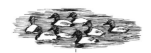

Hatchie River Outfitters

Tipton County, Tennessee

VITAL STATISTICS:

SPECIES: mallards, wood duck, pintail, gadwall, black duck, ring-necked duck, wigeon, hooded merganser
Season: December through January
Hunting Sites: private leases; one blind in flooded rice field in Arkansas, others in 103 acres of flooded timber on Hatchies River, eight miles east of Mississippi River
Accommodations: no private lodging facilities; several good motels within five miles of hunting sites
Meals: breakfast provided as part of daily hunt package; all other meals at local restaurants at hunter's expense.
Rates: $150 per person/day; $650 group rate for up to five hunters; $80 per day for hunters 15 years old or younger
Maximum Number of Hunters: up to five hunters in each of four blinds
Gratuities: guests' discretion
Preferred Payment: cash or check
Getting There: about 38 miles north of Memphis on Tennessee's Hatchie River
Nearest Commercial Airport: Memphis, TN
Dogs and Facilities: no accommodations for guests' dogs
Guides: one guide per maximum of eight hunters
Other Services: duck cleaning; $2 per bird
Other Activities: none
CONTACT:
Bert Combs, Jr.
290 Clowes Rd.
Covington, TN 38019
Ph: 901-476-5787

THE HATCHIE RIVER in west Tennessee has provided migratory habitat for waterfowl for hundreds of years. Well it should, too, as it's only a short hop to the Hatchie's flooded bottoms for ducks following the Mississippi River to wintering grounds farther to the south. Another 80 miles north of the Hatchie River bottoms is Tennessee's historic Reelfoot Lake, where tens of thousands of Mississippi Flyway ducks and geese make migratory stopovers each spring and fall. But the Hatchie harbors its own winter populations of ducks, too; everything from mallards, pintails, black ducks, and gadwalls, to wood ducks and wigeon and, for the collector looking for a mount, hooded mergansers.

Bert Combs operates three blinds on the flooded bottoms of the Hatchie and another blind site on a flooded rice field west of the Mississippi River, 11 miles southwest of Jonesboro, Arakansas. Book with Bert, in other words, and you can arrange for a real sampler of Southern-style waterfowling experiences.

For the waterfowl hunter looking for a quality hunt in comfortable blinds, this is where to find it. Combs' Hatchie River blinds are equipped with heaters, cooking stoves, and restroom facilities. One of the blinds is a massive (14-feet high; 25-foot by 20-foot shooting room with a separate 5-foot by 7-foot bathroom) two-story affair and is even equipped with a battery-operated elevator lift system to accommodate wheelchair-bound hunters. Combs, 33, whose father is disabled and whose late brother-in-law was confined to a wheelchair, built the elevator with these family members and other disabled hunters in mind. "I haven't been to a sports show over the past two years that I haven't met someone in a wheelchair," Combs says. "All of them told me they'd love to hunt more, but couldn't find the right place. I wanted to give them that right place."

On a typical day, Combs or one of his guides will meet you well before dawn and boat you into the Hatchie's maze of inundated backwaters. After an adventuresome ride through the flooded oaks and gum trees comprising the river's floodplain, you'll arrive at a massive, camouflage blind built on the edge of an opening in the trees. In front of the blind, in the "hole," the decoys will already be set. Inside the blind, the heater will be on in short order, so you can shoot in shirtsleeves, even on those bone-chilling days of December and January.

During a lull in the early-morning action, if there is a lull, your guide will hold off on his calling and retrieving duties long enough to fire up the cook stove and provide you and your hunting partners with a hot, down home country breakfast.

You may only be partially finished with the biscuits and gravy course of your morning meal, though, when you have to drop your fork and pick up your shotgun again. And there's no telling what the next duck to drop in for breakfast will be: mallard, pintail, black duck?

Banded Duck Hunt Club

Stuttgart, Arkansas

VITAL STATISTICS:

SPECIES: mallard, pintail, wood duck

Season: mid-November to mid-January

Hunting Sites: flooded rice fields and green timber, Bayou Meto Wildlife Management Area

Accommodations: private lodge, four bedrooms, two baths

MEALS: Southern-style cuisine

RATES: $250 per hunter/day package covers lodging, meals, guided hunt

MAXIMUM NUMBER OF HUNTERS: eight

GRATUITIES: $30-$50 per hunter/day

PREFERRED PAYMENT: cash, check, or credit card

Getting There: 20 miles south of Stuttgart, AR

NEAREST COMMERCIAL AIRPORT: Little Rock, AR

Dogs and Facilities: kennel provided for hunters' dogs

Guides: one guide for four hunters (field shoots); three guides per eight hunters (flooded timber)

Other Services: can arrange for bird processing

Other Activities: afternoon goose hunts; sporting clays; released pheasants and quail; crappie fishing

CONTACT:
James Nelson
Banded Duck Hunting Club
3204 Happy Valley Dr.
Little Rock, AR 72212
Ph: 501-225-9507
Web: www.bandedduck.com

ARKANSAS' BAYOU METO is one of the most famous green timber hunting spots on the continent. It is also huge, covering thousands of acres of sloughs, draws, ditches, and openings in expansive stands of timber that are flooded each fall. Even local hunters occasionally get lost in this maze, which is why, as a visiting waterfowler, you'll definitely need the services of a guide.

Banded Duck Hunt Club can supply the guides as well as lodging and meals. Bayou Meto is one of the club's guides' prime hunting areas. Even though Bayou Meto is open to public hunting, there is plenty of room for an army of hunters, and even with the gunning pressure it receives it provides some of the finest, most productive timber hunting in the world. The ducks are mostly mallards and gadwalls, but you'll have a good chance at bagging pintail, green-winged teal, and woodies.

On a typical day, you'll be motoring into the timber with your guide or guides well before dawn. This could be a boat ride of about three miles. When you reach the chosen spot, which will be an opening in the timber, you'll deploy the decoys there, where passing ducks can see them while flying overhead. Then you'll find a tree to stand beside, which is also your hiding spot. If you have your retriever along, the guides will set up a dog stand so it won't have to stand in the water (you will, but you'll be wearing waders).

As the opening minute approaches, the guides will begin calling, and if you've never heard an Arkansas guide highballing to passing birds, you're in for a real treat. Listening to the expert calling and watching ducks parachuting down through the timber—some may land only a few feet from where you're standing—is an experience every duck hunter should experience at least once in his or her lifetime. As soon as legal shooting time begins and the guide yells "Take 'em," you hear your own shots and those of other hunters in Bayo Meto echo and roll like thunder through the drowned forest.

Hunting in Bayo Meto is only allowed until noon, but you may be limited out and motoring back to the landing well before that. If so, you'll be headed back to the lodge for a big breakast (or lunch, depending on the hour of day) to supplement the coffee, sweet rolls, and biscuit and sausage wakerupper you wolfed down after getting up that morning.

In the afternoon, you have a variety of opportunities. If you've not filled your duck limit, you can spend the afternoon in a rice field pit blind, or the guides can set you up in a field where you can hunt snow and white-fronted geese, which inundate the Stuttgart area each fall and winter. Had enough waterfowling for the day? Upland hunting for released quail or pheasants can be arranged.

In any case, there's plenty to do before Miss Dolly has one of her Southern-style dinners (fried green beans is a signature dish) ready back at the lodge. After that, the bar is open and it will be time to chat with your fellow hunters about all the great shots you made. If you have no braggin' rights that day, you can just listen, watch a duck hunting video, or go to bed.

A giant Canada goose is a tough bird to bring down. The best steel shot load for these huge geese is T size shot fired from a 3½-inch 12-gauge.

Black Dog Hunting Club

Stuttgart, Arkansas

VITAL STATISTICS:

SPECIES: mallard, pintail, teal

Season: mid-November through January

Hunting Sites: acres of reservoirs, flooded rice and soybean fields, sloughs, and cypress breaks

Accommodations: clubhouse with separate guest rooms, daily cleaning service

MEALS: "We take pride in our outstanding home-cooked meals."

RATES: $250 per man/day, includes lodging, meal, and morning hunt; afternoon hunts $75 extra

MAXIMUM NUMBER OF HUNTERS: 16-20

GRATUITIES: $25 per hunter/day

PREFERRED PAYMENT: cash, check, or major credit card

Getting There: 15 miles south of Stuttgart, AR

NEAREST COMMERCIAL AIRPORT: Little Rock, AR

Dogs and Facilities: Dogs are welcome; guests should bring own kennels

Guides: one guide per four to five hunters

Other Services: bird cleaning; taxidermy services

Other Activities: fishing

CONTACT:
Black Dog Hunting Club
P.O. Box 697
Stuttgart, AR 72160
Ph: 870-873-4673 or
1-877-MALLARD

WATERFOWLING is huge in Arkansas, especially around Stuttgart, which is known far and wide as The Duck Hunting Capital of the World. The thousands of hunters descending upon the area are outnumbered only by the hundreds of thousands of ducks and geese on their annual migratory flights. Needless to say, things can get a bit crowded—not only in town or in the few public hunting areas nearby, but even in the many commercial hunting outfits throughout the region.

If you like to share in the big festive atmosphere of waterfowl season but like your hunts to be small and personalized, you'll find just what you're looking for at Black Dog Hunting Club. Located just 15 miles south of Stuttgart, the club seems a world away from the maddening crowds you'll find at some of the other establishments. Family owned and operated since 1986, Black Dog prides itself on its down-home, personalized service. It's a great place to take your family or a small group of close friends.

The club features four guest rooms that sleep up to four hunters per room. The clubhouse is a separate facility, so that guests can be assured of their privacy and quiet time. Though small and quaint, Black Dog is big on Southern hospitality. Owners Todd and Gwen Brittain make sure of that. "We take pride in our outstanding home-cooked meals," says Gwen, who lists steak, seafood, and barbecue as just a sampling of the fare that puts them a notch above many of the other lodges. Meals are served three times a day, and there's an open bar in the clubhouse for afternoon and evening refreshments. There's even daily maid service for your room at no extra charge.

Hunting parties are also small, never more than five hunters per guide. This provides more enjoyable hunting for everyone, and assures you'll get the same hands-on service in the field that you get back at camp. Todd is the top guide and organizes all the hunts, and all of the other guides are professional, knowledgeable, and experienced.

Todd says there's one priority no one at Black Dog ever forgets when it comes to duck hunting. "First and foremost, we hunt mallards in green timber," he says. "If the birds are in the timber, so are we. This is the ultimate waterfowl experience. Nothing else even comes close."

If the ducks aren't likely to be in the timber, you might head out to a flooded rice or soybean field to hunt mallards, pintails, teal, snow geese or specklebellies from a pit, sled blind, or lay-out. All of the fields are well managed and maintained to provide optimal hunting conditions. Moreover, Todd and the rest of the guides work hard in scouting and preparation to put you where the birds are.

"We never have a day when you don't have an option to shoot some ducks and work your dog," says Todd. We shoot ducks of some kind every day, regardless of weather—except, of course, electrical storms. Otherwise, no excuses—just ducks!"

The sign on the highway coming in to Stuttgart says it all: "RICE AND DUCK CAPITAL OF THE WORLD." And folks in these parts are proud of it.

[M I S S I S S I P P I   F L Y W A Y]

Grand Lake Lodge

E u d o r a ,   A r k a n s a s

VITAL STATISTICS:

SPECIES: mallard, pintail, wigeon, gadwall, Canada goose, snow goose, white-fronted goose

Season: mid-November through mid-January

Hunting Sites: 4,000 private acres, primarily rice fields but also some flooded timber

Accommodations: private lodge, four hunters per bedroom; game room, Jacuzzi, bar

MEALS: lodge has fully staffed kitchen, Southern-style meals

RATES: $250 per hunter/day

MAXIMUM NUMBER OF HUNTERS: 10

GRATUITIES: $40 per day, includes two guides per party; $5 additional for each of two cooks per day

PREFERRED PAYMENT: cash or check

Getting There: near Eudora, in southeast corner of Arkansas

NEAREST COMMERCIAL AIRPORT: Monroe, LA, or Greenville, MS

Dogs and Facilities: no facilities for guests' dogs

Guides: two experienced guides per party of four hunters; all guides have trained retrievers

Other Services: bird cleaning and packaging

Other Activities: dove hunting; early-season teal hunting; fishing

CONTACT:
Omar Driskill
Grand Lake Lodge
602 Grand Lake Loop
Eudora, AR 71640
Ph: 870-355-4868

OMAR DRISKILL. Name sound familiar? If you're a retriever trainer, amateur or professional, you may know Driskill as a nationally recognized professional dog trainer and a founder of the National Hunting Retriever Club, Inc. When he's not training retrievers, Driskill manages Grand Lake Lodge, smack dab in the southeast corner of Arkansas. Grand Lake Lodge is a year-round hunting and fishing retreat for 10 club members, but during duck season it opens its doors to other hunters, accommodating 10 nonmembers per day.

Next to the lodge is Grand Lake, 2,700 acres of flooded cypress that act as a duck magnet for birds funneling down the Mississippi Flyway. The big river itself is only a short distance east of the lake. Driskill and his staff of experienced guides maintain three floating blinds on the lake and also hunt three miles of Mississippi River frontage with big boat rigs. The river backwaters hold huge numbers of greenheads, and, later in the season, the river sandbars act as loafing sites for big Canada geese.

The lodge maintains more than 4,000 acres, including the lake and river frontage. The property is encircled by private and national wildlife refuges, making this a hotspot for both wintering and migrating waterfowl. In addition to the lake and river hunting sites, Driskill leases another 2,000 acres of rice fields only 20 minutes from the lodge. The fields have a total of six pit blinds, all 16 feet long with dog boxes, that will each comfortably accommodate five or six people. Surrounding each pit are more than 250 decoys.

Most of the hunting at Grand Lake Lodge is done from the rice field pit blinds, where mallards, pintails, and specklebellies are regular visitors. When large numbers of snow geese are migrating through the area, the guides will lay out a large spread of white decoys, attracting snows, blues, and specklebellies. In late January and February, the guides will also take you to the river sandbars to set up for giant Canada geese.

Wake-up calls at Grand Lake Lodge come early. A full breakfast at 5 a.m. will carry you through to lunch. It's just a short trip to the rice fields, where lodge guides will transport you to your pit blind on a four-wheeler ATV. Hip boots will be all you need to keep your feet dry. Step into the blind and get comfy. You'll have two guides, both of whom are excellent duck and goose callers, with your hunting party, so all you have to do is shoot and reload. All of the guides here have their own retrievers, which are hunting retriever champions, so you'll have the chance of watching some excellent dog work, too.

Hunting lasts until your party limits out or until 1 p.m., whichever comes first. Then it's back to the lodge for lunch. In the afternoon, if time permits, dove or snow goose hunting are options, as is fishing for perch, bass, and catfish on Grand Lake. After that, return to the lodge for a drink and a game of pool before a Southern-style dinner is served at 6 p.m.

[**M I S S I S S I P P I   F L Y W A Y**]

Kenneth McCollum Duck Club

Stuttgart,   Arkansas

VITAL STATISTICS:

SPECIES: mallard, teal, wood duck, gadwall, wigeon

Season: mid-November through mid-January

Hunting Sites: 1,200 acres of privately owned, flooded green timber

Accommodations: two lodges with rooms accommodate from two to 14 hunters

MEALS: home cooked, three meals daily

RATES: $250 per hunter/day, includes guided hunt, lodging and meals

MAXIMUM NUMBER OF HUNTERS: 43

GRATUITIES: 10 to 20 percent

PREFERRED PAYMENT: check

Getting There: 10 miles west of Stuttgart, AR

NEAREST COMMERCIAL AIRPORT: Little Rock, AR

Dogs and Facilities: no facilities, call for more information

Guides: four or five hunters per guide

Other Services: none

Other Activities: released quail; sporting clays (available nearby; extra charge)

CONTACT:
Bud McCollum
McCollum Duck Club
1821 McCracken
Stuttgart, AR 72160
Ph: 870-830-1110 or 870-673-1392

A SHORT DRIVE west of Stuttgart, Arkansas, the "Rice and Duck Hunting Capitol of the World," and next to the famous Bayou Meto duck hole, lies Kenneth "Slick" McCollum's Duck Club. If not the oldest commercial hunting service in the Stuttgart area, the club, in operation for more than 50 years, ranks right up there with the most legendary. On any particular day during the duck season, you might meet here three generations of waterfowlers hunting from the same blind. Chances are that grandpa may have experienced his first duck hunt here with his own father.

Bud McCollum runs the place today, and many of his customers are as familiar to him as an old hunting coat. They keep coming back year after year. That's because, besides Bud's southern hospitality, the club provides consistent hunting, some of the best to be had in this part of Arkansas' "duck heaven."

Bud keeps his clients and ducks coming annually because he owns one of the hottest waterfowl holes this side of Bayou Meto. The bayou itself, when it swells with river overflows each fall, is a natural refuge for hundreds of thousands of ducks, mostly mallards. Some years, though, when the rains don't come, the bayou remains dry. When that happens, there's little green timber hunting—the type for which the Stuttgart area is famous—to be had. But the birds will always gravitate to Bud's place, because there is always water there. He has diked the entire 1,200 acres and, every year, pumps water into it well ahead of the duck season. Inside that block of flooded timber are 10 large openings, or "shooting holes," that draw ducks like magnets.

Duck hunting in Arkansas is a social affair, and so is a stay at one of McCollum's lodges. The place will be packed with hunters and their gear. Come dinner time, they'll be seated around a big table like lumberjacks in a logging camp. The cooks will be carrying small mountains of food to place on the table, and the hungry hunters will be stuffing it in like it was their last meal. Ask for the platter of pork chops to be passed and you may, when it finally gets to you, hand it back to the kitchen for a refill.

You won't go hungry at breakfast, either, unless you sleep through it. Wake-up is early, so get dressed, get fed, and get in the boat. You and the rest of your hunting party will soon be hearing the outboard motor fired up by your guide, who will drive you through what look like impenetrable woods, to your shooting hole. When you get there, you'll find a comfortable, well camouflaged blind. The decoys will already be set. Look up through the hole in the roof of trees. Mallards, silhouetted in the lightening dawn sky, are already passing overhead.

"It's time," your guide says, "but don't shoot until I say so." You load up, and he starts calling. Soon, ducks are landing in the decoys only feet away from you. Many more mallards are spiraling down to the guide's beguiling greeting call. They keep coming and coming. And that's why McCollum's hunters keep returning, too.

Hunting flooded timber is a unique experience, except in Arkansas, where many waterfowlers consider it the only way to hunt ducks.

Pintail Peninsula

S t u t t g a r t ,   A r k a n s a s

VITAL STATISTICS:

SPECIES: mallard, pintail, gadwall, teal, wood duck, wigeon, snow goose, white-fronted goose

Season: ducks: November through January; geese: November through March 1

Hunting Sites: 4,000 acres of private fields and sloughs; 34,000 acres of public green-timber hunting

Accommodations: modern 13,750 square-foot lodge with 14 double occupancy bedrooms and two private bedrooms, all with private baths; spacious great room; bar

Meals: family-style country cooking

Rates: $450 per hunter/day, all inclusive (call for corporate rates)

Maximum Number of Hunters: 32

Gratuities: $25 to $50 per day per guest (suggested)

Preferred Payment: credit card, cash or check

Getting There: 15 miles southwest of Stuttgart, AR

Nearest Commercial Airport: Little Rock, AR

Dogs and Facilities: ten 4' x 10' outside kennel runs with barrel houses for guests' dogs

Guides: one guide for each party of four hunters

Other Services: bird cleaning; airport transportation

Other Activities: automated five-stand sporting clays range; 12-station sporting clays range; professional shooting instructor

CONTACT:

Scott Drummond
Pintail Peninsula Inc.
PO Box 460
Stuttgart, AR 72160
Ph: 888-486-8275
Fax: 870-873-0112
Email: scott@huntark.com
Web: www.huntark.com

IN A DECEMBER 1999 article in *The Wall Street Journal*, correspondent James Sterra, reporting on the great duck hunting opportunities in the Stuttgart area, paid Scott Drummond both a tribute and a left-handed compliment. He described Drummond's new $1.2 million Pintail Peninsula Lodge as a "Taj Mahal of duck hunting." And, he said, "Many locals think he's loco."

Which is to say that Stuttgart, the "rice and duck capital of the world," may be rich in waterfowl, but it's in an economically poor region in a relatively poor state, where million dollar duck lodges may seem out of the ordinary. But Drummond, whose family has been in the commercial hunting business for more than 25 years, is no ordinary fellow. He knows there's a new breed of duck hunter that is looking for comfortable accommodations (without having to sleep in a bunk room with a half dozen of his cohorts), excellent hunting opportunities, and personal service. His attitude before developing the lodge? *Build it and they will come.* Maybe many locals did think he was loco, but since opening its doors in 1997, the lodge has seen near maximum guest capacity.

The lodge is located on 280 acres of prime hunting property nestled between a pecan orchard and the bank of Big Bayou Meto, near the 34,000-acre Bayou Meto Wildlife Management Area. Bayo Meto is best known for its green timber hunting and more importantly for providing refuge for large numbers of ducks on nearly 14,000 acres of flooded green timber. Lodge guides take guests to hunt in the public hunting areas of Bayo Meto as well as the nearby White River Wildlife Management Area, which also has areas open to public hunting.

Both public areas are expansive and, despite the public access, can provide excellent hunting. Pintail Peninsula also offers its guests hunting on 4,000 acres of its private property that is specifically managed for waterfowl. The private acreage includes flooded food plots, harvested fields, and newly planted wheat fields. Says Drummond, "The fields we will be hunting in are prepared for your hunt with the necessary equipment, from the blind to the decoys. Our hunting parties consist of four hunters and a guide. We hunt over various decoy spreads, from large to small, depending on the way the ducks are acting and what set-ups they're most responsive to. Ducks change with the weather, and we're prepared to do the same. We hunt in pits, above-ground blinds, coffin blinds, or standing in flooded timber. In other words, to make your hunt the best that it can be, we go where the ducks are."

Besides ducks, the Stuttgart area is known for wintering amazing numbers of snow and white-fronted geese. During a stay at Pintail Peninsula, you may have the opportunity to harvest either or both. "Our goose hunting is very similar to our duck hunting," Drummond says, "and you may even have the occasional opportunity to shoot geese during your duck hunt. We hunt geese in many of the same fields as our duck hunts, but often have to move to set up where the best opportunity for geese may be. We utilize our coffin blinds to allow us to become hidden in fields that geese are using at any given time."

Great lodge, great hunting. All in all, Drummond doesn't sound so loco after all.

Transportation to and from flooded rice field pit blinds can take on a variety of forms, from shank's mare to 4x4 ATV to swamp buggies and tractor-powered limousines.

[**M I S S I S S I P P I   F L Y W A Y**]

Wild Wings Hunting Club

S t u t t g a r t ,   A r k a n s a s

VITAL STATISTICS:

SPECIES: mallard, gadwall, wood duck, teal

Season: mid-November through late January

Hunting Sites: 1,275 acres—600 flooded timber, 500 flooded marshland

Accommodations: modern lodge, 6,000 square feet, seven spacious bedrooms, dining room, den, bar with satellite TV

MEALS: home-cooked meals

RATES: $300 per hunter, includes overnight stay, meals; $150 per hunter/morning hunt; $120 afternoon hunt

MAXIMUM NUMBER OF HUNTERS: 30

GRATUITIES: hunters' discretion

PREFERRED PAYMENT: cash, check, Visa, or MasterCard

Getting There: five miles southwest of Stuttgart on Highway 79. Turn on Crosby Lane at Wild Wings sign.

NEAREST COMMERCIAL AIRPORT: Little Rock, AR

Dogs and Facilities: dogs welcome; each room has outside door so dog's box can be nearby; kennel runs available

Guides: guides and dogs provided, three to six hunters per guide

Other Services: bird cleaning free for overnight guests

Other Activities: deer, dove, and squirrel hunting for additional fee

CONTACT:
Carlton or Elsie Crosby
1903 Coker-Hampton Dr.
Stuttgart, AR 72160
Ph: 870-673-7604 (home) or
870-673-7813 (lodge)

I F YOU'VE NEVER experienced classic flooded timber hunting in Arkansas, you've been missing out on one of waterfowling's greatest treats. So why deny yourself any longer? The Natural State is centrally located, easy to get to, and the price of hiring an outfitter is truly a bargain when compared to similar services in other parts of the country. And, oh, the ducks! The ducks! The ducks! Few places offer such a glut of flying mallards, teal, wood ducks, gadwall, and other wildfowl.

If you're still not convinced, take Wild Wings Hunting Club as a case in point. Located just 5 miles southwest of Stuttgart, Wild Wings is less than an hour's drive from Little Rock and only about an hour and a half from Memphis. The 6,000-square-foot lodge offers seven spacious bedrooms that can accommodate three to six hunters. An overnight stay includes continental breakfast, a hearty lunch, and a full home-cooked supper. Tea, coffee, and snacks are available throughout the day.

A full hunting package, which includes all of the above and a guided morning hunt, is only $300 per hunter per day. Guided morning and afternoon hunts are offered sans lodging and meals for $150 and $120, respectively. Group and corporate rates are available as well.

What you get could very well be the best waterfowling of your life. You'll head out at 6 a.m. by boat or ATV to a select location on over 600 acres of flooded timber. Your guide will position you and your hunting party to ensure the safest and most productive shooting. You'll stand behind a tree waist-deep in water, waiting for the dawn to bring the first flight birds into the decoys.

A faint light, and the ducks start dropping in like apparitions. Speedy green-winged teal and fast-falling wood ducks. You wait until the guide signals that it's okay to shoot. Meanwhile, the birds are raining down in such profusion that it's a thrill just to watch them. "Take 'em," shouts your guide when it's light enough. Boom! Boom! Boom! Boom! The silence of the morning is shattered by the sudden tumult of the shotguns.

When the world comes back into focus there are a lot of dead birds on the water, but little time to retrieve them as a group of mallards circles overhead. "Stay still," the guide warns, "hug those trees." He blows excitedly and kicks the water with his feet, then falls into a steady cadence as the ducks swing around again and drop suddenly through the cypress. If you've seen anything more spectacular in waterfowling, you can't remember what it was.

Wildlife Farms

Casscoe, Arkansas

VITAL STATISTICS:

SPECIES: mallard, teal, wood duck, gadwall, pintail, wigeon

Season: mid-November to late January

Hunting Sites: 1,750 private acres; five miles of White River frontage, milo fields

Accommodations: private, modern lodge; nine rooms, bar, game room, lounge, hot tub, pool table, large-screen television

MEALS: steak, shrimp, lobster, prime rib entrees

RATES: $400 per hunter/day, includes guides, heated blind, lodging and meals

MAXIMUM NUMBER OF HUNTERS: 34

GRATUITIES: 15% or more, hunters' discretion

PREFERRED PAYMENT: cash, check, credit card

Getting There: on the White River, 14 miles east of Stuttgart, AR

NEAREST COMMERCIAL AIRPORT: Little Rock, AR

Dogs and Facilities: outside kennels

Guides: two guides per blind; four to eight hunters per blind

Other Services: bird processing; airport transportation

Other Activities: goose hunting; chukar, pheasant, and Hungarian partridge hunting; five-stand sporting clays; bird-watching; hiking; fishing; white-tailed deer hunting

CONTACT:
Laura Weatherford
Wildlife Farms Inc.
PO Box 593
Casscoe, AR 72026
Ph: 870-241-3275
Fax: 870-241-9012
Email: wildlife@futura.net
Web: www.wildlifefarms.com

WILDLIFE FARMS is a true sportsman's paradise nestled among 1,706 acres of natural beauty on the White River. The lodge has exclusive hunting rights on an additional 42,000 acres of private farm and timber lands. Acres of habitat for deer, turkey, ducks, geese, Hungarian partridge, chukar, and pheasant also include lakes specially stocked with catfish, bass, crappie, and bream, offering a variety of hunting and fishing opportunities.

The elegant 10,000-square-foot lodge is located near Stuttgart, home to the World Championship Duck Calling Contest and to hundreds of thousands of wintering ducks. It's no wonder, then, that hunters say this area has the best duck hunting in the world. A stay at Wildlife Farms not only exposes you to some of the best duck hunting you can imagine, it will let you do it in comfort and style.

Most of the waterfowl hunting here takes place in flooded timber in backwaters of the White River. Other shooting venues include flooded milo fields and small lakes. But flooded timber hunting is the true allure of the country around Stuttgart, and it is to flooded timber where your guide will most likely take you after an early morning breakfast at the lodge.

After a short boat ride to a floating blind, you'll find yourself in cozy comfort. It will be chilly before sunrise, but all of Wildlife Farms' blinds are heated, so not to worry. When the ducks start flying, the guides will call them in and tell you when to shoot. An hour or two of this can make you hungry. No problem. About midmorning, one of your guides will begin preparing the lodge's famous "duck blind sandwiches," consisting of hot eggs, ham, and cheese, which you can wash down with hot chocolate or coffee. Still hungry? The guides will also serve sweet rolls and other snacks when they're not busy calling at circling birds and retrieving downed ducks. But don't eat too much. There will be a hot lunch served at the lodge at noon.

After lunch, there will be plenty to keep you busy. Wildlife Farms offers upland hunting for planted chukar, pheasant, and Hungarian partridge. Fishing is available on the private lakes. There's five-stand sporting clays to be shot. Guided hunts are available for trophy whitetail bucks. Or take a stroll on the hiking paths and do some bird-watching. If it's Thanksgiving weekend, you can drive to Stuttgart and enjoy the annual Wings Over the Prairie

Festival, featuring duck-calling competitions, beauty contests (Miss Mallard is always a beautiful southern belle), chili cook-offs, and lots of waterfowl gear at manufacturers' exhibits. For those inclined to stay indoors, the lodge has pool tables, gaming tables, and large-screen televisions. Still too much effort? Unwind in front of the lodge's massive stone fireplace or plunk yourself in a steaming hot tub. After all, you've had a pretty tough day. It's a good thing that lodge employees are cleaning and packaging your ducks for you, too. You're worn out.

Beartail Outfitters, LLC

Coldwater, Mississippi

VITAL STATISTICS:

SPECIES: Canada goose, snow goose, white-fronted goose, mallard, pintail, scaup, teal, wigeon, wood duck, gadwall, bluebill

Season: end of November through January

Hunting Sites: 500 acres of flooded corn and milo fields next to the Tallahatchie Wildlife Refuge; 200 acres of flooded corn and milo on the Coldwater River; 50,000 acres of public flooded dead timber and cypress in the Arkabutla flood plain.

Accommodations: private lodge with 16 rooms, two hunters per room; two bunk rooms sleep 6 hunters each

MEALS: steaks and Southern cooking

RATES: $300/day

MAXIMUM NUMBER OF HUNTERS: 32

GRATUITIES: typically 30% of total

PREFERRED PAYMENT: cash, check, or credit card

Getting There: Lodge is 30 miles south of Memphis on the Coldwater River at Coldwater, Mississippi, east of I-55

NEAREST COMMERCIAL AIRPORT: Memphis, TN

Dogs and Facilities: guest dogs welcome; covered outside kennels

Guides: one guide per four hunters; two to eight hunters per blind

Other Services: bird cleaning and packing

Other Activities: sporting clays; gaming at Grand Casino

CONTACT:
Rick French or Gag Coleman
Beartail Outfitters, LLC
5170 Sanderlin, Suite 201
Memphis, TN 38117
Ph: 877-PINTAIL or 601-233-2327
Fax: 901-763-2994
Email: raycoleman@earthlink.net
Web: www.beartailoutfitters.com

SOME 10 YEARS AGO Rick French was looking for land on which to raise cattle. But when he visited 200 acres of land in Coldwater, Mississippi, he knew just what he wanted to do with it, and it didn't have anything to do with beef on the hoof.

"There seemed to be about 10,000 ducks that got up when we drove around," French said. Since then, French has cleared 150 of the 200 acres, leaving 50 in standing timber. He has also built levees, planted crops to flood, and erected a 6,000-square-foot lodge with all the amenities. Operating under the name Beartail Outfitters, the lodge can house up to 32 hunters in two-person rooms and two bunkhouses that sleep six per room. Guests dine on fine steaks and good Southern cooking.

But the main draw at Beartail is ducks and geese, lots of them. "We kill ducks, not time," is the motto of the lodge, and a long string of satisfied guests can attest to the truth of the proposition. Beartail is just 30 miles south of Memphis, Tennessee, on the Coldwater River. Fifteen miles to the west is the Mississippi River, the main artery of the Mississippi Flyway. Beartail Outfitters also has 280 acres near the Tallahatchie National Wildlife Refuge, in the northern portion of the Delta and about a one-hour drive from the lodge. As a further assurance of a steady supply of shooting, nearby there are 50,000 acres of public flooded timber in the Arkabutla floodplain.

Beartail also prides itself on its duck hunting guides, now numbering seven. Together they have some 140 years of experience. Some of the guides start out the season guiding in Canada and South Dakota in September and October and work for Beartail Outfitters in November through January.

The morning of your hunt you'll be driven to the main blind—a double-decker with 504 square feet of room. It is 42 feet long and has heated rooms and a kitchen, with lights, powered by a generator. The big blind can handle 14 gunners. Some 800 decoys surround the blind. From this cozy vantage point you will see ducks of all types—mallards, pintails, scaup, teal, wigeon, wood ducks, gadwalls, and bluebills, plus Canadas, whitefronts, and snows. Other blinds and pits are available elsewhere on the hunting grounds.

"My hardest selling point is reassuring hunters that they will get birds on my place no matter when they come," French says. "I will put you on birds," he adds. "But it's up to you to kill 'em."

Calcasieu Charter Service

L a k e   C h a r l e s ,   L o u i s i a n a

VITAL STATISTICS:

SPECIES: Canada goose, snow (blue and white phase) goose, white-fronted goose; variety of puddle ducks

Season: ducks: November through January; geese: November through February

Hunting Sites: 6,000 acres of leased rice fields

Accommodations: private lodge, five bedrooms (four guests/bedroom), large living area, kitchen, deck

Meals: Cajun-style gumbos, ettoufee, wild game and fish dishes

Rates: $250 per hunter/day includes three meals, lodging, guided hunt; $350 includes guided morning hunt plus afternoon saltwater fishing

Maximum Number of Hunters: 20

Gratuities: $15 to $30 per hunter/day suggested

Preferred Payment: cash, check

Getting There: southwest Louisiana on the east shore of Calcasieu Lake, 18 miles south of Lake Charles, LA

Nearest Commercial Airport: Lake Charles, LA

Dogs and Facilities: guides provide dogs, but will accommodate guests' dogs

Guides: up to three hunters per guide

Other Services: bird cleaning and packaging

Other Activities: afternoon hunts for released quail, pheasants; saltwater fishing

CONTACT:

Captain Erik Rue
Calcasieu Charter Service
210 Bank St.
Lake Chareles, LA 70607
Ph: 337-598-4700
Fax: 337-474-9832
Email: erue@sprynet.com
Web: www.gcaa.com/calcasieucharters

The Cajuns have a saying (actually, the Cajuns have lots of sayings, but this one is particularly poignant) that goes: *If you ain't huntin' or fishin', you ain't doin' nothin'*. If you ain't doing nothin', Eric Rue can take care of that problem. He'll take you huntin' or fishin' and will even guide you to waterfowl in the morning and redfish and speckled trout later in the same day.

Rue's operations are headquartered in Lake Charles at his 2,500-square-foot lodge located adjacent to Herbert's Marina on Calcasieu Lake. On hunt mornings, it's only a 30-minute ride from the comfortable lodge to soybean and rice fields Rue has leased for the exclusive use of his guests. There's 6,000 acres to hunt here, so there's plenty of room to spread out. The fields are adjacent to the Lacassine National Wildlife Refuge, which winters hundreds of thousands of waterfowl, and you can expect plenty of bird action after your guide drives you to your pit blind on his ATV. He'll probably have a trained retriever with him, too, and you can expect him to be an expert caller.

There will be a variety of waterfowl for your guide to call: mallard, teal, pintail, and wigeon, among other ducks, as well as Canada geese, snows, blues, and specklebellies. Any of these can drop into the decoy spread at any minute, so be ready for a memorable experience. Because your next shot can be at ducks or geese, be ready with the right loads in your shotgun, too. Rue recommends only 12-gauge shotguns stuffed with 2¾-, 3-, or 3½-inch magnum loads. Nontoxic shot is required here, as elsewhere in the U.S., so if you are shooting steel shot, a No. 1 or 2 shot size is a good all-around load for decoying ducks and geese.

Your waterfowl hunt will last until about lunch time, shortly before which your guide will take you back to the lodge for cleanup and a Cajun lunch specialty. Your birds will be taken to a local processor for you, allowing you to get on with afternoon activities.

Afternoons are what you want to make of them. Take a nap. Read a book. (In which case, according to Cajun wisdom, you'll be doin' nothin'.) Or grab your shotgun—Rue can arrange for skeet shooting or released quail, pheasant, or chukar hunting at a local private game preserve. Better yet, an afternoon of saltwater fishing is a great way to cap off a morning of duck and goose hunting. Fall and early winter speckled trout and redfish fishing on Calcasieu Lake is second to none.

Giles Island Hunting Club

F e r r i d a y ,   L o u i s i a n a

VITAL STATISTICS:

SPECIES: mallard, gadwall, wood duck, teal

Season: December through January

Hunting Sites: 9,400 acres of private bottomland

Accommodations: five private log cabins

MEALS: Southern-style

RATES: three-day minimum package is $900, including lodging and meals; guide $50/day extra

MAXIMUM NUMBER OF HUNTERS: 12

GRATUITIES: $100/day (suggested)

PREFERRED PAYMENT: cash, check, MasterCard, Visa

Getting There: west bank of the Mississippi River, a fifteen-minute drive from Natchez, Mississippi

NEAREST COMMERCIAL AIRPORT: Baton Rouge, LA

Dogs and Facilities: dogs welcome; outdoor kennel runs

Guides: one guide per four hunters

Other Services: maid service; bird processing and packaging

Other Activities: deer, dove, squirrel, turkey hunting; fishing; horseback riding; sightseeing

CONTACT:

Jimmy Riley
Giles Island Hunting Club
449 Old River Boat Camp Rd.
Ferriday, LA 71334
Ph: 601-431-1412 or 601-431-2002

Seclusion and variety are two things you'll find at Giles Island Hunting Club. Seclusion: Access to the club, surrounded by hardwood forest bottomland, is by ferry service (only a five-minute ride) across an oxbow lake known as Old River. Formerly a working plantation and once attached to mainland Louisiana, the island was formed in 1933 when the U.S. Army Corps of Engineers dredged what is known as the Giles Cutoff, creating a wilderness paradise called Giles Island in the process.

Now privately owned, the island is the site of Giles Island Hunting Club, comprising five log-cabin-style lodges that are air-conditioned and heated, providing queen-size beds and bunkbeds, full baths, and offering guests three sumptuous Southern-style meals each day. Variety: The club manages its land for trophy white-tailed deer. Wild turkeys are also scattered throughout the woods. And the club's main lake, ponds, and flooded timber are magnets for ducks.

Mallard, teal, gadwall, and wood duck gather by the thousands here—just a stone's throw from the main channel of the mighty Mississippi—and club guides can accommodate you with hunting from blinds, jump-shooting, or pass-shooting. Waterfowl hunting is allowed in the morning only at Giles Island, but many visitors opt to fill their afternoons with dove hunting. Fishing on any of the island's eight lakes is another option. Bass up to seven pounds, white perch to three pounds, bream, and catfish are all waiting for you to bait a hook.

But if you'd rather look for a trophy whitetail to bring home, you've come to the right place. The club places a minimum size (eight-pointers only with at least a minimum 16-inch spread) on bucks, but allows does to be harvested at a rate of one per person per day until their management quota is met. Big deer are common here. In addition to the natural vegetation, the club provides supplemental protein in the form of soybeans, protein pellets, minerals, and food plots. The food plots range in size from one-quarter acre to 12 acres and are used by deer and turkey during winter and summer seasons.

If deer hunting doesn't interest you, though, there is plenty to see in the general vicinity. The historic city of Natchez, Mississippi, and its many restored antebellum homes is just a short drive from Giles Island. Just up the pike from Natchez is Vicksburg, site of the famous Civil War siege and home of the Vicksburg National Battlefield and Monument. If you are a Civil War buff or only generally interested in history, the battlefield tour will be an unforgettable experience. But don't plan on taking only a day-trip to appreciate the whole tour or you'll miss too much (the partly restored Confederate ironclad recovered from the bottom of the river is a must-see). An overnighter is highly recommended, and there's legal riverboat gambling available in both Vicksburg and Natchez if you're feeling lucky and have left-over dollars burning a hole in your pocket.

The flooded swamplands of Louisiana are magnets to a variety of species of waterfowl in fall and winter. Transportation here is often in the form of Go-Devil outboard motors mounted on johnboats.

Grosse Savanne Lodge

L a k e   C h a r l e s ,   L o u i s i a n a

VITAL STATISTICS:

SPECIES: mallard, pintail, gadwall, teal, snow goose, white-fronted goose
Season: ducks: November to January; geese: November to February
Hunting Sites: 50,000 privately owned acres, marsh and agricultural fields
Accommodations: 6,000-square-foot, five-bedroom private lodge with fireplace, bar, great room
Meals: Southern- and Cajun-style
Rates: full-service package rates begin at $600 per hunter/day with overnight stay
Maximum Number of Hunters: 10
Gratuities: $20 to $40 per person/guide; $25 for chef and lodge staff
Preferred Payment: cash, check, credit card
Getting There: southeast Louisiana, 20 miles south of Lake Charles, LA
Nearest Commercial Airport: Lake Charles, LA
Dogs and Facilities: no accommodations for guests' dogs
Guides: two hunters per guide; guides provide retrievers
Other Services: airport transportation; bird cleaning and packaging
Other Activities: sporting clays range; bass fishing; saltwater fishing; alligator hunting; marsh tours; golf
CONTACT:
Patrick Milugan
Grosse Savanne Lodge
1730 Big Pasture Rd.
Lake Charles, LA 70607
Ph: 337-598-2357
Fax: 337-598-5359
Email: pmilugan@sweetlake.com
Web: www.grosssesavanne.com

BOOK A HUNT at Grosse Savanne Lodge and you're in for a first-class experience. Grosse Savanne, located just east of the state's famous Calcasieu Lake, is Louisiana's only Orvis-endorsed wingshooting lodge. This is prime waterfowl hunting territory. During the fall and winter months, millions of ducks, geese, and other migratory waterfowl arrive in southwest Louisiana's coastal wetlands, prairies, and farm fields to feed on residual grains, invertebrates, aquatic plants, and seeds not available elsewhere. Fifty thousand acres of that type of habitat is owned and maintained by Grosse Savanne for its waterfowl hunting clientele.

The lodge building here is a piece of architectural art. It has five semi-private bedrooms, each with its own bath. Beautiful artwork adorns the lodge interior, including its focal point great room. The room features a marble fireplace, a wet bar stocked with top-shelf spirits, a hand-crafted card table, and a large-screen television. The adjoining dining room features a cypress and pinewood decor.

Duck hunts here are morning affairs beginning with a wake-up and a continental breakfast. Hunters are taken to blinds in either freshwater or saltwater marshes or flooded rice fields by truck, ATV, or boat, as dictated by terrain. A lodge guide, who does the calling and handles a retriever to pick up his guests' ducks, accompanies each pair of hunters. The birds here can be pintails, mallard, wigeon, teal, or any of a variety of divers, depending upon the lateness of the season and which type of water you choose to hunt on a given day.

After the morning hunt, your guide will return you to the lodge for a Southern-style brunch. This is when you plan your afternoon activity, and there is plenty to do. Snipe or goose hunts are in the offing. The lodge staff offers some excellent guided fishing in freshwater or saltwater. The lodge property borders some of the finest speckled trout, redfish, and flounder waters in the state. A marina is only minutes away where 24-foot and 21-foot Kenner boats are available for charter for snapper, cobia, and other pelagic fishes. In addition, Grosse Savanne has over 15,000 privately managed acres to fish for largemouth bass.

Skeet shooting is another afternoon option, as are nature tours and marsh boat tours. The marsh boat tour takes you into the heart of the coastal wetlands. A guide will take you through thousands of acres of habitat containing herons, pelicans, ducks, otters, alligators, and a host of other wetland creatures. If the alligators intrigue you, you can even arrange an alligator hunt.

At the end of the day, it's time to retreat to the lodge dining room for a five-course Cajun gourmet country dinner. After dinner, if you're still mobile, you can take an evening drink to the nearby bird-watching tower and view the coastal marshes at sundown. If you don't feel up to the climb, sit out on the great room's screened porch and listen to the ghostly noises as the marsh comes alive with nocturnal animals. There will be sounds you'll never forget.

Hackberry Rod and Gun Club

Hackberry, Louisiana

VITAL STATISTICS:

SPECIES: white-fronted goose, snow goose, pintail, gadwall, wigeon, teal, other duck species

Season: ducks: November 1 through January; geese: November 1 through mid-February

Hunting Sites: 15,000 acres of leased, brackish water marshland

Accommodations: condominium-style lodge with large clubhouse, dining room

MEALS: Cajun-style dinner and lunch; continental breakfast

RATES: package rates are $300 per hunter/day, includes meals, lodging, guide; two hunters per guide

MAXIMUM NUMBER OF HUNTERS: lodge accommodates up to 36 hunters, but two hunters per blind at 1,000 acres per blind

GRATUITIES: $40-$50 per day suggested

PREFERRED PAYMENT: check or cash

Getting There: 16 miles south of Sulphur, LA

NEAREST COMMERCIAL AIRPORT: Lake Charles, LA

Dogs and Facilities: no accommodations for dogs

Guides: one guide per two hunters

Other Services: bird cleaning available locally

Other Activities: saltwater fishing for redfish, speckled sea trout; sightseeing at Holly Beach Creole Nature Trail and Sabine National Wildlife Refuge; riverboat casinos

CONTACT:

Terry Shaughnessy
Hackberry Rod and Gun Club
485 Lake Breeze Rd.
Hackberry, LA 70645
Ph: 337-762-3391
Fax: 337-762-3791
Web: www.hackberryrodandgun.com

CAMERON PARISH, Louisiana, should be on every waterfowl hunter's "top ten places I'd like to hunt before I get too old" list. Maybe the top five. Not only is this the heart of the wintering grounds for a variety of ducks and geese, it's a stopover for others on their way farther south to Mexico and South America. Not only are there many species of waterfowl here, there are, collectively, hundreds of thousands of representatives of each of their feathered tribes: pintail, wigeon, gadwall, teal, ringnecks, and snow and specklebelly geese the most numerous.

And if you do make it to Cameron Parish before you get too old to hunt there, you absolutely can't go wrong by hunting with Terry Shaughnessey at his Hackberry Rod and Gun Club, located on the west shore of fabled Calcasieu Lake. Terry, a former Green Beret and professional football player before he started guiding full-time 22 years ago, has plenty of stories to tell and plenty of quality duck hunting to offer. He leases 15,000 acres of wetlands around the lake, allowing only one blind per thousand acres and two hunters (plus a guide) to each blind. This ensures that ducks and geese will work the decoys (from 120 to 400, depending on the blind) and with little pressure from nearby hunters. He also enforces a 10:30 a.m. shooting cutoff to allow the birds respite from hunting pressure and to come back into the marsh ponds to feed and rest.

Terry's is a three-step operation. In the morning, over coffee and rolls, you'll be introduced to your guide. A bit later, you'll step (1) into his vehicle and ride to a boat dock where you'll step (2) into a johnboat powered by a Go-Devil outboard for a trip through a maze of marsh grass. Eventually, you'll arrive at a dry, camouflaged, sunken fiberglass blind, which you'll step (3) into from the boat. You're there. The decoys are already set, so all you have to do is sit back and wait. The guide will do the calling and collect the ducks and geese you shoot.

But you won't just be sitting there waiting to snap a cap. The variety of bird life—from ibises and roseate spoonbills to ospreys and shorebirds—will amaze you. Your guide, meantime, will be whistling to wigeon and pintails, quacking at gadwall, mottled ducks and teal, and yodeling to speckelbellies. You might even hear him squeal at one of the tree ducks not too uncommon on these hunting grounds. By the cutoff time, your sensory as well as your bag limits should be filled.

Well, almost filled. You'll be heading back to the lodge to savor some of Mrs. Shaughnessy's Cajun gumbo, a taste sensation unto itself. And if you think the gumbo is great, wait until the evening meal, another sensational Cajun concoction from Mrs. Shaughnessey's list of specialties (she has had a recipe book of these published, if you're interested). Meanwhile, your guide will tag your birds and take them to a local processor if you don't care to take care of the chore yourself.

So what do you do in the afternoon? Nap, play cards, read. But as long as you're here, you owe it to yourself, if you're so inclined, to take it to the limit and sample some of the area's near-shore saltwater fishing. During duck season, it may be a little early for sea trout, but redfish are available here all year and are great fun to catch on light tackle. The redfish don't come black-ened, by the way, but Terry's wife has a recipe for that, too.

Louisiana Flyway Lodge

K a p l a n ,   L o u i s i a n a

VITAL STATISTICS:

SPECIES: mallard, pintail, teal, wigeon, gadwall, white-fronted goose, snow goose

Season: duck: November to January; geese: through February

Hunting Sites: flooded and drained rice fields owned or leased for exclusive use of guests

Accommodations: private lodge with three bedrooms, two bunkhouse rooms, all with private baths

Meals: gourmet Cajun-style cooking; duck gumbo with deer sausage, pot-roasted specklebelly goose, dove fricassee are favorites

Rates: $325 per hunter/day, includes meals, lodging, guided hunt

Maximum Number of Hunters: 20

Gratuities: hunters' discretion

Preferred Payment: cash, check, credit card

Getting There: in southwest Louisiana, 20 miles north of the Gulf of Mexico

Nearest Commercial Airport: Layfayette, LA (40 minutes by car)

Dogs and Facilities: well mannered dogs welcome; outside kennels provided

Guides: one guide for up to four hunters; some guides prefer to hunt with their own dogs, others allow hunters to bring their own if they are proficient and well behaved

Other Services: bird cleaning and packaging for travel (extra charge)

Other Activities: sporting clays; bass fishing in private ponds; sea trout and redfish fishing in saltwater estuary

CONTACT:

Josette Hanks
Louisiana Flyway Lodge
21602 Dewberry Rd.
Kaplan, LA 70548
Ph: 337-785-0087
Fax: 337-783-1198
Email: speckcall@aol.com
Web: www.laflyway.com

THE FIRST CAJUNS to arrive in southwestern coastal Louisiana found freshwater marsh and wetland prairie to homestead. From the 1880s on, the terrain was converted to flooded rice fields as a vast system of canals was dredged to drain, contain, and control floodwaters. Today, deep-water wells supply the water flow more efficiently. The proper cultivation of rice requires that type of precision in flooding and draining the crop. Of course, the flooding is also perfect for waterfowl, especially when there's plenty of waste grain left after the harvest for hungry waterfowl.

Located only a short duck or goose flight from the Gulf of Mexico, and in the middle of that rice country, is Louisiana Flyway lodge. The accommodations spread over 5,000 renovated square feet and range from private to group relaxation. You can choose to socialize in the large recreational area, with a bar, satellite TV and pool table, or escape the crowd in your own private space. Between hunts, you can watch geese through the lodge windows, which overlook a private preserve, or fish for bass or bream on a private lake, or practice your shooting skills by gunning clay birds. When the fishing is hot, the lodge staff can also arrange a trip for speckled trout and redfish on a nearby saltwater estuary.

But your main reason for being here is specklebelly geese and greenhead mallards, not speckled trout and redfish. The lodge folks will have no problem helping you find what your looking for. The folks are just that, folks: an extended family operation—husbands, wives, sons, daughters, brothers, sisters, and cousins who have hunted and guided here for more than 40 years. According to lodge manager Josette Hanks, "Our guides were not only born to hunt, some were born hunting. All live nearby and speak Cajun French, Cajun English, Cajun duck, and Cajun goose, but not necessarily in that order. Some are even supposed to have webbed feet, but we can't guarantee it."

Hunting is for dabbling ducks and geese over natural crop cover and from comfortable pit blinds sunk into rice field levees. Transportation from the lodge to the blinds is by truck and customized duck buggy, pulled by tractor or an all-terrain vehicle. Because the lodge staff can control water levels on each side of a blind, they can attract a variety of species, and ducks and

81

geese are often hunted from the same blind. All the guides are proficient callers of ducks and geese, especially the local favorite specklebelly goose, which works decoys beautifully and, as the Cajuns say, "takes the call good."

On a typical hunt day, according to Hanks, "The guides wake you for coffee, then join you for a short breakfast before taking you to your blind. In the predawn hour, as soon as legal shooting time starts, you'll usually have action right away, often from zooming teal, love-lost mallard drakes coming to a hen call, to what look like B-52s but are actually geese lumbering in to the decoys. After sunup, just about any hungry duck or goose that likes water may show up—mallards, pintail, mottled ducks, wigeon, greys, teal, shovelers, scaup, snow geese, or specklebellies."

As the Cajuns say, *it don git no better an at.*

Pin Oak Mallards Lodge

Rayville, Louisiana

VITAL STATISTICS:

SPECIES: mallard, gadwall, wood duck, teal, wigeon, pintail

Season: mid-November to late January

Hunting Sites: 800 acres of flooded timber; 2,000 acres of agricultural fields

Accommodations: private lodge: four private rooms sleep two each; two bunk rooms sleep six each

Meals: home-style and Cajun

Rates: $300 per hunter/day; group discounts available

Maximum Number of Hunters: 18

Gratuities: $20 daily for cooks and pluckers; $50 to $100 daily for guides (unsalaried)

Preferred Payment: cash or check

Getting There: northeast Louisiana, 12 miles from Monroe

Nearest Commercial Airport: Monroe, LA

Dogs and Facilities: dogs welcome if they are trained hunters; kennels available

Guides: one guide for up to four hunters; all guides have trained retrievers

Other Services: birds cleaned, packed and frozen

Other Activities: sporting clays; crappie and bass fishing; white-tailed deer hunting

CONTACT:
Ace Cullum
Pin Oak Mallards Lodge
711 Hwy. 15
Rayville, LA 71269
Ph and Fax: 318-248-3549
Web: www.pinoakmallards.com

ACE CULLUM proudly calls it "the best damn duck club in Louisiana." Ace is six-feet-five-inches tall and close to 300 pounds, so you might not want to argue that point with him. Most people who've hunted at Pin Oak Mallards Lodge don't either, but not because of Ace's imposing size. They love this place for its great hunting, its accommodations, and the cordiality of the staff and guides.

Built in 1990, Pin Oak Mallards Lodge is located on the water's edge and in the middle of Cullum's hunting acreage. The lodge overlooks a reservoir and is surrounded by flooded green timber and dead timber. With federal, state, and private rest areas for waterfowl nearby, the hunting areas boast excellent shooting opportunities for novice and experienced hunters alike.

The hunting areas include 2,000 acres of agricultural fields that, when flooded, provide pit blind hunting for mallards, pintails, and geese. But this is pin oak country, hence the name of the lodge, and hunting in the flooded oaks is something to behold. Ace has strategically placed blinds in the flooded timber where wood ducks, mallards, teal, and wigeon are regular guests. By mid-November, as many as 20,000 mallards work the flooded timber here, and their numbers increase as the season progresses. Spots where you might be waiting for them to decoy through the trees include "The Sweet Hole," "Meadow Blind," "Southwest Hole," "Yukon Jack," "Gator Hole," "Woods Hole," or "Hook Hole." Each has a history and its own stories about it.

A typical hunt at Cullum's lodge begins with an early wake-up call and a buffet breakfast. Before sunrise, you'll be transported by boat or ATV to your hunting area. That could be a heated stick blind in the woods, a pit blind in a field, or you might just be standing in flooded timber (waders are a good idea). Hunts last until noon, and then it's back to the lodge for a hearty lunch.

Afternoons are free. You can kick back in the lodge in front of the fireplace, read a book, watch satellite TV, or play pool. Or you can shoot five-stand sporting clays or fish for crappie and bass in front of the lodge. Later you can grab an adult beverage at the bar and watch the "sundown flight" of ducks through the glass-fronted lodge. By the time the last duck has flown, a hot Cajun-style dinner will be awaiting you.

Cullum also offers deer hunts. Bottomland whitetails here can grow large, and some sport impressive antlers. Afternoon hunts are from 2 p.m.

until sunset. A guide will take you to a deer stand, probably by four-wheel ATV. He'll pick you up at sunset and return you and, if you're lucky, your buck to the lodge. Deer hunting fees are extra, and if you score a really big buck, there's also a trophy fee to consider.

Ace Cullum's spacious Pin Oak Mallards Lodge ("the best damn duck club in Louisiana," he claims) overlooks a refuge reservoir where, in the evenings, guests sip cocktails and watch mallards and other ducks make their sundown flight to a peaceful night roost.

CENTRAL FLYWAY

MONTANA, NORTH DAKOTA, SOUTH DAKOTA,
NEBRASKA, COLORADO, OKLAHOMA, TEXAS

THE DAKOTAS, OF COURSE, are in the heart of the Prairie Pothole Region, the nation's "duck factory." Hunting here, primarily for dabbling ducks, can be spectacular. Prairie potholes and marshes are the place to go for ducks, while the agricultural fields are the place to hunt for Canada geese and snow geese.

Mountain vistas, trout, mule deer, elk, antelope. And, yes, ducks and geese, too. Most people may not know it, but the West offers excellent waterfowl hunting opportunities. The agricultural fields that flank the Front Range of the Rocky Mountains in Colorado provide a huge wintering ground for mallards and Canada geese. Rivers, potholes, and farm fields offer hunting that often rivals what the Dakotas can offer, albeit at slightly lower autumn and winter temperatures.

Montana is a great venue for duck and goose hunters, even after winter sets in. Geese and ducks hold out on open waters on big rivers such as the Bighorn, where huge concentrations of mallards stay well into December. Seasons are long and bag limits are generous in this country, and hunting pressure is just about nil. To top it off, you can mix up your opportunities by chasing upland birds—pheasants, sharptails, Hungarian partridge—or try a "cast and blast" and fish for trout after a morning bird hunt.

Texas, big as it is, deserves its own paragraph. Along the Gulf Coast as well as in the central and northern parts of the state, agricultural areas are magnets for Canada geese, snow geese, and specklebellies. Many pintail and redheads winter here, especially along the coast, and good numbers of mallards are found in the central and northern agricultural plains. What a place. You can hunt geese in the morning, ducks in the afternoon, and finish the day with a bowl of chili con carne and a mesquite-grilled steak.

Lodges:

Montana

1 BEAVER CREEK GUIDES, SACO

2 EAST SLOPE OUTFITTERS, BILLINGS

North Dakota

3 CLUB NORDAK, STREETER

4 SHELDON'S WATERFOWL AND UPLAND BIRD HUNTS, STREETER

South Dakota

5 BIG BEND RANCH, ABERDEEN

6 BUSH RANCH, PIERRE

7 FLYWAY GOOSE CAMP, PIERRE

8 FORESTER RANCHES, OACOMA

9 HIGH PRAIRIE OUTFITTERS, SIOUX FALLS

10 THE OUTPOST LODGE, PIERRE

11 SOUTH DAKOTA HUNTING SERVICE, HERRICK

Nebraska

12 RIVERFRONT HUNT CLUB, TEKAMAH

Colorado

13 MT. BLANCA GAMEBIRD & TROUT LODGE, BLANCA

14 SCENIC MESA LODGE, HOTCHKISS

15 STILLWATER GUN CLUB, BRIGHTON

Oklahoma

16 TRIPLE H RANCH & HUNTING LODGE, FREDERICK

Texas

17 74 RANCH RESORT, CAMPBELLTON

18 BAY PRAIRIE OUTFITTERS & LODGE, MIDFIELD

19 COASTAL WATERFOWL, KATY

20 THE FARRIS HOTEL, EAGLE LAKE

21 GREYSTONE CASTLE SPORTING CLUB, MINGUS

22 H & H GUIDE SERVICE, PORT LAVACA

23 LARRY GORE'S EAGLE LAKE AND KATY PRAIRIE OUTFITTERS, KATY

24 NORTH TEXAS WATERFOWL, DALHART

25 PO' BOYS OUTFITTERS, BAY CITY

26 THIRD COAST OUTFITTERS, BAY CITY

27 TOTAL OUTDOOR ADVENTURES, CONROE

28 W.S. SHERRILL WATERFOWL HUNTING, WHARTON

29 WEBFOOT CONNECTION, ROCHESTER

Beaver Creek Guides

Saco, Montana

VITAL STATISTICS:

SPECIES: mallard, pintail, gadwall, Canada goose
Season: October to January
Hunting Sites: 10,000 acres of leased land for upland bird hunting; 1,000 acres on Beaver Creek for waterfowl hunting
Accommodations: private, six-bedroom three-bathroom lodge; private bedrooms, satellite television, bar
Meals: home-cooked, family-style
Rates: $450 per hunter/day (guided); $350 per hunter/day (self-guided)
Maximum Number of Hunters: six
Preferred Payment: cash or check
Getting There: northeastern Montana, 230 miles from Billings, MT
Nearest Commercial Airport: Glasgow, MT
Dogs and Facilities: dogs welcome; outside kennels provided
Guides: three hunters per guide; dogs available for lease
Other Services: bird cleaning (fee)
Other Activities: upland bird hunting for Hungarian partridge, sage grouse, sharptails, pheasants, dove; white-tailed and mule deer hunting
CONTACT:
Joe Taylor
Beaver Creek Guides
PO Box 167
Saco, MT 59261
Ph: 406-527-3339
Fax: 406-527-3340
Email: jtaylor@nemontel.net
Web: www.jaytaylor.com

NORTHEASTERN Montana's bird hunting has been a well-kept secret among wingshooters for more than a generation. The rolling prairie here is vast, distant from population centers, receives very little hunting pressure, and is crawling with upland game. Given its proximity to the Canadian prairies, the birthplace of hundreds of thousands of ducks and geese, it's also a hotspot for waterfowl.

Jay Taylor's lodge near Saco is one of the very few available to hunters visiting this part of Big Sky Country. His Beaver Creek Guides business caters to wingshooters who like to combine early morning waterfowl hunts with afternoon upland hunts. All the hunting is on land privately leased for the exclusive use of his guests, and plenty of land there is, all within a 50-mile radius of his comfortable lodge.

Hunts for Canada geese take place on agricultural fields, wheat being the primary crop here. Western Canadas, a large subspecies almost as big as the giant Canada goose, are the most common geese in the area. Otherwise, for ducks, Taylor or his guides can set you up in a blind on Beaver Creek. Mallards, pintails, and gadwalls are the primary duck species. Jump shooting the same ducks is also an option for those hunters who get impatient waiting for their game to come to them or are disinclined to adventure forth on predawn waterfowling forays.

Walking up to your targets can provide a lot of surprises besides ducks in this terrain. Agricultural fields, ditches, cattail sloughs, and hay fields surround the creeks. All of these varied types of cover can hide, in addition to ducks, wild pheasants (one of the largest populations outside the Dakotas), sharp-tailed and sage grouse, and coveys of Hungarian partridge. Walk far enough and bust enough cover and you can expect a mixed bag comprised of several species on any given day.

Taylor offers two options to visiting gunners. First, they can hunt with a guide and one or more of the lodge's dogs. Second, hunters who bring their own dogs can take to the fields on a self-guided hunt. Or you can mix the options and hunt with a guide and your own dog, if you wish. Once you get to know the country a little better, and no offense to the guides, you can pretty well go it alone. (If you do, though, bring a compass and map with you, and know how to use them. An extra ration of water for you and the dog are a good idea, too. And don't forget, you'll have to carry all those birds by yourself. Hmmm . . . maybe having a guide along is a good idea after all.)

If a couple of days of bird hunting wears you out, Taylor can arrange for a walleye fishing trip on Nelson Reservoir, only 10 miles from the lodge. Or, if you have big game on your mind, he can, with plenty of advance notice to coordinate licenses and so forth, guide you on a mule or white-tailed deer hunt.

So many choices, so little time.

Sharp-tailed grouse inhabit the grasslands and woodlot fringes of the prairies and offer wonderful wingshooting opportunities in the afternoons on prairie outfitters' hunting lands.

[C E N T R A L   F L Y W A Y]

East Slope Outfitters
B i l l i n g s ,   M o n t a n a

VITAL STATISTICS:

SPECIES: Canada goose, mallard, gadwall, wigeon, pintail, teal, bufflehead, goldeneye

Season: October 1 through January 6

Hunting Sites: leased agricultural fields, Bighorn River, Yellowstone River bottoms

Accommodations: private lodge, motel, cabin

MEALS: beef, fowl, pork, seafood

RATES: packages start at $1,395 for three days, four nights; call for details

MAXIMUM NUMBER OF HUNTERS: eight

GRATUITIES: guests' discretion

PREFERRED PAYMENT: cash or check

Getting There: areas hunted are near Billings, MT

NEAREST COMMERCIAL AIRPORT: Billings, MT

Dogs and Facilities: outside kennel available for guests' dogs

Guides: up to three hunters per guide

Other Services: bird cleaning and packaging

Other Activities: upland bird, preserve pheasant, and turkey hunting; trout fishing

CONTACT:
Jim Laughery
East Slope Outfitters
1130 Nugget Place
Billings, MT 59105
Ph/Fax: 406-254-6565
Email: eastslope@mcn.net
Web: www.eastslopeoutfitters.com

JIM LAUGHERY'S outfitting operation in eastern Montana is sort of a moveable feast. That is, where you stay when you book with him depends upon what time of the season you travel there and what you're hunting for. And there's plenty to hunt, from ducks, geese, upland game, and wild turkey to deer and antelope. Then there's fishing on the Bighorn River, one of North America's premier trout rivers, which holds more than 7,000 rainbow and brown trout per mile.

Laughery begins his season in September, guiding upland bird hunters to native sharp-tailed grouse and Hungarian partridge in the country's brush-filled draws and grain fields. Doves are on the hunt menu here in September, too, as are licensed game preserve pheasants, which inhabit the rolling hills, brushy coulees, and river bottoms. Sage grouse provide additional opportunities for upland hunters.

Upland hunting is available once the waterfowl season opens in October, too. Duck hunting is available in Loughery's Yellowstone River camp outside of Forsyth, some 95 miles east of Billings, or at his Bighorn River Camp south of Billings. Goose hunting can also be quite productive at the Yellowstone River camp. The river flows through very productive agricultural lands where corn, sugar beets, barley, alfalfa, and wheat are major farm crops. From the mouth of the Bighorn River to the east boundary of Rosebud County, the Yellowstone River is closed to waterfowl hunting within the river bed. This provides a major rest area for 70,000 to 90,000 Canada geese each fall. Laughery hunts the fields located just off the river and spread throughout the valley. Early season ducks are abundant here as well. Mallards, teal, and wigeon work the same grain fields in the mornings and afternoons with geese, or they can be hunted over floater decoys along sloughs and creeks.

Early season ducks provide good decoy hunting on the Bighorn River, too, but here the best action begins in November, when the northern migration begins and the river fills with many species of ducks—predominantly mallards but also gadwall, green- and blue-winged teal, pintail, wigeon, goldeneye, bufflehead—and Canada geese. It's not uncommon here to fill a bag limit by selectively shooting drake mallards.

The Bighorn River camp is also where you can experience a Montana cast and blast. Sportsmen travel from across the globe to experience the excellent trout fishing in the tailwaters below the river's Yellowtail Dam. This fishery remains open all year, courtesy of the constant flow of water and water temperatures that keep the river flowing throughout the winter months. In November and December, it is not uncommon to hook 30 or more fish per day on a fly rod.

The open water also creates a wonderful rest stop for waterfowl when temperatures freeze all the surrounding lakes and potholes, and also freezes out the fair weather anglers of summer and early fall. So, you can float the river, stopping to fish for trout here and hunt ducks and geese there. Along the way, you can try for wild pheasants that winter on the river's many islands, using the dense river bottom growth of Russian olives, buffalo berries, and snow berries for food and cover.

Floating the Bighorn River for a combination duck hunt and trout fishing trip—a true Montana "cast and blast"—is an adventure not to be missed.

Club NorDak

Streeter, North Dakota

VITAL STATISTICS:

SPECIES: mallard, pintail, other puddle ducks, Canada goose, snow goose
Season: October 6 to November 15
Hunting Sites: 25,000 private acres of agricultural fields, lakes, pot-holes
Accommodations: house/lodge with three semi-private bedrooms, two baths
MEALS: home-style
RATES: $1,495 for four nights lodging, meals, and three days hunting
MAXIMUM NUMBER OF HUNTERS: six
GRATUITIES: $20 to $25 per hunter/day
PREFERRED PAYMENT: check
Getting There: near Streeter, ND
NEAREST COMMERCIAL AIRPORT: Bismark, ND
Dogs and Facilities: dogs welcome; outside kennel runs available
Guides: one guide per three or four hunters on goose hunts
Other Services: airport pickup; bird cleaning and processing
Other Activities: upland bird hunting for pheasants, sharp-tailed grouse, Hungarian partridge
CONTACT:
Charles Arndt
Fin & Feather Safaris
1400 Montgomery Hwy., Second Floor
Birmingham, AL 35216
Ph: 205-824-0833 or 800-320-7117
Fax: 205-824-1411

YOU CAN'T GET much closer to the heart of the Central Flyway than Streeter, North Dakota. It's as close to the center of the Prairie Pothole Region, the continent's "duck factory," as you can get. The area is laced with grain fields and Conservation Reserve Program grasslands, potholes, and sloughs. Not only does this country produce a lot of ducks, it attracts tens of thousands of migrant ducks and geese from farther north, in Canada, each fall.

The plethora of waterfowl here is what prompted Mark and Penny Dokter to establish Club NorDak some years ago, and has prompted many hunters to visit their camp since then. The Dokters have converted a prairie farmhouse to a lodge that will accommodate up to six hunters during a three-day (four nights of lodging) guided hunt. The lodge is located atop a hill over-looking many of the potholes their clients use for duck hunting and the fields they tromp to find wild pheasants, sharptails, and Hungarian partridge. With 25,000 acres of private land under NorDak's control, hunting competition on their properties is nonexistent.

NorDak's guides vary hunting opportunities during your stay there. Over the course of a three-day program, you'll have the opportunity to request your preferences. You can hunt geese, ducks, and upland birds. Each day, there will be two separate hunts, one in the morning and one in the afternoon. The morning hunt, depending upon the weater, is usually a goose ambush. Greater and lesser Canadas are targets early in the season, snows and blues later in the season. For these hunts, the guides use Final Approach layout blinds and full-bodied and silhouette decoys. The guides will do the calling, but you are welcome to join in.

Duck hunting opportunities are unlimited, considering the dozens of potholes on Club NorDak's properties. Some of the potholes are within walking distance of the lodge, others only a 10-minute drive away. The guides will set out decoys for you and strategically place one or two hunters on a pothole, spreading other shooters out on surrounding potholes to keep the ducks moving. Waders will be required here, because you may have to hide in emergent vegetation on the rim of the pothole. Bring your duck call and your retriever, and prepare for a great shoot. Club NorDak doesn't guarantee limits, but waterfowl are plentiful here in the fall, and upland bird hunting success depends on the amount of walking you are willing to do.

On mornings of early hunts, a light breakfast will be available before you sally forth to greet the dawn. Depending upon the hour you return from your morning hunt, Penny Doktor will have either a big breakfast or lunch awaiting you. Evening meals are preceded by regional hors d' oeuvres and followed by one of Penny's mouth-watering homemade desserts.

And following the after dinner conversations, before you turn in for the night, you can step outside and hear a chorus of coyotes bid you goodnight.

This jubilant, smiling hunter has just scored a double on Canada geese. The scene? A prairie in central North Dakota.

Sheldon's Waterfowl and Upland Bird Hunts

S t r e e t e r ,   N o r t h   D a k o t a

FOR THE HUNTER who likes to mix it up, do a little or a lot of everything, there's Sheldon's Waterfowl and Upland Bird Hunts in Streeter, North Dakota. Sheldon's specializes in full-day combination hunts. And when they say *full*, they mean it. Where else can you hunt geese in the morning, upland birds in the afternoon, and if you're still up for it, ducks or doves from late afternoon until dark?

Greater and lesser Canada geese, snow geese, a wide variety of ducks (mallards, pintails, redheads, canvasbacks, teal, wigeon, gadwall, greater and lesser scaup), sharp-tailed grouse, doves, pheasant, Hungarian partridge, tundra swans, sandhill cranes, snipe—you name it, they hunt it.

This is pothole country, so waterfowl have plenty of roosting areas. And when it comes to food, owner Sheldon Schlecht plants 26 10- to 12-acre plots of unharvested corn, sunflowers, millet, milo, and oats around his 41,000-acre farm. What this means is an abundance of birds—wild birds, for the most part, though Sheldon's occasionally supplements with planted pheasants.

The bounty, however, doesn't end with the birds. A three- to six-day hunting package at Sheldon's comes with a wealth of services, including airport pickup, three daily guided hunts, lodging, daily maid service, all meals and snacks, guides, dogs, and even bird cleaning, packing, and storage. Groups of four or more get their own 6-bedroom house. Hunters are encouraged to bring their dogs, which can stay in the house or in separate kennels.

A typical day starts out with a light breakfast before you head out to set the goose decoys for field hunting. After an exciting goose hunt, it's back to the lodge for lunch and a rest. Then you'll head off to hunt sharptails, pheasant, Huns, or a combination, in the unharvested crops or in the fallow grass, weeds, and brush thickets that offer great cover for these wild birds. You'll end the day on a perfect note, hunkered down in a blind as a wide variety of ducks fall into the decoys in a beautiful little pothole at dusk.

For the big-game enthusiast, Sheldon's offers a combination deer, waterfowl, and upland bird hunt. Local deer are big, and for $2,500 you'll get a guaranteed shot at a buck (or a $500 "bad luck" refund) plus six days and seven nights of hunting. This includes three hunts per day for deer, waterfowl and upland birds. For the hunter who wants to do it all, this hunt can't be beat.

White camouflage clothing and a large spread of decoys are just the ticket for hunting snow geese, from northern Canada to Mexico.

[C E N T R A L   F L Y W A Y]

Big Bend Ranch

A b e r d e e n ,   S o u t h   D a k o t a

VITAL STATISTICS:

SPECIES: Canada goose, mallards
Season: November through December
Hunting Sites: 3,500 acres of private grainfields and ranch lands, stock dams, ponds
Accommodations: private, modern lodge; eight semi-private bedrooms, each with bathroom; satellite television, smoking lounge, dining room, great room
MEALS: fine dining: steaks, grilled seafood, roast pheasant; homemade breads, desserts
RATES: $2,700 for three-day, four-night package, including airport transportation, lodging, meals, shells, guides and dogs, bird cleaning, some licenses, sporting clays
MAXIMUM NUMBER OF HUNTERS: 16
GRATUITIES: appreciated but not expected; range from 5% to 15% of package rate
PREFERRED PAYMENT: check
Getting There: in central South Dakota, 30-minute drive from Pierre
NEAREST COMMERCIAL AIRPORT: Pierre or Sioux Falls, SD
Dogs and Facilities: guests' dogs welcome; 12 outdoor kennel runs with heated dog houses
Guides: guides and dogs provided
Other Services: rate package is all-inclusive
Other Activities: ring-necked pheasant, Hungarian partridge hunting; fishing in private trout pond; sight-seeing, including bison herd tour; tribal casino gambling

CONTACT:

Alex and Annie Falk
Big Bend Ranch Hunting Inc.
1301 N. 4th
Aberdeen, SD 57401
Ph: 605-229-3035 or 606-875-3445 (during hunting season)
Fax: 605-229-1888
Web: www.bigbendranch.com

RICH IN HUNTING tradition, Big Bend Ranch sprawls along high bluffs overlooking the Missouri River. Although primarily managed as a pheasant hunting operation, Big Bend also offers excellent opportunities for the waterfowl hunter. Adjacent to a state waterfowl refuge and roosting water on the "Big Mo," the ranch's 3,500 acres of farmland—corn, winter wheat, and milo—provide food for hungry geese and mallards that stage on the river each fall.

Hundreds of thousands of Canada geese, many of them the large western variety that rivals the giant Canada in size, gather on the river during their southern migration. The geese leave their refuge on the river every morning and cross the bluffs to feed in Big Bend's fields, offering fantastic shooting over decoys. Given appropriate winds and weather, pass-shooting from the edge of the bluffs can also be unbelievable. Although Canada geese greatly outnumber other species here, snow geese and white-fronted geese also occasionally provide shooting opportunities, either over decoys or pass-shooting. The ranch's many stock dams attract migrating mallards and offer another opportunity to hunt over decoys.

Waterfowl populations hit their peak around the ranch from November through December. Most hunting for mallards and geese takes place from sunrise to about 10:30, and in the afternoon from 3:30 until sunset. Between morning and afternoon waterfowling forays, guests can scour Big Bend's upland cover—shelterbelts, weed patches, food plots, and grasslands— intensively managed for pheasants and Hungarian partridge. Both species are abundant here, and a midday hunt may be all you need to significantly diminish your shell supply.

For a change of pace, Big Bend Ranch, South Dakota's only Orvis-endorsed wingshooting lodge, also offers guests a chance to shoot sporting clays or catch a rainbow trout from its private pond.

After an exhilarating day afield, it's time to retreat to your lodge room, rest, and clean up for dinner. Big Bend has two lodges, and no effort has been spared on the buildings, dining, and amenities. One lodge overlooks Two Deer Lake to the east, the other the Missouri River to the west. Ready for dinner? First, head to the great lodge for cocktails and hors d'oeuvres. While snacking and sipping, relax outside on the deck or watch from inside through the smoking lounge windows as the evening spectacle of pheasants flying back to their roosts unfolds against a magnificent South Dakota sunset.

The last bird is snuggled in for the night. Let's head for the dining room. Dinner may begin with grilled seafood soup and strawberry spinach salad. Tonight, the main course just might be prairieland pheasant baked in vermouth sauce, with a side of Minnesota wild rice. For dessert, how about homemade creme brulee or chocolate praline layer cake?

Quite the meal, wasn't it? And quite the day, too. You may just want to return to your room and snuggle into your own roosting cover pretty soon. A hearty country-style breakfast awaits you in the morning, well before sunrise and the first goose flies.

Retrievers get double duty workouts on upland game birds as well as waterfowl on South Dakota's Big Bend Ranch.

Bush Ranch, Inc.

Pierre, South Dakota

VITAL STATISTICS:

SPECIES: Canada goose
Season: October 20 through December 16
Hunting Sites: 12,000 acres of private land; agricultural fields, native grasses, shelterbelts, freshwater marshes
Accommodations: individual, double-occupancy cabins; rustic private lodge with steakhouse dining area, bar with TV, game room
Meals: home-cooked walleye, beef, chicken
Rates: $1,590 for three-day package including lodging, meals, guided hunts, bird cleaning, shells, airport transportation
Maximum Number of Hunters: 20
Gratuities: $100/hunter (suggested)
Preferred Payment: cash, check, money order
Getting There: in central South Dakota, 27 miles north of Pierre
Nearest Commercial Airport: Pierre, SD
Dogs and Facilities: hunters' dogs welcome; indoor and outdoor kennels available
Guides: three to four hunters per guide
Other Services: bird cleaning included in package rate
Other Activities: pheasant hunting
CONTACT:
Jeff Bush
Bush Ranch Inc.
18467 282 Ave.
Pierre, SD 57501
Ph: 605-264-5496
Fax: 605-264-5435
Email: jeff@bushranch.com
Web: www.bushranch.com

THE 12,000-ACRE Bush Ranch rests on a peninsula surrounded on three sides by Lake Oahe, an immense impoundment of the Missouri River. The lake is a waterfowl refuge where, from September through December, huge numbers of Canada geese reside most of the day. When not on the lake, though, the big birds are looking over local fields, searching for something to eat.

The ranch has plenty of food to entice the hungry honkers: milo, corn, and small grain crops. It is in these harvested fields that ranch owner Jeff Bush tows his portable 24-inch auger to drill goose pits. Sort of like being buried standing up, except the hole is only four feet deep instead of six; each hunter has his own pit for the morning shoot. Several holes are dug in a row, to accommodate hunters and guides. Around the pits, Bush spreads an array of Carry-Lite, Big Foot, and Outlaw goose decoys, strategically placing a landing zone for the big birds in the line of the hunters' fire.

The morning starts with hot coffee and a sumptuous country-style breakfast. You and your hunting party will be in your holes well before dawn. When the first flock of Canadas appears, a guide will do the calling. If everything works according to plan, the big birds will be wing-cupped and feet down soon enough. No need to hurry shooting a limit. The daily bag here is only two per hunter, but big western Canadas are common in this country. Might as well pass up shots at the smaller subspecies and pick out a couple of these giants. Between goose flights, especially when the northern mallards come through later in the season, you may have a smokin' gun day.

When your morning shoot is over, you'll return to the clubhouse to change into upland gear. After lunch, and maybe also a change from a 12 gauge to a 20, you'll be guided to some of the best pheasant cover in South Dakota. Hunting with one of Bush's pointing Labs or your own dog, there will be plenty of cover to push, too. And there will be plenty of birds hiding there. Like other large pheasant hunting operations in this country, Bush plants hundreds of pheasants to supplement the huge natural population of roosters that lurks in his crops, shelterbelts—cedar, green ash, plumb and chokecherry—and CRP fields of native grasses. The preserve status of the ranch allows pheasant hunting to begin in September, weeks before the statewide pheasant season begins. The ranch habitat also harbors sharp-tailed grouse and Hungarian partridge as a bonus, but these can't be hunted until state seasons begin later in October.

How good is the hunting on the Bush Ranch? When Kevin Costner was on location in the state, filming *Dances with Wolves*, he brought his family here to hunt pheasants and geese. But it wasn't only the hunting that attracted Costner. Take a look at a prairie sunset from the front picture widow of the main lodge. A majestic view of the Missouri River at sundown was another great reason for him—and for you—to visit here.

Upland hunting for wild or released pheasants is a pleasant afternoon adjunct to morning waterfowl hunts on many South Dakota outfitters' operations.

Flyway Goose Camp

Pierre, South Dakota

I N HUNTING, as with any outdoor sport, there is no such thing as a sure bet. But if you're a goose hunter, you can come pretty close to those odds if you're near Pierre, South Dakota, during the goose migration along the Central Flyway, hunting in the company of Brian Tracy and his guides. Geese pour through here like the steady current of the Missouri River, and Brian's Flyway Goose Camp is perfectly situated on 16,000 choice acres of farmland where the corn and wheat fields act like goose magnets.

Flyway Goose Camp has been guiding hunters to these prime fields since 1992; prior to that these fields were a strictly private camp. Brian works in conjunction with a variety of lodging outfits nearby so that he can concentrate solely on the hunting. But there are very nice cabin-style lodges available, or clean and well-run motels, if you prefer. The action begins each morning about 6:30 a.m. when the hunters gather at the Flyway Goose Camp clubhouse at the center of the property. Over coffee the guides will lay out the game plan, selecting the best hunting spots for the day. You and your group will head for fields where geese have been feeding and settle in to lined goose pits while the guides put out a substantial set of decoys. It is not long before the action begins, as the geese are drawn into the decoys by skillful calling and flagging. Most hunters have shot their limit and are ready for lunch and a rest by noon.

Rested and fed, you may well be ready for more hunting action, and Brian and his guides can certainly oblige. After all, you're also in the heart of some of the country's best pheasant hunting. Or if you want a complete change of pace, there is walleye fishing on the famed Oahe Reservoir of the Missouri River.

Brian and guide Bruce "Wickerbill" Crist are also to be commended for putting together the Annual Wickerbill Youth Goose Hunt. Each year, a fortunate group of kids gets the opportunity to hunt from the pit blinds over hundreds of decoys. Last season they bagged nearly 200 geese. It's a great way to introduce a new generation to the joys of sitting in a blind and watching the sky fill with honkers.

Forester Ranches

Oacoma, South Dakota

VITAL STATISTICS:

SPECIES: mallard, Canada goose
Season: ducks: October and November; Canada geese: November to January; snow geese: March and April
Hunting Sites: 130,000 private acres: prairie potholes, Missouri River and agricultural fields
Accommodations: private lodge: four double occupancy bedrooms
MEALS: home-style steaks, chops, chicken
RATES: $1,895 package includes three days hunting, four nights lodging, meals, shells, guide service, dogs, bird cleaning and packaging
MAXIMUM NUMBER OF HUNTERS: eight
GRATUITIES: hunters' discretion
PREFERRED PAYMENT: cash or check
Getting There: in south-central South Dakota, near Chamberlain
NEAREST COMMERCIAL AIRPORT: Sioux Falls, SD
Dogs and Facilities: use of personal dogs not encouraged
Guides: usually two hunters per guide (have own dogs) for ducks; four or more hunters per guide for geese
Other Services: bird cleaning and packaging included in package rate
Other Activities: upland bird hunting for pheasants, prairie chicken, sharp-tailed grouse, Hungarian partridge, bobwhite quail, dove
CONTACT:
John or Lance Forester
Forester Ranches
Box 102
Oacoma, SD 57365
Ph: 800-982-6841
Fax: 605-734-5508
Email: visitus@midstatesd.net

HUNTERS HAVE BEEN visiting John Forester for 35 years. His ranchlands (in South Dakota, there is a big difference between a *rancher* and a *farmer*, by the way, so be careful how you address your host) are near Oacoma, just west of Chamberlain and the I-90 bridge where it crosses the Missouri River. Those lands are home to pheasants, mostly wild ones, as well as prairie grouse, Huns, and bobwhites. Short pastures and huge tracts of native grasses are just what these birds prefer.

Three-day-hunt packages are available here beginning in September, but those are only for upland game. In October, combination packages for waterfowl and upland game become available as seasons open for migratory waterfowl. Arranged properly, these hunts can include ducks and geese in the morning and a different upland hunt each afternoon, targeting either pheasants, sharptails, or Huns. Later in the season, goose hunting may become a day-long affair.

True, this is the heart of South Dakota pheasant country, but it's also a good bet for ducks and geese. Lake Sharpe, an impoundment of the Missouri River upstream of Chamberlain, has become a major staging area, and in some years, a wintering area for Canada geese and mallards. A stretch of the river known as "Big Bend," surrounded by the Crow Creek and Lower Brule Indian reservations, serves as a roosting area for many thousands of these birds. While those ducks and geese may see considerable gunning pressure north of Chamberlain, the river south of town, near Oacoma, and the potholes on Forester's property and agricultural fields he leases, see much less and therefore attract considerable air traffic.

When there are plenty of South Dakota potholes filled with water, ironically, duck hunting can sometimes be a crapshoot. The birds have plenty of places to sit, especially during the balmier days of October. Good hunting here under those conditions requires daily scouting to see which potholes the ducks are using, then being there, decoys set and you well-camouflaged in whatever cover you can find, before sunup the following morning. The same holds for scouting fields that geese are using for feed. Left undisturbed on their late afternoon/early evening feeding binges, the geese will usually return to the same fields the next morning.

John and his staff can do the scouting for you, but part of the fun of waterfowling is finding these hotspots and deciding which ones to use on your own. The great part about it is that you can do this while on an afternoon hunt for upland birds, that is if you can pay attention long enough to scout waterfowl instead of shooting at flushing game.

After your daily fun afield, you can return to the intimate lodge John maintains for his guests. All the bedrooms have private baths. You don't have to worry about much, either, because his package rate includes meals (steaks, prime rib, chops, wild game), guide services, dogs, shells, bird cleaning and field transportation. What more can you ask for? (Okay, within reason.)

Good reflexes and sharp shooting bagged this hunter a sharptail and a Hungarian partridge on a trek across a stretch of South Dakota prairie.

High Prairie Outfitters

Sioux Falls, South Dakota

VITAL STATISTICS:

SPECIES: mallard, Canada goose, snow goose

Season: ducks: October through December; geese: September through January; snow geese: February through May

Hunting Sites: 100,000 acres throughout the state of South Dakota

Accommodations: private lodges, motels, and cabins in various locations; tent and trailer if in remote areas

Meals: three meals per day, including light breakfast, deli-style lunch, and hearty evening dinner

Rates: $1,500 per person for three-day waterfowl/pheasant combination hunt; $900 per person (four-hunter minimum), $600 per person (six-hunter minimum) for three-day spring snow goose hunt; $1,500 for three-day turkey hunt; add 5 percent sales tax to all prices, call for other packages

Maximum Number of Hunters: one to six for waterfowl; one to four for turkey; one to twenty for pheasant (smaller groups preferred)

Gratuities: "Let your enjoyment level be your guide"

Preferred Payment: cash, check, or money order

Getting There: Sioux Falls, South Dakota

Nearest Commercial Airport: Sioux Falls, Rapid City, or Pierre

Dogs and Facilities: Hunters encouraged to bring dogs; kennel run available at base; three kennels available on the road

Guides: outfitter provides personalized guide service with trained dogs

Other Services: bird cleaning and packing; taxidermy; sight-seeing; sporting clays; any special food items customer would enjoy

Other Activities: turkey hunting; trout fishing; sight-seeing; big game hunting; upland bird hunting; pike and walleye fishing

SIOUX FALLS, South Dakota, in the southeast corner of the state, has long been known as the Gateway to the Plains. Likewise, a similar appellation could be applied to Dave Ciani's High Prairie Outfitters. Call it the Gateway to Plains Hunting—because that's exactly what it is. Whether you're looking to hunt Canada geese, snow geese, mallards, pheasant, prairie chickens, sharp-tailed grouse, turkey, deer, antelope, trout, pike, walleye, or any combination of these, High Prairie has the key to unlock a whole world of Great Plains adventure.

That's because Dave is as flexible and as itinerant as a guide-outfitter can be. His motto is: We Go Where the Game Is. And that's no lie. He has a degree in fish and wildlife management, as well as extensive experience in the field, so he knows where the game is. And that's exactly where he'll take you, which could be any of dozens of spots throughout South Dakota and parts of Nebraska, depending on the species you're after and the time of year.

"We hunt the whole state of South Dakota," says Dave. "Over 100,000-plus acres of owned or leased land, marshes, fields, potholes, lakes, rivers, and the Missouri River throughout our range."

Because of this, accommodations can be at any number of lodges, cabins, or motels throughout the region, many of which will have a hot tub and swimming pool, because Dave is always looking out for the comfort of his guests, and because after a hard day of hunting you'll need some time to relax. When hunting in a remote area, however, you might even camp out in a tent or in Dave's 29-foot custom hunting trailer, which comes equipped with a kitchen, generator, freezer, stove, heater, toilet, ATV, boat, bunks, blinds, decoys, and a decoy sled.

If you're looking for a customized hunt, no problem. In fact, Dave encourages his customers to dream and plan a special hunt of their own. His job, as he sees it, is to help you make your dreams come true. He'll do whatever it takes to personalize your hunt and make memories that will last a lifetime.

Toward that goal, he also recommends—nay, encourages—his clients to bring their dogs. "It's always a wonderful experience for dog and master to work together and to work with my experienced dogs," he says. "I really enjoy exposing dogs and their owners to positive hunting experiences."

Service is the name of the game, says Dave, who will be happy to pick

103

CONTACT:
Dave Ciani
49 N. Knoll Drive
Sioux Falls, SD 57110
Ph: 605-338-2377
Fax: 605-335-6774
Email: highprairie@basec.net
Web: highprairieoutfitters.com

up supplies such as dog food, ammo, licenses, cooler, special food requests—anything that might cut down on your load when you're flying in. He also offers bird cleaning, taxidermy, and sporting clays, if desired.

If you're hunting ducks or geese in the morning, you might choose to hunt pheasants, prairie chickens, or sharptails in the afternoon. Or you might choose to fish at a number of blue-ribbon trout streams that sluice through the region. Whatever you decide on, Dave will plan to make your trip as exciting and memorable as possible. And why not, since his tipping policy is: Let your enjoyment level be your guide.

Huge decoy spreads, sometimes employing more than a thousand snow goose "rags," are the order of the day for South Dakota prairie hunts for this species.

The Outpost Lodge

Pierre, South Dakota

VITAL STATISTICS:

SPECIES: Canada goose, mallards

Season: November through January

Hunting Sites: leased acreage on five different ranches

Accommodations: 12 modern cabins accommodating from two to 20 guests

Meals: guests may prepare own meals in cabin kitchenettes or dine in lodge restaurant

Rates: packages include meals, lodging, guides and dogs, and bird cleaning; waterfowl package: $250 per person/day; waterfowl/pheasants: $450 per person/day

Maximum Number of Hunters: varies

Gratuities: hunters' discretion

Preferred Payment: check

Getting There: lodge is 15 miles north of Pierre on bluffs overlooking Lake Oahe

Nearest Commercial Airport: Pierre, SD

Dogs and Facilities: Dogs are allowed to stay in cabins with their owners

Guides: one guide per two to ten hunters, depending on type of hunt

Other Services: fishing available on Lake Oahe

Other Activities: pheasant hunting

CONTACT:

Brad Garrett
18857 Benelli Place
Pierre, SD 57501
Ph: 605-264-5432
Email: bstkgarrett@sullybuttes.net

THE OUTPOST LODGE sits on a bluff overlooking Lake Oahe, and you can often stand there in the evening and look down on the roosting birds you'll be hunting the next day. Huge numbers of geese—many of them the large western Canada subspecies that rivals the giant Canada goose in size—congregate on the lake and tailwaters of the Missouri River in fall and winter.

In the morning, the geese lift off their roosting water and fly up over the bluffs of the Missouri, looking for feed in the broad expanse of picked cornfields and wheat stubble of farms on higher ground. Hunt here with Brad Garrett or one of his guides and you'll probably find yourself in a goose pit on one of the five farms (or ranches, as South Dakotans prefer to call them) Garrett leases, encompassing anywhere from 5,000 to 10,000 acres each.

Garrett's pits are surrounded by decoys, and your guide will call and shake his goose flag, simulating honkers landing in the spread, to attract the passing flocks of Canadas. Across the vast prairie sky, you'll witness skeins of the big gray-and-brown birds flying to breakfast. Don't start daydreaming, though, because while you watch the geese, a dozen mallards may streak over the decoys, catching you unawares. If nothing else, the sounds of your hunting partners' shotguns will snap you out of your reverie.

Canada geese are abundant here, but Garrett's hunters also get the occasional opportunity to bag white-fronted geese and snow geese. And then there's the huge population of wild pheasants to consider. But, because of state regulations, you can't begin hunting these upland birds until after noon during the first two weeks of the open season, and until after 10 a.m. thereafter. So, the best thing to do in those idle hours of dawn and early morning is to hunt waterfowl.

If you feel too confined in a goose pit, you can hide in grass cover along the bluffs and pass-shoot geese on their early morning and late afternoon feeding flights. Still, your best bet for bagging a brace of honkers is to hunt from the pits and over decoys.

Most of Garrett's hunters opt for his waterfowl/pheasant package, which combines a morning waterfowl hunt with afternoon pheasant forays. He or one of his guides will take you from cover to cover on private lands leased exclusively for Outpost Lodge guests. You'll hunt a variety of cover including prairie grasses, cornfields, shelterbelts, and whatever else can hide a gaud rooster. Along the way, you may flush sharp-tailed grouse or the occasion covey of Hungarian partridge. But pheasants are the main game here, an you'll find plenty of them.

Return to the lodge at the end of the day and relax with a drink in th lounge. No need to worry about cleaning and packing birds—that's done fo you as part of the hunt package. After a great dinner at the lodge's Lake From Steakhouse, what you do is up to you. But I suggest a good night's sleep because tomorrow you'll have to get up early and do it all over again.

This happy waterfowler has bagged an exceptional example of an adult blue goose, a color phase of the lesser snow goose.

South Dakota Hunting Service

Herrick, South Dakota

VITAL STATISTICS:

SPECIES: mallard, pintail, wigeon, gadwall, blue- and green-winged teal, redhead, bluebill, Canada goose, white-fronted goose, snow goose, sandhill crane

Season: ducks and geese: October through December; cranes: October through November

Hunting Sites: 8,000 acres of lake beds, potholes, and agricultural fields leased for guests' private use, plus hundreds of miles of Missouri River backwaters

Accommodations: eight-bedroom lodge with shared baths

Meals: home cooking

Rates: $350/day for waterfowl; $450/day for waterfowl and pheasant

Maximum Number of Hunters: 12 to 16

Gratuities: hunters' discretion

Preferred Payment: cash or check

Getting There: drive or fly to Pierre, SD, and rent a car

Nearest Commercial Airport: Pierre, SD

Dogs and Facilities: dogs are welcome and may be kept in room; outside kennels available on request

Guides: two hunters per guide; trained dogs available

Other Services: bird cleaning and freezing; transportation and airport pick-up

Other Activities: hunts for turkeys, wild pheasants, sharp-tailed grouse, prairie chickens; walleye fishing; trophy deer hunting

CONTACT:
Mike Moody
South Dakota Hunting Service
P.O. Box 324
Herrick, SD 57538
Ph: 605-654-2465

THERE ARE few places better suited to experiencing the resurgence of ducks in the Central Flyway than the traditional marshland of the South Dakota prairie. And it would be difficult to come up with a person better qualified to getting you into ducks and geese than Mike Moody. For over a dozen years Mike's South Dakota Hunting Service has been guiding waterfowlers to what is certainly some of the country's best prairie duck hunting. When not guiding for ducks and geese, he is busy taking hunters on some excellent upland bird and trophy deer hunts.

Early in the season, Mike directs duck hunters to the action on over 8,000 acres of lake and potholes that are literally teeming with ducks. Wading in before dawn to the dry-land blinds situated on little hummocks in the marshes, you are likely to hear the unmistakable sound of flushing wings—lots of them. But when the pre-dawn sky lightens a bit, you'll not only hear them but also see them by the hundreds, flocking into the wetlands surrounded by alternating patches of CRP grass and grainfields. For ducks, it is a veritable feasting ground. For duck hunters, it is more like paradise. You'll not only have a chance to shoot plenty of mallards, but pintails, wigeon, gadwalls, teal, redheads, and other species as well. Later in the year, after freeze-up, which usually comes in November, Mike moves his decoys and hunters to the big water of the Missouri River for combination goose and duck hunts. There are literally hundreds of miles of backwaters available to the waterfowler here.

Enjoy some of the home-cooked food at the comfortable lodge after you've completed your morning hunt, and rest up a bit, because you have the opportunity to chase wild pheasants, sharp-tailed grouse, and even prairie chickens in the afternoon. Remember, you're not only in the midst of the heartland's greatest waterfowl hunting, you're at the epicenter for the ring-neck resurgence. You'll be hunting wild birds, not pen-raised ones, on some of the thousands of acres of CRP land, croplands, sloughs, and thickets available to South Dakota Hunting Service guests. If you don't have your own upland pointer or flushing dog, Mike can provide you with a well-trained canine companion.

The emphasis at South Dakota Hunting Service is on personalized service for family and small-group hunts. Each outing is tailored to meet the client's individual needs.

[**C E N T R A L   F L Y W A Y**]

Riverfront Hunt Club

T e k a m a h ,   N e b r a s k a

VITAL STATISTICS:

SPECIES: mallard, Canada goose (95% greater)
Season: November through February 5
Hunting Sites: in eastern Colorado along the South Platte River
Accommodations: motel available in Julesburg, CO
Meals: four fine restaurants and steakhouses within 10 miles
Rates: $125/day
Maximum Number of Hunters: 18
Gratuities: hunters' discretion
Preferred Payment: cash or check
Getting There: northeast of Denver near I-76 and the Nebraska state line
Nearest Commercial Airport: Denver, CO
Dogs and Facilities: dogs provided; no guest dogs
Guides: one guide per six hunters; friends can hunt together
Other Services: bird cleaning available
Other Activities: prairie dog hunting
CONTACT:
Raymond (Rick) Olson
Riverfront Hunt Club
4800 CR E
Tekamah, NE 68061
Ph: 402-374-2582 or
970-474-9942 (from Oct. 25-Jan. 31)

EACH FALL waves of ducks and geese follow the contours of the Platte River from central Kansas to the eastern plains of Colorado, using this great waterway on their migration south. And each autumn for over 35 years Rick Olson has been there, too, with well-trained dogs, seasoned guides, and loyal clients waiting for the great migration to unfold. There's a rhythm and predictability to it that soothes the soul, but like all hunting, it takes the experience and guidance of a master to deliver consistent results day in and day out.

Rick maintains two blinds on the South Platte River, 12 miles apart, for duck and goose hunting. And a bit back from the river he maintains four field pit blinds for hunting the big Canadas. The pit blinds are a comfortable haven even when bone-chilling winds whip the prairies. Each blind has a gas grill for heat and for cooking. A hunt at the Riverfront Hunt Club is an all-day affair, and Rick and his guides do a great job of making it a comfortable and productive outing. On a typical hunt, you will follow the guides out to the parking area near the blind you will hunt that day and then make a 100 to 200 yard walk to the blind, which will be buried six feet deep and level with the ground. The blind is constructed of welded steel and has four gas heaters with a sliding roof. With dawn, you'll begin to see the flocks of geese moving along the river. Even late in the season when these geese have had plenty of experience dodging gunners, the guides expert calling and flagging will pull small groups of Canadas from the large flock and bring them into the blocks. The geese continue to lift off the river and head over the pit blinds throughout the day, providing continual shooting for the waiting waterfowlers.

When you're ready for a morning break, the guide will fire up the stove and scramble some eggs, with hot salsa and bratwurst, and wrap them in a burrito shell for a true southwestern breakfast treat. Along the river, mallards move back and forth, and Rick's clients may move to one of the duck blinds tucked into the banks of the Platte. When the sun begins to set, it is time to help pick up decoys and head back to the motel in Julesburg, Colorado, and head for one of the fine steakhouses or restaurants nearby.

Mt. Blanca Game Bird & Trout Lodge

B l a n c a ,   C o l o r a d o

VITAL STATISTICS:

SPECIES: mallard, pintail, Canada goose

Season: between October and January

Hunting Sites: 6,000 private acres including four lakes, agricultural fields

Accommodations: private, eight-bedroom lodge with hot tub, sauna, lounge, restaurant

MEALS: gourmet regional and game cuisine

RATES: $99/night (double occupancy) plus waterfowl guiding fee of $225 per hunter/half day

MAXIMUM NUMBER OF HUNTERS: 16

GRATUITIES: 15%-20%; guests' discretion

PREFERRED PAYMENT: cash, check, credit card (Visa or MasterCard)

Getting There: one and a half hours by car from Colorado Springs, CO

NEAREST COMMERCIAL AIRPORT: Colorado Springs, CO

Dogs and Facilities: guests' dogs welcome; outside kennels available

Guides: four hunters per guide; guides have dogs

Other Services: bird cleaning and processing

Other activities: upland bird hunting for pheasant, chukar, quail, Hungarian partridge; lake and stream fly-fishing; sporting clays; skeet

CONTACT:

R.L. McDonald
Mt. Blanca Gamebird and Trout Lodge
11228 Rd. FF
PO Box 236
Blanca, CO 81123
Ph: 800-686-4024
Fax: 719-379-3843
Email: mtblanca@fone.net
Web: www.mtblanca.com

HERE'S A PLACE where you can do it all, in style, and do it while surrounded by breath-taking scenery. Mt. Blanca Gamebird & Trout Lodge is located in south central Colorado. This full-service resort has secluded duck hunting on four private lakes, and along the 1,200 acres it owns on Trinchera Creek. Canada goose hunting is available on the many agricultural fields on its properties.

Mourning doves, ducks, and geese are wild here, and there are a fair number of wild upland game birds, too. The lodge operators supplement the wild upland birds by releasing quail, pheasant, chukar, and Hungarian partridge prior to Colorado's upland bird season. Part of the property is managed as a licensed shooting preserve, though, so hunters are not hindered by state seasons and bag limits.

Waterfowl hunts are half-day affairs. After spending a pleasant evening in the lodge, a guide will arrive to discuss strategies and safety procedures before you depart for a nearby hunting area. Your guide will have decoys in place and will do the calling, too, if you wish, so that you and your party can sit in your blind and enjoy maximum shooting opportunities. Mallards and pintails are the most common waterfowl here, but Canada geese also utilize the lodge's stubble fields, so keep an eye out for a flock of the big birds—they can slip into the decoys, unannounced, at any minute.

After a morning waterfowl hunt, you will return to the lodge for lunch and perhaps a siesta while your birds are cleaned and packaged for you. Afternoons are wide open. The lodge features five-stand sporting clays, skeet, and a full-fledged sporting clays range. Having trouble hitting those clay birds? Lodge personnel also offer personalized gun-fitting services and a shooting school.

If shooting clays doesn't excite you, a guide can take you to chase uplands birds across the rolling terrain surrounding the lodge. You can take your own dog, of course, but the lodge will provide Labs or pointers for upland hunters who choose to leave their own dogs at home. When chasing a dog across the uplands in search of birds, though, it will do you well to understand that you are at almost 8,000 feet above sea level here. If you're a flatlander or out of shape, that can mean an ugly, lung-sucking afternoon. (Especially if, the previous evening, you availed yourself of one of the lodge's house specialties, the 20-ounce Hunter's Choice prime ribeye stuffed with shallots, sweet peppers, and mushrooms.)

So, instead, you might consider something less aerobic for your afternoon enjoyment. Try breaking out the fly rod and visiting the lodge's stocked ponds, for example, and play with the rainbow trout there. They range up to three or four pounds. Or have one of the guides take you on a lake or stream fly-fishing trip. That can be arranged, too.

If this all sounds too strenuous, remember you can soak in the hot tub or sweat your way to relaxation in the lodge's sauna after dinner. Then, I suggest, you go directly to bed.

Scenic Mesa Ranch

H o t c h k i s s , C o l o r a d o

VITAL STATISTICS:

SPECIES: mallard, teal, wigeon, pintail, goldeneye, and Canada goose
Season: December through January
Hunting Sites: exclusive use of blinds along six miles of the North Fork River
Accommodations: lodge features three rooms with two single beds in each with private baths, game room, and large dining area; clubhouse has two rooms and loft with two single beds in each and shared bath
MEALS: meals customized to guests' needs
RATES: $250/day for guided waterfowl hunt; $750/day for guided two-day combination waterfowl and upland bird hunt
MAXIMUM NUMBER OF HUNTERS: six
GRATUITIES: 10-15%
PREFERRED PAYMENT: cash, check, or Visa
Getting There: Fly to Grand Junction or Montrose and rent a car
NEAREST COMMERCIAL AIRPORT: Montrose or Grand Junction, CO
Dogs and Facilities: guests' dogs encouraged; dogs may stay inside clubhouse; lodge guests may place dogs in housed kennel with outside runs
Guides: one guide and blind per two hunters
Other Services: bird cleaning and freezing for shipment
Other Activities: upland bird shooting for released, naturalized pheasants and for wild chukars; trap shooting; horseback riding; fishing; hiking; big game hunting

CONTACT:
Stan Stockton
Scenic Mesa Ranch
P.O. Box 370
Hotchkiss, CO
Ph: 970-872-3078
Fax: 970-921-3378
Email: ranch@scenicmesa.com
Web: www.scenicmesa.com

THE FERTILE BOTTOMLANDS along the North Fork of the Gunnison River—rich in willows, reeds, and springs—provide an ideal habitat for migrating ducks and geese along the western slope of the Rocky Mountains. It is here that Scenic Mesa Ranch offers waterfowlers a comfortable opportunity to hunt the fall flights.

This 8,000-acre working ranch, where bison still roam much as they did when the Dominquez-Escalante expedition traversed this unique high desert country in 1776, provides some of the West's most scenic country as well as an incredible variety of sporting opportunities. Duck and goose hunters have access to six miles of the North Fork of the Gunnison for their exclusive shooting, as well as 10 acres of wetlands and ponds. Warm-water springs along the river's edge attract mallards, teal, wigeon, pintails, and goldeneyes, especially late in the season.

After a morning duck hunt, you'll return to the clubhouse for lunch and then have the chance to hunt wild and naturalized chukars and pheasants over pointing or flushing dogs in the afternoon. At the end of the day, your birds will be cleaned, frozen, and packed for you, or shipped if you choose. Enjoy a country gourmet evening meal prepared family-style and served in the great room, and don't pass up a chance to sample the ranch-raised bison. Evenings can be spent in the game room or relaxing in the Lodge's great room among the collections of Indian pottery, arrowheads, and beautiful buffalo rugs.

Guests can also enjoy the Ranch's relatively close proximity to the resort towns of Aspen, Telluride, and Crested Butte or enjoy the splendor of the new Black Canyon of the Gunnison National Park and the Grand Mesa National Forest.

Stillwater Gun Club, Inc.

B r i g h t o n ,   C o l o r a d o

VITAL STATISTICS:

SPECIES: Canada goose, mallard, teal, gadwall, wigeon

Season: ducks: first week of October through mid-January; geese: October through first week of February

Hunting Sites: leased farmland, sloughs, ponds, lakes

Accommodations: local motels (amenities vary from basic to elaborate)

MEALS: local restaurants

RATES: $175 per hunter daily for duck hunts; rate varies for goose hunting, depending on number of hunters

MAXIMUM NUMBER OF HUNTERS: October and November: eight; December: 12; January and February: 16

GRATUITIES: $20 to $30 per hunter/day

PREFERRED PAYMENT: cash, check, or credit card

Getting There: Front Range of Colorado 20 miles north of Denver

NEAREST COMMERCIAL AIRPORT: Denver, CO

Dogs and Facilities: no facilities for guests' dogs

Guides: one guide for up to four hunters; guide provides retrievers

Other Services: sporting clays, trap, and skeet ranges available (extra charge); bird cleaning available (extra charge)

Other Activities: upland bird hunting; horseback riding; hiking; skiing

CONTACT:
Mark Beam
Stillwater Canada Goose Hunting
16588 Telluride St.
Brighton, CO 80601
Ph: 303-659-8665
Fax: 303-659-6824
Email: stwgcinc@aol.com
Web:
www.sportsmansdream.com/stillwater

MAYBE COLORADO doesn't sound like a goose hunting destination to the average waterfowler, who might think the state is more suited to elk and deer hunting, but the Front Range, from Denver north to the Wyoming border, is a wintering area for tens of thousands of the big birds. The short grass prairie population of lesser Canadas and the highline population of greater Canadas may spend as many as four months here before returning north in spring. Farmers in this region raise corn, wheat, millet, milo, and sorghum, providing a literal smorgasbord for hungry honkers, to say nothing of the multitudes of ducks that also freeload on the nutritious grains.

Mark Beam of Stillwater Gun Club, Inc, operates his Stillwater Guided Goose and Duck Hunts business out of Brighton, just 20 miles north of Denver. He leases hunting rights on more than thirty farms distributed over a 70-mile-long stretch of the Front Range, where the majority of geese winter in Colorado. That way, Beam can move his hunting opportunities as various flocks move up and down the range during winter. Some newly acquired properties along with his traditional areas allow him to rotate hunt sites and keep gunning fresh fields throughout the hunting season. His hunts take place near Fort Collins, Windsor, Brighton, and Denver.

Beam's hunts are day trips; that is, he doesn't provide lodging and meals, just guide services, decoys, and blinds. Depending on the time of year that you book, he can assist you in arranging for comfortable rooms, licenses, and stamps. Each morning, he or one of his guides will meet you at a predesignated restaurant. From there, you follow the guide to the daily hunting site and help set up the decoys and, if goose hunting, ground blinds. Goose hunts will normally take place in agricultural fields, and if not hunting from ground blinds, you may hunt from pit blinds. Beam limits goose hunting to three parties, with four guns to a pit maximum, until the last few weeks of January.

You can elect, however, to hunt ducks, geese, or a combination hunt for both. Duck hunts are available from October to mid-January and take place on ponds, sloughs, and lakes, as well as on the South Platte River. These are either morning or afternoon hunts (or both), and the species most commonly taken are mallard, teal, wigeon, gadwall, and redhead. Duck hunts require a two-gun minimum, three-gun maximum.

A combination hunt for geese and ducks is what Beam calls his "water-fowl buffet." The day will start at the crack of dawn for early flights of ducks at a pond, slough, or river. After the early morning shoot, you'll relocate for field shooting for Canada geese. If you're still up for it and haven't limited on ducks in the morning, you'll head back to the water site for an evening duck hunt.

If you book a trip with Beam from November on, be sure to bring along your woolies. This is mile-high country, after all, and you may be hunting in snow and near-freezing or freezing temperatures. *Brrr*.

Mallards and geese are common visitors to the wetlands and farm fields of Colorado's Front Range in fall and winter.

[C E N T R A L   F L Y W A Y]

Triple H Ranch & Hunting Lodge

F r e d e r i c k ,   O k l a h o m a

VITAL STATISTICS:

SPECIES: mallard, pintail, greater and lesser Canada goose; occasionally canvasback, gadwall, blue- and green-winged teal, wigeon, redhead

Season: ducks: November to early December, and mid-December through mid-January; geese: late October to early December, and mid-December through early February

Hunting Sites: 20,000-plus acres of hunting land, including lands along the Red River, North Fork of the Red River, Salt Marsh Lake, and private lakes and ponds; 95 percent is for exclusive use of guests

Accommodations: two lodges: one sleeps 11; the other six to eight; bunkhouse sleeps 12

MEALS: Mexican, broiled steak, fish

RATES: from $175/gun

MAXIMUM NUMBER OF HUNTERS: 31

GRATUITIES: 10% of guide's fee

PREFERRED PAYMENT: cash or check

Getting There: far southwest Oklahoma, bordering the Red River

NEAREST COMMERCIAL AIRPORT: Lawton, OK, or Wichita Falls, TX

Dogs and Facilities: guests' dogs welcome; enclosed kennel with dog runs.

Guides: trained dogs and guides

Other Services: birds cleaned and packed for travel

Other Activities: hunting for wild quail, doves, turkey, sandhill cranes; fishing for bass, catfish, crappie, and perch

CONTACT:
Joe E. Horton, M.D.
Triple H Ranch & Hunting Lodge
608 Cedar Lane
Frederick, OK 73542
Ph: 580-335-5385 or
800-874-9080 + 35 access code

WHEN IT COMES TO bird hunting, Oklahoma may be one of the best-kept secrets in the country. The Sooner State is among the nation's leaders in quail and pheasant harvests, has three species of wild turkey, and offers great mourning dove hunting statewide. Not surprisingly, with dozens of state Wetlands Development Areas, a number of national wildlife refuges, thousands of acres of agriculture, and plenty of lakes, rivers, and marshes, Oklahoma also offers top-notch waterfowl hunting.

Nowhere is this truer than in the southwest corner of the state. Waterfowl gather from points north on the Central Flyway to winter and feed on the area's abundance of winter wheat and milo. To the north is 60,000-acre Wichita Mountain Wildlife Refuge, a haven for migrating waterfowl. To the south is the famous Red River, on the Oklahoma-Texas border, marking the corridor of the Great Western Trail, where millions of heads of cattle were driven from Texas to the Kansas stockyards and then farther north.

Here, in the heart of Oklahoma's Great Plains Country, Triple H Ranch & Hunting Lodge is one of 40 area outfitters that have thrived by putting sportsmen in touch with the region's bountiful wildlife. With more than 20,000 acres of hunting lands along the Red River, Salt Marsh Lake, and other lakes and ponds, Triple H offers excellent duck hunting over decoys. Duck species include mallard, pintail, gadwall, blue- and green-winged teal, wigeon, redhead, and canvasback. The daily bag limit is six ducks, including no more than five mallards, three scaup, two wood ducks, two redheads, one canvasback, and one pintail.

Geese are hunted in wheat, milo, and peanut fields, and the primary species are lesser and greater Canadas. The daily bag limit for Canada geese is three. Also on the menu is sandhill crane, which has a three-bag limit as well.

If you'd like to mix in upland bird hunting, Triple H offers a trifecta of quail, turkey, and dove. This area is home to some of the best quail hunting in the country, and they're all wild birds. For the itinerant hunter who can't wait to stretch his legs after a day in the duck blinds or goose fields, quail can be the ideal quarry. For those not so keen on chasing the state's most popular game bird through tall-grass prairie, turkey and dove round out the options.

Triple H also offers white-tailed deer hunting, and plenty of good fishing for bass, catfish, crappie, and perch.

74 Ranch Resort

Campbellton, Texas

VITAL STATISTICS:

SPECIES: teal, pintail, gadwall, wigeon

Season: early teal in mid-September; split duck season: end of October to end of November and mid-December to late January

Hunting Sites: 27,000-acre private ranch with over 100 stock tanks and some 20 miles of river and creeks

Accommodations: 12 private rooms with 2 queen beds in each and private baths; 3-bedroom VIP cabin

MEALS: executive chef prepares cuisine ranging from gourmet to country cooking

RATES: from $250/day

MAXIMUM NUMBER OF HUNTERS: 15 to 30

GRATUITIES: varies with hunt

PREFERRED PAYMENT: cash, check, or major credit cards

Getting There: one-hour drive south of San Antonio, TX

NEAREST COMMERCIAL AIRPORT: San Antonio, TX; 3,800-foot paved, lighted runway at ranch

Dogs and Facilities: trained Labs, pointers, German shorthairs; no guest dogs

Guides: yes

Other Services: game cleaning and vacuum sealed packing; lighted 5-stand sporting clays with 80-foot tower, 12-station sporting clays; trap and skeet fields and rifle/pistol range

Other Activities: private exotic animal park for viewing and photography, featuring African, South American, Asian, and European hoofstock that roam freely; quail, deer, spring turkey, dove, and alligator hunting in season

CONTACT:
Milo Abercrombie
74 Ranch Resort
P.O. Box 38
Campbellton, TX 78008
Ph: 830-579-7474
Fax 830-579-4222
Web: www.74ranch.com

EVER HANKERED to live like an oil baron or captain of industry? Well, that may be beyond the reach of most of us, but if you want to sample the good life for at least a few days, a trip to 74 Ranch Resort is in order. After all, legendary oilman "Mr. Jim" Abercrombie once owned this 27,000-acre south Texas hunting ranch and exotic game preserve, and it has hosted its share of the country's movers and shakers.

Here the gunning enthusiast can hunt quail in a style once reserved for the few. Following some of the nation's top pointing dogs, you'll experience classic Texas-style hunting on some of the most intensively managed quail-shooting property in the country. But often overlooked in the south Texas hunting experience is some downright excellent duck shooting that can rival and often exceed the plains outside of Houston or the Gulf Coast. George Robinson, owner of 74 Ranch Resort, and hunt manager Milo Abercrombie, have built more than 100 stock tanks (man-made ponds to Northerners), many created especially for waterfowl.

Most waterfowl hunters arrive the afternoon preceding the hunt so they can be in the blind before dawn. Getting to the blinds here doesn't involve any treacherous airboat rides or long walks through mud. You will be driven to within 100 yards of the blind at most of the lakes. Teal are hunted in the September early season and again during the duck season, which starts in late October or early November. Many guests often combine the early teal hunting with dove, or even alligator, hunting in the afternoon. The split duck season extends through January and provides an excellent opportunity to pair waterfowl hunting in the morning with quail in the afternoon.

Prior to or following your morning duck hunt, you can also sharpen up your shooting on some world-class sporting clays layouts, including a lighted 5-stand setup and a full 12-station course. Want more shooting? Try the skeet or trap layouts. And if you want a break from hunting, or you've brought along a nonhunter, the ranch is also home to an amazing array of free-roaming, exotic animals for viewing and photography (not hunting).

And since you are going to shoot like an oil baron, you might as well eat like one as well. The folks at 74 Ranch have an executive chef on hand, and there's a fine wine cellar, as well. And why not retire to the game room after dinner for a cigar and a touch of cognac to get you in the mood for the following morning's flights of ducks?

Bay Prairie Outfitters & Lodge

M i d f i e l d ,   T e x a s

VITAL STATISTICS:

SPECIES: snow goose, blue goose, white-fronted goose, Canada goose, Ross' goose, pintail, redhead, wigeon, teal, sandhill crane

Season: snows, blues, Ross': November through February; Canadas and specks: November through January; ducks (split season): November through January

Hunting Sites: 30,000 acres in five-county area of Texas Rice Belt

Accommodations: private motel that can hold two to three hunters per room, plus three private cabins-all equipped with cable TV and private baths

MEALS: buffet breakfast and lunch

RATES: $190/day, includes lodging, breakfast, morning hunt, lunch, bird processing and storage

MAXIMUM NUMBER OF HUNTERS: 60

GRATUITIES: $10 per day

PREFERRED PAYMENT: cash, check, or major credit cards

Getting There: 80 miles southwest of Houston

NEAREST COMMERCIAL AIRPORT: Houston Intercontinental or Hobby Airport

Dogs and Facilities: dogs welcome for private parties of four or more hunters; building first-class dog run

Guides: one guide per four to five hunters

Other Services: bird processing and storage

Other Activities: upland bird hunting for released quail, chukar, and pheasants

CONTACT:
Mike Ladnier
Bay Prairie Outfitters & Lodge, Ltd.
P.O. Box 35378
Houston, TX 77235
Ph: 713-728-8646 or 800-242-1374
Fax: 361-588-6565
Email: mladnier@texas-goose-hunting.com
Web: www.texas-goose-hunting.com

THE TEXAS GULF COAST is home to a wide variety of wildlife, everything from alligators to whooping cranes. But an abundance of marshes and agricultural fields make it the perfect haven for wintering geese and ducks. Honkers, especially, gather in huge flocks to roost in the area's waters and feast on rice, corn, milo, soybean, and rye grass. Once the geese have been to a particular field, there's no mistaking the signs of their presence: the crops are stomped down flat, as if an army had goose-stepped through them.

Predicting where the birds will be the next day is no small matter, especially if you want to be there bright and early. That's why, for Bay Prairie Outfitters in Midfield, Texas, scouting is key. "Good scouting is the difference between a professional guide service and a day-lease operation," says Bay Prairie owner Mike Ladnier.

Because the geese move daily, Bay Prairie moves its spreads daily to put you in the middle of the best action. The guides do the scouting the afternoon before the hunt. The morning of the hunt, you'll help your guide place the hundreds of rags, windsocks, kites, and flyers in the fields. The guide will position everyone to ensure the best and safest shooting. He will also call the birds and the shots. And before you know it, all that preparation will pay off as the geese whirl in—snows, blues, Canadas, and specklebellies—to decoy within shooting range.

A full-service operation, Bay Prairie has its own motel, the Bay Prairie Lodge, with 16 private rooms that hold two to three hunters each. There are also four new private cabins that hold parties of four or more hunters. Both the motel rooms and cabins come with air-conditioning, color TV, and a private bath. The lodge also has a restaurant that serves breakfast and lunch as part of the hunting package. Bird processing and storage are also included.

Bay Prairie is building a first-rate 10-run dog kennel and encourages parties of four or more to bring their own dogs, though dogs are provided if you'd rather leave yours at home. Individual or groups of less than four hunters will join with other parties and are not encouraged to bring dogs.

Bay Prairie offers hunting on more than 30,000 acres over a five-county area in the famed Rice Belt of Texas. Most hunts are within 30 to 40 minutes of the lodge. The outfitter offers afternoon hunts for sea ducks on Matagoda Bay, and upland gunning for released quail, pheasants, and chukar.

Coastal Waterfowl

K a t y ,   T e x a s

VITAL STATISTICS:

SPECIES: pintail, redhead, wigeon, gadwall, bluebill, goldeneye, ring-neck, green-winged teal, snow goose, blue goose, white-fronted goose, Canada goose, Ross' goose

Season: ducks: November through third week in January; geese: November through February

Hunting Sites: 100,000 acres of salt marshes around Matagorda Island; 20,000 private acres of farmland around Port O'Conner

Accommodations: area motels with kitchenettes, private baths, and queen-size beds

Meals: breakfast and lunch included

Rates: $350/day, includes morning and afternoon hunts/fishing, lodging, breakfast and lunch

Maximum Number of Hunters: 25

Gratuities: $10-$25 person/day

Preferred Payment: cash, check, or major credit cards

Getting There: 2-1/2 hours southwest of Houston on the Texas Gulf Coast

Nearest Commercial Airport: Houston

Dogs and Facilities: dogs provided, but clients' dogs welcome and can stay in motel rooms with their owners

Guides: one guide per four to five hunters/anglers

Other Services: bird cleaning and storage; stamps and licenses; shells

Other Activities: wildlife viewing and fishing

CONTACT:
Mark Teeman
Coastal Waterfowl
P.O. Box 1343
Katy, TX 77492
Ph: 888-618-4868

PORT O'CONNER and surrounding environs on the southwest coast of Texas are home to one of the richest estuaries in the state. Its many marshes, bays, sloughs, and flats make it one of the largest wintering areas for waterfowl in the Central Flyway. Kris Kelley and Mark Teeman of Coastal Waterfowl like to say that sometimes there are so many ducks in the region, you almost have to shoot them in self-defense.

While that might be a bit of an exaggeration, the sentiment is right. What self-respecting waterfowler, after all, wouldn't feel compelled to swing a shotgun at the clouds of redheads, pintails, and wigeon, as well as a dozen or more other species of ducks trading across the area's bays and flats?

Kelley and Teeman will help you answer that question by putting you in the thick of things in the more than 100,000 acres of salt marshes around Matagorda Island. Few know the area better than these two, because when they're not guiding hunts, they're guiding fishing trips in many of the same places. In fact, their specialty is a combination hunting and fishing expedition.

A Coastal Waterfowl blast-and-cast begins with a morning duck hunt. If you don't get your limit of ducks in the morning, you can choose to duck hunt in the afternoon as well. Kelley and Teeman are very flexible, and understand that avid waterfowlers may want to fill their limits. Those who are accustomed to shooting ducks only in the morning will be surprised at how many ducks may be moving through the bays and marshes of this region. If conditions are right, afternoon shoots can be just as productive as morning shoots.

If you shoot your limit of ducks in the morning, you can opt for an afternoon of fishing for redfish, speckled trout, and flounder. Kelley has years of experience fishing the area's many bays and reefs and can put you on to trophy-sized fish. Whether you choose to wade and cast a fly rod or toss bait and artificial lures from the boat, personalized service and a great time on the water are guaranteed.

Coastal Waterfowl also offers goose and sandhill crane hunting packages, which can be reserved for groups of four or more hunters and a minimum of three hunting days. These big birds are hunted on 20,000 private acres of the nearby Texas rice prairie, which is famous for attracting huge flocks of wintering snows, blues, specklebellies, Canadas, and Ross' geese. Since goose hunting is more weather-sensitive than duck hunting, you can always switch to the latter if the right weather conditions don't prevail.

117

*Coastal Texas waterfowlers commonly shoot pintail,
wigeon and teal from bayleaf blinds erected in
shallow feeding areas near shore.*

The Farris Hotel

Eagle Lake, Texas

VITAL STATISTICS:

SPECIES: Canada goose, white-fronted goose, snow goose, mallard, pintail, teal, wigeon

Season: ducks: November 1 through January 25; geese: November 1 through February 15

Hunting Sites: ponds, marshes, agricultural fields

Accommodations: hotel (see text description)

MEALS: country gourmet, buffet-style

RATES: $120 per person/day, includes hotel lodging, three daily meals, snacks, setups; guide fees additional

MAXIMUM NUMBER OF HUNTERS: hotel accommodates 66

GRATUITIES: none expected nor accepted

PREFERRED PAYMENT: cash, check

Getting There: 50 miles west of Houston, TX

NEAREST COMMERCIAL AIRPORT: Houston, TX

Dogs and Facilities: guests' dogs welcome; outside kennels and runs

Guides: see text

Other Services: none

Other Activities: released pheasant and chukar hunting

CONTACT:
Toy Kurtz
The Farris Hotel
201 N. McCarty
P.O. Box 99
Eagle Lake, TX 77434
Ph: 409-234-2546
Fax: 409-234-2548
Email: farrishotel@elc.net
Web: www.farrishotel.com

IT ISN'T REALLY a guide service, and it isn't an outfitter's operation either. The Farris Hotel is a goose hunting lodge that's been in operation for a quarter of a century. Hotel owner Toy Kurtz will provide you with lodging and meals and all the information you need on local guides, though, and coordinate your goose hunting and pheasant hunting if you're on your first trip to the prairies surrounding Eagle Lake, winter home of "the world's largest concentration of wild geese."

On a daily basis, those geese feed in agricultural fields—predominately harvested rice and soybean fields—near Eagle Lake. The birds are mostly snow geese but include good numbers of white-fronted geese and smaller races of Canada geese. Goose hunting here is traditionally done "Texas rag style," employing huge layouts of white cloth decoys. Tremendous flocks of snow geese, especially, can circle a spread like this several times each morning, but most of the birds will remain out of range. Still, enough will come in for a closer look, and if you're laying in the spread in white camouflage, 10 or 12-gauge in hand and loaded with 3- or 3½-inch shells, you'll have plenty of opportunities to bring home the bacon.

There will be opportunities to shoot ducks, especially pintails, while hunting geese on the leased farmlands. If you're more interested in duck hunting, local guides can set you up in marshes or on a small lake where wigeon, teal, pintail, and a few mallards are likely to come to decoys set over water.

But let's get back to the lodging accommodations. A visit to the Farris, built in 1912 and on the Texas Historic Register, begins with arrival the evening before the hunt. After settling in at the main lodge or guest house—both carpeted throughout and adorned with unusual antiques—you can relax in one of the lounge areas and enjoy tidbits from cheese trays and a drink before dinner. The evening meal is the highlight of the day. Chef Trinita Thomas will prepare two or three entrees with an array of vegetables and side dishes, home-made breads, and a salad selection second to none. Lunch after the morning hunt is relaxed. Chef Thomas' special soups are served with an array of salads, desserts, and hot selections of country cooking at its best.)

You'll also enjoy a wonderful breakfast at the hotel, but it's served very early—your wake-up call comes at 4 a.m. Your guide will be joining you for breakfast and to fill you in on what to expect during the upcoming hunting event. Soon you'll be off on the great adventure.

[C E N T R A L   F L Y W A Y]

Greystone Castle Sporting Club

M i n g u s ,   T e x a s

VITAL STATISTICS:

SPECIES: mallard, wigeon, gadwall, teal, canvasback, ringneck

Season: October through February

Hunting Sites: 4,000 acres with 19 bodies of water from two to 20 acres

Accommodations: elegant 24-room (nine double occupancy, 15 singles) English-style castle

MEALS: gourmet prime rib, mahi mahi, pork loin, venison, quail, etc., served with fine wines

RATES: $750 per hunter/day, includes lodging, meals, guides, dogs, bird processing; other packages available (call for rates)

MAXIMUM NUMBER OF HUNTERS: 33

GRATUITIES: guests' discretion, based on service

PREFERRED PAYMENT: cash, check, credit card

Getting There: 75 miles west of Dallas/Fort Worth, 20 miles west of the Brazos River

NEAREST COMMERCIAL AIRPORT: Dallas/Fort Worth International

Dogs and Facilities: because of liability concerns, guests are not permitted to bring dogs

Guides: maximum of three hunters per guide; dogs provided

Other Services: gun shop; catered sporting clays tournaments

Other Activities: upland hunting for released pheasant, partridge, and quail; golf; big game hunting; bass fishing; sporting clays with instruction; fly-fishing with instruction

CONTACT:
Bill Honza
Greystone Castle Sporting Club
PO Box 158
Mingus, TX 76463
Ph: 800-399-3006
Fax: 254-672-5971
Email: billhonza@aol.com
Web: www.greystonecastle.com

A CASTLE? IN TEXAS? You've got to be kidding. No. It's there, on top of a 1,200-foot mesa overlooking 4,000 acres of native prairie grass savannas and hardwood brushland about an hour's drive west of Dallas/Fort Worth. Of course, it's not centuries old and the former home of royalty. It's modern but with an Old World setting, and it's a multiple opportunity destination for game bird and big game hunters. As you can see by the rates in the statistics column, this Orvis-endorsed wingshooting lodge may not be a destination for everyone. But where else can you hunt, sleep in a castle, and have gourmet meals, cocktails and cigars thrown into the package rate?

Greystone Castle offers two types of duck hunting. The club's 19 lakes are a natural attraction for Central Flyway ducks using the Brazos River corridor. Wood duck, mallard, wigeon, teal, pintail, and gadwall are abundant. The club provides guides and retrievers for these hunts.

In addition to hunting for wild birds, the club offers flighted mallard shoots, a method of pre-stocked mallard shooting that was developed and refined in the Chesapeake Bay area. These hunts are guided by expert callers, and the ducks decoy to shoreline blinds.

Guests may also hunt upland game birds—pheasant, chukar, and quail—on the rolling hills and open meadows of the club property. A guide and well-trained dogs ensure that each hunting party will have an exciting day afield.

Don't feel like walking over hill and dale? How about a continental pheasant shoot? You can experience the finest of European-style driven pheasant hunts here, too. Participants are assigned a stand in the drive area and move to different locations during this half-day event. The rolling terrain where these shoots take place provide a variety of challenges for the gunners. Continental shoots are held monthly or a large group can arrange for its own private shoot.

Before trying a driven hunt, though, you may wish to hone your shotgunning skills a bit. You can do this at the club's five-stand trap and skeet course located next to the castle. This five-stand, fully automated combination course is one of the few multilevel courses in existence. Or, how about sporting clays? The club maintains two 100-round courses that incorporate the varied topography and beautiful views of the mesa country. The valley course and the castle course offer a variety of presentations for any level of shooter.

Big game hunting is also available at Greystone Castle. Although the ranch maintains herds of exotic aoudad sheep, antelope, and various imported deer for selective harvest, the primary focus of the big game program here is on the development of a superior trophy white-tailed deer herd. If you want to try for one of the castle club's trophy bucks, or one of their exotic animals, call ahead for rates and reservations.

However you and your group want to mix up your activities at the club, the staff will accommodate specific needs and custom-coordinate your trip. In other words, they will treat you like visiting royalty. Long live the King! (That'd be you.)

❖ *A Willow Creek Guide* ❖

───
North America's GREATEST Waterfowling Lodges
───
[C E N T R A L   F L Y W A Y]

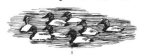

H & H Guide Service

P o r t   L a v a c a ,   T e x a s

VITAL STATISTICS:

SPECIES: snow goose, Ross' goose, blue goose, white-fronted, lesser Canada, redhead, pintail, teal, gadwall, bufflehead, bluebill, goldeneye, mottled duck, shoveler

Season: ducks: October 30 to November 28 and December 11 to January 23; geese: October 30 to January 23, special season snows after January 23

Hunting Sites: 30,000 acres, including rice fields, row-crop fields, rye grass and wheat fields, and pasture; bay hunts in Matagorda Bay

Accommodations: private accommodations and motels in the area

MEALS: seafood, Mexican food, and American meals available locally

RATES: $100 per person for morning goose hunt; $85 bay hunt for ducks, morning or evening; $100 combination hunts, ducks and geese

MAXIMUM NUMBER OF HUNTERS: 20

GRATUITIES: $20 per guide/day

PREFERRED PAYMENT: cash

Getting There: 10 miles north of Port O'Connor and 10 miles east of Seadrift, TX

NEAREST COMMERCIAL AIRPORT: Houston, TX

Dogs and Facilities: guest dogs discouraged due to alligators; outside kennels are available

Guides: one guide for up to six guns on goose hunts; one guide and dog per four guns on bay hunts

Other Services: breasting birds and packaging with a wing; pickers available for additional charge

Other Activities: bay fishing; offshore fishing; sporting clays; upland game hunts

CONTACT:
Kevin Henke
H & H guide Service
546 FM 2541
Port Lavaca, TX 77979
Ph: 361-552-2892
Email: kbhenke@txcr.net
Web: www.hhguideservice.com

WHEN IT COMES TO hunting ducks and geese along the Texas Gulf Coast, even many of the local hunters turn to a pair of lifelong residents of Calhoun County— Kevin Henke and Cory Housworth. That's because Henke and Housworth and their H & H Guide Service bring with them 40 years of waterfowl hunting experience in the Port Lavaca area. Quite simply, they have the expertise and the equipment to put you on the birds.

And birds there are. Their goose hunts, for example, are conducted near four major roosts. The largest is a 3,000-acre U.S. Fish and Wildlife freshwater wetland project that is maintained year-round and holds one of the largest concentrations of waterfowl along the Gulf Coast. Snow geese are abundant all season long into late February. Specks are more predominant in the early season, and lesser Canadas reach their greatest numbers in the later season. Your guides will scout the fields to find where the birds are actively feeding, which may be plowed ground or fields of rice, rye grass, or grain. Once a field is located and a good flight path is established from a roost to the field, they will set up the evening before your hunt with decoys that range from full body to silhouettes and windsocks. They're also likely to throw in a few goose magnets to give the spread the most lifelike appearance.

If it's bay ducks you're after, H & H will take you to Matagorda Bay, leaving from either Port Alto, Port O'Connor, or Seadift. You'll have plenty of shooting for redheads, pintails, wigeon, green-winged teal, scaup, buffleheads, goldeneyes, and mergansers. Your guides will be U.S. Coast Guard-approved captains and they'll have blinds and decoy spreads waiting. Even a spate of rough weather won't spoil the hunt, since the guide service has plenty of private wetlands and flooded rice fields that hold mallards, gadwalls, wigeon, pintails, blue-winged teal, and occasionally different species of tree ducks.

Or why not get the best of both worlds and book a combination goose and duck hunt on H & H's private wetland projects or flooded rice stubble. You'll be comfortably transported to your blind on a trailer or six-seat all-terrain vehicle. Once you have a chance to hunt these wetland restoration projects, you'll appreciate the land management skills that brought these conservationists a Texas Parks and Wildlife Land Steward Award.

Larry Gore's Eagle Lake and Katy Prairie Outfitters

Katy, Texas

VITAL STATISTICS:

SPECIES: pintail, gadwall, wigeon, teal, mallard, tree duck, snow goose, Ross' goose, white-fronted goose, lesser Canada goose, sandhill crane

Season: ducks: November to January
geese: November to February
sandhill crane: January to February

Hunting Sites: 50,000 private acres: cropland, flooded flats, reservoirs

Accommodations: several options, call for types and rates

MEALS: depends on lodging option, call for more information

RATES: goose and duck (morning hunt only) $125/hunter; afternoon duck hunt $75/hunter; afternoon pheasant/chukar hunt $125/hunter; multiple-day package rates available

MAXIMUM NUMBER OF HUNTERS: unlimited; groups of up to 20 hunters

GRATUITIES: hunters' discretion

PREFERRED PAYMENT: money order, cash or check

Getting There: southeast Texas, 25 miles southwest of Houston

NEAREST COMMERCIAL AIRPORT: Houston, TX

Dogs and Facilities: dogs welcome; several lodging options are pet friendly

Guides: four to six hunters per guide

Other Services: bird cleaning (extra charge)

Other Activities: sporting clays course available in area

CONTACT:
Gordon Johnston
Larry Gore's Eagle Lake and Katy Prairie Outfitters
PO Box 0129
Katy, TX 77492-0129
Ph: 281-391-6100
Fax: 281-391-6114
Email: elkpo@pdg.net
Web: www.larrygore.com

THE SMALL TOWN of Katy is only a Texas-long stone's throw from the huge metropolis of Houston. But it's far from the maddening crowd—of people, that is, not geese. Katy is smack dab in the Texas rice belt, a region that winters approximately one to one and a half million white geese: snows and Ross' geese. Tack on more than a half million specklebellies and about 300,000 lesser Canadas; add thousands of wintering pintail, gadwall, wigeon, teal, mottled ducks, black-bellied tree ducks, and assorted divers and you have what's known as crowded airspace, a target-rich environment, a die-hard waterfowl hunter's destination.

The Eagle Lake/Katy Prairie area is no secret to waterfowlers, either. This is where the famous "Texas rag" hunt for snow geese originated. This is where you can begin hunting ducks in September, during the state's early, two-week teal season, hunt ducks again from the end of October until late January, and hunt sandhill cranes from New Year's day till January 23. And now a special "conservation season" for white geese extends into March.

These extensive hunting opportunities have not been lost on local outfitters. Larry Gore's Eagle Lake and Katy Prairie Outfitters has been guiding wingshooters in this country since 1977. These Texas boys know how to "do the right thing," too. They rotate the goose fields and blinds they hunt, restrict goose hunting beyond noon, and maintain refuge roost ponds for geese over a 50,000-acre area, to allow the birds to feed and rest between hunts.

Accommodations here will usually be area motels, with meals available at local restaurants. It's at one of these designated eateries that you'll meet your guide in the morning and get the lowdown on which field you'll be in by sunup. The guide will have scouted that field the previous evening, so you can be well assured geese will be meeting you there with the dawn.

But first, there's work to be done. After breakfast, you'll drive to the field, hike in, and help your guide place the white spread, which may consist of anywhere from 500 to 1,000 decoys—rags mostly, but maybe a dozen or so shells. Next, squirm into a white parka and lay down in the spread. You are now a giant-sized snow goose decoy. Hear that huge pack of dogs yipping in the distance? They're not dogs. They're snow geese. Thousands of them. The fun is about to begin.

Fun's over at noon. By then, on a mediocre day, everyone in your party will have bagged anywhere from two to five birds. On a good day, the personal bag can be anywhere from 10 to 23! Bring lots of shells. Most of the shots will be at white geese, but you'll have opportunities to bring down ducks, specklebellies, and small Canadas, too.

After lunch, if you so desire and have paid the outfitter's fee, a duck hunt may be in order. Afternoon duck hunts are fully guided and take place over flooded fields, ponds, and reservoirs. Box blinds, pit blinds, and natural blinds are used, depending on the species of duck you are pursuing—pintails are numerous here—and which areas they are using at that time of the season.

If you prefer upland game, your guide can, for an additional charge, also arrange a preserve hunt for pheasant and chukar. There's some bass fishing on a local lake, too. Or, late in the season, a chance to bag a sandhill crane. There's just no end to it.

A guide calls and his retriever waits for a flock of circling snows to come within shotgun range.

North Texas Waterfowl

Dalhart, Texas

VITAL STATISTICS:

SPECIES: Canada goose, snow goose

Season: November 1 to February 4

Hunting Sites: 260,000 acres of leased agricultural fields

Accommodations: local motel (room furnished in hunting rate)

Meals: local restaurants

Rates: from $300 per hunter for a two-day hunt

Maximum Number of Hunters: 15

Gratuities: hunters' discretion

Preferred Payment: cash or check

Getting There: in the Panhandle of Texas, 80 miles north of Amarillo

Nearest Commercial Airport: Amarillo, TX

Dogs and Facilities: dogs welcome to stay in motel with owners

Guides: two to six hunters per guide; guides furnish dogs

Other Services: bird cleaning

Other Activities: prairie dog shooting; duck hunting; pheasant hunting (in season)

CONTACT:
Tom Sanford or Randy White
North Texas Waterfowl
PO Box 492
Dalhart, TX 79022
Ph: 806-249-8477 or 806-244-8043
Email: ntwfhunt@xit.net

HEADQUARTERS for Tom Sanford's and Randy White's guide service, North Texas Waterfowl, is based in Dalhart, Texas, just 80 miles north of Amarillo and in the heart of the Central Flyway. For years, the wheat- and corn-producing region of Dalhart has been the winter home of lesser and greater Canada geese, as well as snow geese and white-fronted geese. Sanford and White began their business in 1987, leasing 64,000 acres of agricultural fields from local farmers for the exclusive use of their clients. Today the pair has 260,000 acres under lease.

Although Canada geese are the primary quarry here, Sanford and White also guide snow goose hunters, duck hunters, and pheasant hunters. The pair also offers combination duck and goose hunts. They also guide during the Texas early teal season in September.

Goose seasons are long in north Texas, and bag limits generous. The season on dark geese (Canadas and whitefronts) runs from November 1 to mid-February, and allows five geese per hunter per day. The season on snow geese runs concurrent with the dark goose season, but bag limits are 20 light geese per day. Conceivably, then, a hunter can take up to 25 geese per day, combining the light and dark goose daily bag limits. While this is hardly ever accomplished, it would make one heck of a lot of goose sausage.

The early teal season usually lasts for two weeks, starting about September 11, and allows six birds in the daily bag; the general duck season runs from the end of October to late January. To top it off, pheasants are legal targets for two weeks in December, too, allowing hunters to take three roosters a day in addition to their waterfowl limits.

Sounds like a hard day of hunting, and a multi-species combination hunt can especially be taxing. So, let's just concentrate on a goose hunting day.

"Our full-service guided hunt normally begins at 4 a.m. at a designated meeting location," says Sanford. "We ask our hunters to follow us in their own vehicle to the field we'll be hunting that morning. It's customary for the hunters to assist the guide in placing the decoys, and picking them up at the end of the hunt, at about 11 a.m. The guide is responsible for calling the birds as well as the shots. Our hunters are welcome to call, too, if they desire. If you don't get all the birds you want in the morning, we'll take you out again in the afternoon. The afternoon hunts are pass-shooting at geese leaving their roost for their evening feed.

"Also," Sanford says, "we don't mix parties. Lots of hunters don't like being thrown in with other hunters that they don't know. All we need is a minimum of two hunters. Then it's just you, your partner and your guide."

North Texas Waterfowl also provides unguided hunts on their leased properties. "Our unguided hunts are designed for experienced waterfowlers who only need property on which to hunt," says Sanford. "All unguided hunts take place on the same lands on which we conduct guided hunts, but unguided parties must provide their own decoys and do their own calling."

Winter wheat acts like a magnet for hungry geese. This field has been all but decimated by grazing Canadas and specklebellies. Ranchers and farmers who own these fields often ask hunters to come on their lands and shoot the pesky critters.

Po' Boys Outfitters

B a y   C i t y ,   T e x a s

ONE THING you can say about the Texas Gulf Coast is that it has no shortage of birds, either in numbers or varieties. Freshwater and brackish marshes provide habitat for all types of resident and wintering fowl, and ducks, especially, like the lodging and accommodations these wetlands provide. Puddlers include blue- and green-winged teal, pintail, gadwall, wigeon, mottled duck, wood duck, northern shoveller, and black-bellied whistling duck. Divers range from canvasback and redhead to lesser and greater scaup, bufflehead, and goldeneye. Geese, too—snows, blues, Ross', specklebellies, and some smaller races of Canadas—all winter here.

There's plenty of room open to public hunting, plenty of waterfowl, but relatively few hunters. Why? Because, as Po' Boys Outfitters' chief guide, Dennis Kelly, can tell you, all those coastal marshes aren't easy to get to, especially at low tide. That's why Kelly and his crew of guides travel by shallow-running airboats to and from their hunting spots.

Most of those spots are around Big Boggy and San Benard national wildlife refuges and the bays east and west of Matagorda, a huge chunk of seaside real estate, most of which sees surprisingly little hunting pressure.

To arrange yourself a hunt with Po' Boys, you'll need to get to Bay City and find a motel room. Food is on your own in local eateries. Dennis or one of his guides will contact you before the morning hunt and explain logistics. After that, it's up to you to be at the local boat ramp at 5 a.m. Bring your gun, shells, waders, a thermos of coffee, and don't forget a camouflage face mask (and, if you've never ridden in an airboat, I'd suggest a pair of earplugs).

The ride to the blind can be a short or long one, depending on where the birds are working best. When you arrive, the guide would appreciate some help deploying the 40 to 50 decoys (per person in the blind). Once the decoy set is in order, it's into the blind and get ready. Shooting starts a half hour before sunrise, and flocks of teal will be bombing the stool by the time you get loaded and prepared to shoot. Teal are numerous here, and you can shoot a whole limit of them in short order, but there will be plenty of other species to keep you occupied, too.

The hunt will last no later than 11; then it's back to the dock. If, however, you haven't taken a limit of birds, your guide will take you out again in the afternoon at no extra charge. If you have limited in the morning, Po' Boys can arrange an afternoon of shallow-water fishing for speckled trout and redfish. Or, if you've brought along a rifle or bow, they can also set you up on a bait pile where you can await the arrival of a wild hog. In other words, while hunting with Po' Boys, you can cover the basic food groups: fowl, fish, and "the other white meat."

A duck hunter reflects on a successful morning's shoot as he leaves his blind on the Texas coast. Green-winged teal, wigeon, and pintails have graced him with a full bag limit.

Third Coast Outfitters, Inc.

Bay City, Texas

VITAL STATISTICS:

SPECIES: snow goose, blue goose, Ross' goose, white-fronted goose, lesser Canada goose, pintail, green-winged teal, mottled duck, spoonbill, gadwall, wigeon, redhead, bluebill, bufflehead, blue-winged teal (early season)

Season: ducks: November to January
geese: November to February

Hunting Sites: over 40,000 acres in three Texas-size counties-Matagorda, Jackson, and Wharton-on fields of rice, corn, soybeans, milo, rye grass, and wheat; also hunting on marsh, ponds, flooded flats, and reservoirs

Accommodations: motel with one to two hunters per room

MEALS: home-cooked meals at local restaurant

RATES: $150/day for morning goose and duck hunts; $100/day for evening duck hunts; $570 for 3-day package with morning hunt, motel room, breakfast, bird cleaning and storage

MAXIMUM NUMBER OF HUNTERS: 40

GRATUITIES: $10 to $50 per hunter

PREFERRED PAYMENT: cash

Getting There: 80 miles south of Houston, TX

NEAREST COMMERCIAL AIRPORT: Houston, TX

Dogs and Facilities: no accommodations for guests' dogs

Guides: experienced guides with dogs

Other Services: bird cleaning, packaging, and storage

Other Activities: saltwater fishing and hunting for quail, pheasants, and chukar; sporting clays

CONTACT:
Bobby Hale
Third Coast Outfitters Inc.
P.O. Box 1351
Bay City, TX 77404-1351
Ph: 888-894-3373 or 409-245-3071
Web: www.third-coast-outfitters.com

AFTER FLYING into Houston and driving 80 miles south to the Gulf Coast town of Bay City, Texas, you check in to your motel and tuck in early because the next morning you're up at 4 A.M. and gathered at the Cattlemen's Restaurant next to the motel to meet your guide. There's time for a hearty breakfast and a chance to get the Thermos filled. Then you follow your guide to a field that's been scouted the day before. All hands help in setting the decoys under the expert guidance of the guide. After the spread has been set, your guide will position you on the downwind side of the spread, and he'll issue you white waterproof parkas and camo makeup for your face. Hunters are positioned in a straight line on their backs, feet and guns pointed downwind.

You wait, but not for long, before geese and ducks start filling the sky and setting wings for your decoy spread. These fields of rice, corn, soybeans, milo, rye grass, and wheat are a magnet for birds that have spent the night on the natural roosting areas of the marshes along the Texas Gulf Coast and its bays, as well as on the many man-made ponds inland. Waterfowl have been migrating to these areas for centuries.

"Take 'em," your guide hollers, breaking your early morning reverie. Suddenly you are sitting upright with your companions, the safety off, tracking the big birds as they come in. On command, your guide's dog retrieves the downed birds, and you reload, recline, and get ready for the next wave.

After the hunt, you, your companions, and the guide go back to the Blessing Hotel or the Cattlemen's Restaurant for the all-you-can-eat home-cooked meal and compare notes. Today, in addition to snows and a few specklebellies, you were fortunate to take a few pintails, mallards, and teal. On other outings, hunters have taken mottled ducks, fluvous ducks, and black-bellied whistling ducks in the goose decoys. Tomorrow, you all concur, you'll hunt puddle ducks on the saltwater bays.

And so it goes at Third Coast Outfitters, where the waterfowl hunting opportunities are many thanks to some 40,000 acres of leased land that is ripe with the food ducks and geese love—milo, corn, rice, rye, soybeans, wheat—plus the endless miles of Gulf Coast habitat. It is no wonder that this area has been dubbed a "waterfowl mecca" and has been written about with great respect by leading sportsman's magazines.

Total Outdoors Adventures

C o n r o e ,   T e x a s

VITAL STATISTICS:

SPECIES: snow goose, blue goose, Ross' goose, white-fronted goose, mallard, pintail, wigeon, teal, shoveler, gadwall, wood duck, bluebill, redhead, and canvasback

Season: snows, blues, and Ross': October 30 through February 13; Canadas and ducks: October 30 through January 23

Hunting Sites: over 40,000 acres throughout the Texas rice belt

Accommodations: one lodge and two bunkhouses, each sleeping up to 8 hunters

Meals: dinners built around theme meals, including Texas, Cajun, and Fiesta nights

Rates: $245 per person/day, getting cheaper with each day stayed

Maximum Number of Hunters: up to 24 hunters at lodge, 16 at other facilities; no more than five groups of eight total

Gratuities: hunters' discretion

Preferred Payment: cash or check

Getting There: an 85-mile drive southwest of Houston, TX

Nearest Commercial Airport: Houston, TX

Dogs and Facilities: dogs welcome

Guides: trained dogs and guides

Other Services: bird processing and storage included

Other Activities: sporting clays

CONTACT:
David Pruett
Total Outdoor Adventures
P.O. Box 3520
Conroe, TX 77305
Ph: 800-569-0839
Email: toa@lcc.net
Web: www.texasgoose.com

NOVEMBER THROUGH mid-February is a hot time in the rice belt of southwest Texas. If you're thinking in terms of ambient temperature or spicy food, think again. Think geese—as in snow goose, blue goose, Ross' goose, and specklebellies—flock after flock raining in on your big decoy spread. Your pump or repeater growing hot in your hands. That kind of hot.

David Pruett, owner and chief guide of Total Outdoor Adventures, will almost guarantee you great goose hunting action if you mosey on down to Texas. Heck, he will guarantee it. That's because Total Outdoors offers a guaranteed kill with each one- to five-day hunting package that includes lodging, meals, and guided hunt(s). If your party (four hunter minimum) does not get at least one bird per hunter per day, your group gets a free guided hunt the following season.

That's no ordinary guarantee. But then TOA is no ordinary outfitter. It boasts a hunter success ratio that puts it in the top 5 percent of all waterfowl outfitters in the region. Which means you're not likely to get a free day of hunting. Which in turn means hold on to your Stetson.

Located just 85 miles southwest of Houston, TOA has access to over 40,000 acres of privately owned farmland in the middle of the Texas rice belt. The lodge itself is located on a picturesque thousand-acre pecan orchard just north of El Campo, Texas. The 2,000-square-foot main house comes equipped with two bathrooms, air-conditioning, and a covered porch. In addition, there are two newly constructed bunkhouses complete with the same amenities, which sleep up to eight hunters each.

Mornings began at 4 a.m. with a hardy breakfast of eggs, pancakes, sausage, ham, bacon, hash browns, biscuits, toast, coffee, and juice. After breakfast you'll head out to a prescouted field planted with rice, soybean, or rye grass. After a few words on safety, your guide will ask you to help set out the decoys—up to 1,500 if you're hunting snow geese. "Peering out over an 800- to 1,500-piece spread is an amazing sight," says Pruett, "but not nearly as amazing as what's about to unfold."

You'll put on a white parka and disappear into the spread with the other hunters to the sounds of thousands of geese waking up on nearby roosts. Then get ready for some hot shooting, as your guide calls the flocks over the decoys and the shots, too.

Back at the ranch, you'll be treated to a buffet-style dinner with a different theme every night. There's Texan Night, of course, featuring 16- to 18-ounce ribeye steaks. There's Cajun Night, with deep-fried turkey and all the fixins. And what would a few days in Texas be without a Fiesta Night filled with festive music, fajitas, tamales, Mexican rice, and refried beans?

Total Outdoor Adventures is, as the name suggests, about more than goose hunting. It also offers seaduck hunting in one of four Texas bays, as well as flooded roost and flooded pond hunting. There's even sandhill crane hunting from early January to around mid-February.

CENTRAL FLYWAY]

W.S. Sherrill Waterfowl Hunting

Wharton, Texas

VITAL STATISTICS:

SPECIES: snow goose, Canada goose, white-fronted goose, Ross' goose, blue goose, teal, pintail, gadwall, wigeon, and other duck species

Season: ducks: early November through late January; geese: early November through late February

Hunting Sites: 50,000 acres composed primarily of croplands, with 34 flooded roosts for a total of 1,300 acres of water

Accommodations: two first-class private hunting lodges with full amenities, accommodating 20 and 24 hunters, respectively

MEALS: lodge stays include three home-cooked meals per day, snacks, refreshments and cold drinks

RATES: $145 per hunter/day (four hunter minimum); $125 per person/day for lodging

MAXIMUM NUMBER OF HUNTERS: 44

GRATUITIES: $60-$100 per day per guide

PREFERRED PAYMENT: cash, check

Getting There: approximately 50 miles southwest of Houston

NEAREST COMMERCIAL AIRPORT: Bush Intercontinental Airport and Hobby Airport, Houston, TX

Dogs and Facilities: dogs provided by guides

Guides: at least four hunters per guide

Other Services: bird processing and cold storage available in Wharton

Other Activities: sporting clays available in Houston

CONTACT:
W.S. Sherrill Waterfowl Hunting
1702 Garrett Ct.
Wharton, TX 77488
409-532-1789

THE RICE PRAIRIE southwest of Houston is home to some of the best snow goose hunting in the country. Not surprisingly, it is also home to a number of outfitters, including W.S. Sherrill Waterfowl Hunting, which claims to offer the "finest waterfowling in Texas." Sherrill backs up its boast with numbers: more than 80 square miles of hunting property from Eagle Lake Prairie to the Gulf Coast; over 1,300 acres of flooded roosts; and more than 3,300 guided hunts in over 20 years in the business, which comes out to about 13,000 hunters.

Owner Bill Sherrill says many of those hunters have been repeat customers. "Customer satisfaction is the name of the game," he says. "Your success is our number one goal. We want your business this year, and we want it next year, too. And we've been fortunate so far in building a loyal clientele."

Word of success spreads fast, and though W.S. Sherrill doesn't spend much money on advertising—"no fancy color brochure, just fancy hunting," according to their flier—word has gotten out. The outfitter has been featured recently on ESPN's *Suzuki Great Outdoors* and on Fox Sports' *Outdoor Adventure Series*. That means you'll need to book early if you want to reserve a hunt for the upcoming season. What it doesn't mean, however, is that you'll be crammed in on a crowded hunt, or that the down-home service they've staked their reputation on has changed in any way.

Most hunts are in groups of four, which is the minimum per guided hunt. Five-, six-, and seven-man groups can be accommodated, but eight-man groups are usually split into two groups of four. Each group will have its own guide as well as its own field.

What sets W.S. Sherrill apart from other area outfitters can be summed up in one word: water. Bill Sherrill takes special pride in the flooded roosts he establishes to hold large concentrations of waterfowl. "This year we plan to establish 34 roosts, ranging in size from 10 to 100 acres. About half of all the roosts on Eagle Lake Prairie belong to our club. It's expensive, pumping in water and building levees, but it's well worth the cost."

All this preparation means that the Sherrill properties sometimes hold 150,000 birds or more throughout the entire season. That's a lot of snow geese, blue geese, specklebellies, and Canada geese, which you can hunt from early November through late February. That's also a lot of ducks, such as pintail, wigeon, gadwall, and teal, which are in season from early November to late January. Goose limits are a generous 22 per hunter per day (20 snows and 2 darks), while duck limits are six birds per hunter per day.

The two lodges, Cow Camp Hunting Lodge and Caney Creek Lodge, come with full accommodations, including three full, home-cooked meals per day, snacks and refreshments. Cow Camp is located in the heart of a 32,000-acre private ranch, and includes six bedrooms and five baths, plus a den with billiard and card tables, a gun-cleaning room, and rustic porches. Caney Creek is located one mile from the town of Wharton and includes eight bedrooms and eight and one-half baths, a den with fireplace, wet bar, decks, gun-cleaning room, and a private lake.

[C E N T R A L   F L Y W A Y]

Webfoot Connection, Inc.

R o c h e s t e r ,   T e x a s

VITAL STATISTICS:

SPECIES: Canada goose, white-fronted goose, snow goose, mallard, pintail

Season: geese: November 1 through February 15; ducks: November 1 through January 23

Hunting Sites: leased milo, wheat, and peanut fields; private lakes

Accommodations: lodge has six bunkrooms that sleep four each and two cabins that sleep 10 each; rates include three meals per day in restaurant on site

Rates: $250 per hunter/day; includes meals, lodges, guided morning hunt

Maximum Number of Hunters: six to eight hunters per hunt; lodge accommodates 24 maximum

Gratuities: $20 per hunter/day

Preferred Payment: cash, check, credit card

Getting There: 60 miles north of Abilene, TX

Nearest Commercial Airport: equal distance from Abilene, Lubbock, and Wichita Falls, Kansas, airports

Dogs and Facilities: outside kennel runs; dogs must be obedient and trained

Guides: two guides per group of six to eight hunters; guides have trained retrievers

Other Services: birds cleaned, frozen, packed for travel

Other Activities: released pheasants, wild quail; afternoon duck hunts; wild hog hunts

CONTACT:
Smokey and Kathy Rathbun
Webfoot Connection Inc.
PO Box 130
Rochester, TX 79544
Ph: 888-326-3248
Email: webfootconnection@westx.net
Web: www.webfootconnection.com

DRIVE THROUGH a good portion of north-central Texas and you wouldn't think there would be a duck or goose within hundreds of miles. There's plenty of desert, the kind that reminds you of a John Wayne western movie. But tucked away down near the small town of Rochester is an agricultural outlier that encompasses almost two counties. Wheat, milo, and peanuts are the main crops, and fields of these commodities attract thousands of hungry, wintering waterfowl. The birds roost on several lakes, reservoirs, and on the nearby Brazos River.

In predawn light, the geese lift off the water and head for the fields to feed. But which fields? The guides at Webfoot Connection will have that sorted out for you. They'll have spent the previous afternoon and early evening hours scouting the countryside to determine which fields the geese are using at that time and will no doubt return to the next morning.

You will probably arrive at the lodge about the time the scouting is going on. Relax, unpack your gear, and kick back in the lodge until dinnertime. The roomy main lodge has a wide-screen television and plenty of hunting videos to help you pass the time. Or enjoy a game of pool with a friend. Forget some small item of hunting gear? There's also a small inventory in the sporting goods section: duck and goose calls, face masks, camouflage clothing, and other goodies to choose from. Enjoy a drink at the bar. Then walk next door to the Branding Iron restaurant for dinner. Mesquite-broiled steaks are a specialty.

The next morning at breakfast (also at the Branding Iron), you'll meet your guides for the morning hunt. The drive to the field may take anywhere from 10 to 40 minutes, but you'll arrive well before sunup. Help the guides stake out a couple of hundred silhouette decoys, get covered up in camo netting, and wait.

Hopefully, the wait won't be long. Depending on the timing of the migration, the first flock into the decoys could be small Canadas, Canadas mixed with whitefronts, or, later in the season, snow geese. Whichever they may be, the guides will expertly call the geese, working them into the ambush. Don't move a muscle until the birds are in range and the guide yells "Take 'em!" The rest is up to you.

What might drive you crazy here are the flocks of mallards and pintails that also come to the field sets. You may have a couple dozen ducks hovering 20 yards over your head, but if there are geese anywhere in sight, the guides won't call the shot on ducks. And there are usually geese somewhere in sight.

If you do want to hunt ducks, though, Webfoot will arrange an afternoon hunt for you on a canyon lake along the Brazos River. Otherwise, if sitting around the lodge is a bit too little to do, the guides will also schedule an afternoon of hunting for released pheasants or wild quail. Looking for a little action at night? Forget about the Dallas Cowboy Cheerleaders. How about an encounter with a wild hog that could go up to 400 pounds? That can be arranged, and much more easily, too.

A satisfied group of clients poses with their guides and morning bag of geese taken in a peanut field near Rochester, Texas.

ALASKA

THE LAST FRONTIER. EVERYONE should make a trip to Alaska sometime in their lives. For the waterfowler, I'd suggest that be in fall or winter. The scenery is sensational, there are loads of ducks and geese, and every hunt is an adventure. Alaska is a nesting ground for huge numbers of waterfowl. In years when the prairies are dry, most of the continent's pintails nest here. So do plenty of scaup and wigeon, and, along the expansive coastline, sea ducks. Pacific brant and white-fronted geese nest here, as do Aleutian Canada geese.

On the mainland, you'll want to plan your trip in early fall. Early cold weather here can send ducks and geese flying south in a hurry. But along the coast, where the Japanese Current keeps ocean temperatures moderate throughout the winter, you can hunt ducks well into December and January. Most of those will be sea ducks—oldsquaw, harlequins, scoters, and eiders—but don't be surprised to discover mallards and greenwings here in the middle of winter. Some local mallard populations in coastal waters on Kodiak Island, for example, are nonmigratory. The birds are some of the biggest you'll ever encounter. And speaking of encounters, rare ones, the island is possibly the only place you'll have an opportunity to bag a king eider or see a whale in your decoy spread. Want a go at it? Read on.

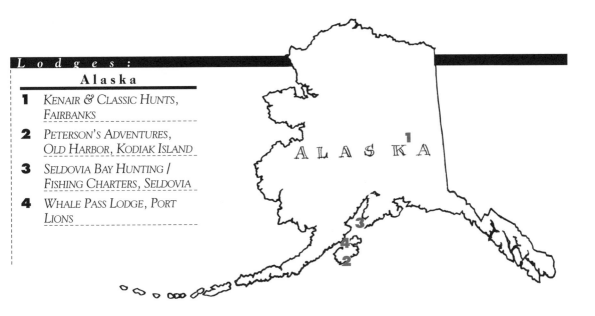

ALASKA

[A L A S K A]

Kenair and Classic Hunts

Fairbanks, Alaska

VITAL STATISTICS:

SPECIES: mallard, pintail, wigeon, scaup, teal, Canada goose, white-fronted goose, sandhill crane

Season: September

Hunting Sites: Minto Lake, sloughs, ponds, and surrounding lakes

Accommodations: fly-in outpost camp, all-weather shelters with cots, gas lighting and heaters; food and cooking gear provided for clients' use

Meals: camp fare, but good and nourishing

Rates: $1,175 for first four days of duck season, $974 thereafter; all hunts four-day packages

Maximum Number of Hunters: 12

Gratuities: hunters' discretion

Preferred Payment: cash or check

Getting There: 30-minute float plane trip from Fairbanks, AK

Nearest Commercial Airport: Fairbanks, AK

Dogs and Facilities: dogs welcome

Guides: one outpost camp guide transports hunters to selected blinds with decoys

Other Services: none

Other Activities: wildlife watching; fishing

CONTACT:
Rafe Russell
KenAir
500 Roberts Roost Rd.
Fairbanks, AK 99712
Ph: 907-488-8848
Fax: 907-488-8848

BORN TO BE WILD? Looking for adventure or whatever comes your way? Keep your motor running with a fly-in duck hunting trip to interior Alaska. The Minto flats, 50 nautical miles west of Fairbanks, is one of Alaska's most productive waterfowl breeding areas. The expansive flats (800 square miles) include Minto Lake, sloughs, ponds, and other small lakes that teem with ducks and other wildlife, including moose, beaver, fox, and eagles.

But don't think you can trailer your duck boat there, and don't look for a luxurious lodge on the shore of Minto Lake. The only way to get to the flats is by float plane, and the only accommodations there is an outpost camp with portable living shelters. But you won't find a lot of competition from other duck hunters, either.

KenAir charter flights of Fairbanks and professional waterfowl guide Mick Davis of Classic Hunts have teamed up to provide adventurous waterfowlers with the unique experience of hunting the flats. KenAir gets you in and out of the fully equipped camp, and Davis helps you out while you're there. This isn't quite a do-it-yourself hunt, but it's close to it. Davis shows you to your living quarters, complete with cooking facilities and food, ferries you to and from your duck blinds via Go-Devil boat and motor (decoys are already there and set), and shows you everything else you need to know.

These are four-day hunts, but allow yourself extra days on either end, because weather in Alaska determines when you get in and out of camp. Allow yourself at least one whole day in Fairbanks when you arrive there, to rest up and acclimate before the next day's float plane trip into camp. The next morning, you'll fly with an experienced bush pilot aboard a Cessna 185 to camp. Be prepared to travel light. The weight limit for your gear is 60 pounds.

If the weather cooperates, you'll be in camp in the morning and hunting that afternoon. If you are there during the first four days of the state's duck season, you'll probably have the opportunity to hunt sandhill cranes, which are in the area along with millions of other waterfowl during the summer. After the first four days, cranes may migrate off the flats, but migrating ducks start to build up (yes, the "great northern flights" even appear as far north as Alaska) with the summer resident ducks and geese.

Day two and three in camp are devoted to separate morning and afternoon hunts. You may want to take a couple of hours, though, to fling a spoon or spinner in the shallow water for northern pike. These "water wolves" are here in great numbers, and some grow to more than 20 pounds. Day four is a morning hunt, after which (again, depending on weather) your pilot will pick you up and return you to Fairbanks.

When you get back to the city, be sure to allow yourself a day or two to see the sights. Head out on the highway. Your friendly bush pilot can recommend a variety of things to do and see.

In many parts of Alaska, the only transportation in and out of the best hunting and fishing areas is by float plane. The flights offer passengers a chance to see spectacular scenery.

Peterson's Adventures

O l d   H a r b o r ,   A l a s k a   (K o d i a k   I s l a n d)

VITAL STATISTICS:

SPECIES: king eider, Barrows goldeneye, oldsquaw, harlequin, scoter (three species), green-winged teal, bufflehead, mallard, pintail, mergansers, others (18 species total)

Season: November through January

Hunting Sites: Kodiak Island coastal waters

Accommodations: modern 10-room lodge with private rooms and full baths, or bed-and-breakfast lodge

Meals: full breakfast, lunch; dinner: steaks, chops, seafood

Rates: $1,590 for four-day package; $2,555 for seven-day package; both include guide services, lodging, and meals

Maximum Number of Hunters: six

Gratuities: hunters' discretion

Preferred Payment: cash or check

Getting There: 65 miles southeast of the city of Kodiak, Kodiak Island, Alaska

Nearest Commercial Airport: Kodiak

Dogs and Facilities: due to remote location, clients are not encouraged to bring dogs

Guides: one guide for four to six hunters

Other Services: bird cleaning and packaging

Other Activities: deer hunting; fishing; kayaking; sight-seeing

CONTACT:
Jeff Peterson or Naomi Klouda
Peterson's Adventures
PO Box 141
Old Harbor, AK 99643
Ph: 907-286-2252
Fax: 907-286-2316
Email: fishunt@alaska.net
Web: www.kodiakcombos.com

"NO CROWDS, guaranteed." That's what native Alaskan Jeff Peterson will tell you about hunting and fishing near Old Harbor. Given its location, you wouldn't expect to have to put up with any gunning pressure. Old Harbor is located on Kodiak Island's protected east side, 65 miles southeast of the city of Kodiak. Accessible by a three-hour boat ride or a 25-minute daily scheduled charter flight (about $50 per person) from Kodiak, Old Harbor, an Alutiq Native village, is one of Alaska's oldest towns. There isn't even a crowd in town, as the population is 325.

Given the area's moderate temperatures (summer days are 50 to 70 degrees Fahrenheit, winter temperatures above 30 degrees), it's a great place for year-round outdoor activities. Whale-watching for migrating gray, humpback, and killer whales adds to the unique opportunities of wildlife viewing here. The terrain itself is something to behold, varying from rolling alpine tundra to steep, alder-choked mountains and rugged coastlines. The island also boasts the highest Sitka black-tailed deer populations and biggest bucks in North America. To say nothing of the island's famous brown bears, which can grow to 1,200 pounds. For the duck hunter, though, the unique wildlife of greatest interest are the sea ducks, the rarity and variety of which are available in few other places in the world. Barrows goldeneye, oldsquaw, harlequin, common and red-breasted mergansers, and scoters are common here, and this is one of the few places where collectors can add a king eider to their trophy room. Common duck species include mallard, pintail, green-winged teal, and greater scaup.

Peterson grew up in Old Harbor and is intimately familiar with the terrain, waters, and wildlife. He prides himself in his ability to accommodate his clients' wishes. That is, if you only want to hunt ducks, he'll not only guide you exclusively for ducks, he'll set you up in a location for the particular species you'd like to hunt each day. If you'd like to combine the multiple sporting experiences the island has to offer, he'll accommodate that, too. He's even trademarked the name "Kodiak Combos" to demonstrate to visiting sports that they can combine hunting and fishing opportunities—halibut fishing and winter king salmon fishing with duck and blacktail hunting. So be prepared to bring your shotgun, rifle, bow, and fishing rods to experience all he has to offer.

A day with Peterson starts with a full breakfast prepared by the lodge cook, who will also pack you a lunch to take aboard his 24-foot Seaport boat. Then it's off to selected bays, depending on which species of ducks you'd like to hunt that day. Upon arrival, Peterson sets out the decoys and assigns each hunter a spot to shoot from, which could be stony beach blind, a coastal lagoon, or a saltwater slough. After lunch, you'll pick up and change hunting locations, or, if you'd like to, fish for halibut (some go more than 200 pounds) or troll for king salmon. So much to do, and each day has the potential for what Peterson has coined (he hasn't trademarked this, yet) "a Kodiak moment."

Barrow's goldeneye and harlequin ducks are two of several sea duck species common to Kodiak Island.

Seldovia Bay Hunting/Fishing Charters

Seldovia, Alaska

VITAL STATISTICS:

SPECIES: harlequin, oldsquaw, Barrow's and common goldeneye, scoter, greater scaup, bufflehead, mallard, wigeon, pintail, green-winged teal, Canada goose, black brant

Season: September 1 through December 16

Hunting Sites: Pacific coastal waters, marshes, and bays near Seldovia

Accommodations: apartment-style housekeeping

MEALS: lunch provided; otherwise, cooking facilities in apartment lodging or nearby restaurant in Seldovia

RATES: $175 per person/day for party of four or more; $200 per person/day for party of less than four; lodging additional $20 per person/day

MAXIMUM NUMBER OF HUNTERS: six

GRATUITIES: hunters' discretion

PREFERRED PAYMENT: check deposit, remainder cash

Getting There: Seldovia is on the Kenai Peninsula, 15 miles west of Homer and 200 miles south of Anchorage

NEAREST COMMERCIAL AIRPORT: Seldovia, AK

Dogs and Facilities: hunters' dogs welcome in apartment-style housing

Guides: Warren "Buck" Brown guides all parties

Other Services: fish and bird cleaning and packaging

Other Activities: ptarmigan and grouse hunting; fishing for halibut and king salmon

CONTACT:
Warren Brown
PO Box 77
Seldovia, AK 99663
Ph: 907-234-7498
Email: buck@xyz.net

WARREN "BUCK" BROWN is a one-man waterfowling operation, and what an operation it is. He's been in business for 10 years in the Seldovia Bay area of Alaska's Kenai Peninsula and knows the waters and wildlife well. And if you're looking for a mixed bag that includes ducks, geese, salmon, and halibut, Seldovia Bay will more than fit the bill.

The town of Seldovia itself is the last, southernmost habitation of any size on the Kenai Peninsula. Head out of the protected waters of Seldovia Bay into expansive Kachemak Bay, and it's a 15-mile boat ride to Homer. Turn left out of Seldovia Bay on a west-southwest heading, and you'll reach the tip of Kodiak Island, if you don't run aground on the aptly named Barren Islands first, in a few hours (weather and tides permitting).

But, thankfully, Brown won't have to take you far from Seldovia Bay to immerse you in spectacular Alaskan scenery and introduce you to a cornucopia of fish and game. Every day of your hunt will bring you to a different, secluded bay or marsh, the big waters of Hachemak Bay, or even shore blinds for brant and sea duck hunting. Variety is the spice of life, of course, and Brown will provide some of that on a daily basis; Alaska will provide the rest.

Brown's best hunting starts after the middle of October, but he guides parties early in the season (September 20 to October 20) to Cold Bay to hunt ducks, geese, and brant. Cold Bay offers isolated pond hunting for ducks and field hunting for geese, as well as brant hunting from blinds built along the wilderness shore. If there is a slowdown in the waterfowling action, you merely have to take a short hike inland to flush ruffed grouse and ptarmigan, using your own dog or Brown's bird dog. But, grouse and ptarmigan being subject to population ups and downs, you may also spend time soaking a line—and make sure it's a strong one—for Alaskan king salmon in a nearby tributary stream.

Later in October, Brown focuses his operations on sea duck hunting from floating blinds. For hunters looking to expand their collection of mounted ducks, this is the best time to bag a harlequin, oldsquaw, Barrow's goldeneye, or any of the three species of scoters common in Alaska but rarely found in the Lower 48.

Don't forget to spend at least part of a day with Brown fishing for halibut. These tasty fish can run from 20 to 200 pounds or more, so if you do hook one, you're in for a battle. But, then, a single fish, cleaned and filleted, can fill an ice chest. Still, make room for a few Pacific cod, also great "eaters," which you'll often hook while fishing for halibut.

So, you better bring two ice chests: one for ducks, geese, brant, and grouse; the other for halibut and salmon. Maybe a third one for transporting home all the film you should be exposing of Alaskan scenery and the many memories you'll want to preserve of a memorable time in "The Last Frontier."

Whale Pass Lodge

P o r t   L i o n s ,   A l a s k a

VITAL STATISTICS:

SPECIES: sea ducks, divers, mallards, wigeon, green-winged teal
Season: early October through late January
Hunting Sites: rivers, bays, straits, and coastal waters of Kodiak Island
Accommodations: private, remote three-bedroom lodge
MEALS: field lunch and two hot, home-cooked meals per day
RATES: six nights lodging with five days hunting: $1,950 per person; group rates available
MAXIMUM NUMBER OF HUNTERS: six (prefer four)
GRATUITIES: guests' discretion
PREFERRED PAYMENT: cash or check
Getting There: fly to Kodiak, then charter flight to Port Lions, AK
NEAREST COMMERCIAL AIRPORT: Kodiak, AK
Dogs and Facilities: guests are not encouraged to bring their own dogs because of travel logistics
Guides: one guide per four hunters; guides have trained Chesapeake Bay retrievers
Other Services: birds cleaned and packaged for shipping
Other Activities: bear hunting; fishing; bird and whale watching; sightseeing

CONTACT:
Bob May
Whale Pass Lodge
PO Box 32
Port Lions, AK 99550
Ph: 800-4-KODIAK
Email: bob@whalepasslodge.com
Web: www.whalepasslodge.com

I MAGINE sitting in this comfortable lodge and having your morning coffee. Looking out the picture windows, overlooking the strait known as Whale Pass, you can often watch whales porpoising and flocks of sea birds flying low over the water. That is, if the eagles flying by the front of the lodge don't obscure your view.

Whale Pass Lodge is located on one of the breathtakingly beautiful, moutainous and remote islands that make up what is commonly referred to, singularly, as Kodiak Island. Yes, the island, or more correctly, islands, of the big brown bears. And of sitka black-tailed deer, halibut, Pacific cod, salmon, steelhead, dolly varden trout and a host of other creatures. For ducks, this is a collector's paradise. The tides keep most of the coastal waters here ice free during fall and winter, providing perfect habitat for three species of scoters, Barrow's goldeneye, oldsquaw, harlequin, bufflehead, eider, common and red-breasted mergansers, as well as mallard, wigeon, and green-winged teal.

And getting to this island paradise is not as difficult as you might expect. Commercial flights from Anchorage arrive and depart the city of Kodiak a couple of times a day. From there, as many as four scheduled charter flights a day will take you to Port Lions, 28 miles west of Kodiak. From there, Bob will pick you up and take you another seven miles to the lodge aboard his 24-foot cruiser, which will also be the mother ship for your daily hunting forays.

Those forays include a leisurely start in the mornings, because there is no need to get up at the crack of dawn (which, this far north, is late anyway). After breakfast, depending on the species you decide to pursue that day, it's back into the cruiser for a ride to the hunting grounds, which can be a bay, beach, pothole, marsh, or what have you, but the scenery will be spectacular. You'll pack in a full day's hunting and see plenty of ducks, too, more than you could possibly imagine. (What you won't see here, though, are other duck hunters.) Wear warm, waterproof clothing, but don't be too surprised to discover that winter here isn't all that bad. The warming effect of the Japanese Current keeps the islands more temperate than, say, northern Wisconsin or Minnesota, even in December and January.

You'll be back at the lodge before dark and in time to savor a regional tradition: a Russian-Aleut style steam bath, or *banya*. Then it's time to share a bottle of wine or indulge in a cocktail (it's BYO here, for insurance reasons), before a hot dinner, possibly a halibut Wellington, one of the house specialties.

If you care to, Bob will even take you fishing so that you can take some halibut home. There are also Pacific cod in the same deeper waters of the bays, and there's always the chance to catch salmon and steelhead, and Bob can arrange for that, too. With advance notice, he'll also combine a deer hunt with your duck expedition.

Whatever you choose to do at Whale Pass Lodge, you'll be in the hands of an experienced, trustworthy outfitter who is intimately familiar with the waters and wildlife of the islands. Bob May and his Whale Pass Lodge simply can't be beat if you are considering an Alaskan duck hunt. And you should consider it. In fact, you owe it to yourself.

Bob May, chief guide and proprietor of Whale Pass Lodge, waits for ducks on a Kodiak Island slough.

CANADA EAST

NOVA SCOTIA, QUEBEC, MANITOBA

F ROM MANITOBA TO THE EAST coast of the Island of Newfoundland is quite a stretch. But for our purposes here, the division of eastern and western Canada is quite arbitrary. In the provinces east of Manitoba, you're looking at forested habitats and big water, and a diversity of hunting opportunities. Black ducks and mallards, sea ducks, Canada geese, and greater snow geese are the draw here, and the hunting takes place in some unique habitats, from the tundra lowlands of Ontario's James Bay to the craggy shores of Newfoundland and Labrador. Here, you can even enjoy a historic method of waterfowl hunting banned in the U.S.—sink box shooting.

The Province of Manitoba, from Hudson Bay to the southern prairies, offers its own grand diversity of hunting styles and target species. Just about every species of waterfowl in North America can be hunted here, depending on where you set your decoy spread. There's big water hunting for canvasback and redheads on lakes Winnipeg and Winnipegosis, mallards in the Portage La Prairie surroundings, and untold numbers of Canada geese and lesser snow geese near Oak Hammock Marsh and in the Interlake region. In the north, the prairies and boreal forests around The Pas offer a mixture of mallard and diver duck hunting on agricultural areas and pristine wilderness lakes. Yes, Manitoba has it all, eh?

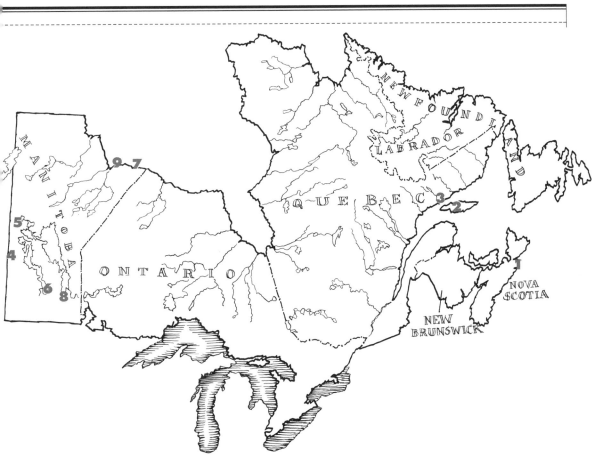

Lodges and Outfitters:

Nova Scotia

1 GOLDENEYE GUIDE SERVICE, HALIFAX

Quebec

2 SÉPAQ-ANTICOSTI, ANTICOSTI ISLAND

3 ROGER GLADU GUIDE SERVICE, ST. IGNACE DE LOYOLA

Manitoba

4 BEAR VALLEY OUTFITTERS, SWAN RIVER

5 CARPENTER'S CLEARWATER LODGE, THE PAS

6 CROOKED CREEK LODGE, ST. AMBROISE

7 KASKATTAMA SAFARI ADVENTURES, KASKATTAMA RIVER DELTA

8 MASSEY GUIDES AND OUTFITTERS, LOCKPORT

9 NANUK LODGE, HUDSON BAY

Goldeneye Guide Service

H a l i f a x ,   N o v a   S c o t i a

LOOKING FOR a unique waterfowl hunting experience? Not afraid of cold, damp quarters? How about a sink box hunt? Outlawed long ago in the United States, sink boxes are still legal for duck hunting in parts of Canada, including Nova Scotia. Imagine yourself sitting eye-level with the decoys, bobbing in the North Atlantic, watching a flock of scoters or oldsquaw lined out, heading your way and only a foot or two above the water. They're at the outside edge of the blocks now, but wait, still too far. A couple of wingbeats later and they're only 25 yards out, moving fast. You rise and shoot, sending a spray of ocean water erupting 15 feet behind the bird you aimed at. Shoot again. Only eight feet behind this time. Shoot again.

So it goes, as any experienced sea ducker can tell you. You're going to spend some time and ammunition before you figure out the correct lead on these fast-flying ducks. And shooting out of the cramped confines of a sink box won't help your shot-to-kill average, either. *How in the heck*, you might be asking yourself, *did the old time market gunners ever make a living doing this?* That would be a good question for Brian Mason. He's been guiding hunters on sink box shoots off Nova Scotia's eastern shore for 11 years.

But Mason doesn't confine his hunters to sink boxes. Depending on wind, tide, and migrations, he might have you hunting over decoys, or "tollers" as they're called here, from a rock blind on a point of land, in a stick blind in a salt marsh, on an offshore rock ledge, or maybe even in a "gunning tub." The tub is another waterfowling feature unique to this area. It consists of a plywood blind sunk in the mud at low tide that has its sides shored up with rocks. At high tide, the blind is submerged, but as the tide goes out, the blind is bailed out and the hunters jump in to gun the ducks and geese that come to feed on the surrounding, shallow flats.

The sink box hunt is different. Mason tows the sink box to the shooting area, anchors it, and sets out strings of decoys. Once the box is loaded with iron ballast to sink it to water level, you climb in . . . alone. Don't worry, Mason won't be too far off and will be keeping on eye on you. After an hour stint in the box, you'll rotate with another hunter. You can sit in the tender and have a cup of coffee, or you might be ferried to a shore blind.

If the weather doesn't cooperate for sink box gunning, Mason and his guides have plenty of back-up areas to hunt for black ducks and Canada geese. Or, if you prefer a hunt for a trophy whitetail, Mason can arrange that, too.

Sépaq-Anticosti

VITAL STATISTICS:

SPECIES: black duck, common eider, surf scoter, green-winged teal, pintail, Canada goose

Season: mid-September to mid-October

Hunting Sites: freshwater marshes, island coastal areas

Accommodations: private lodge (call for additional information)

MEALS: American style with French influence

RATES: $1,899 (Cdn) includes seven nights lodging, all meals, six days guided hunting

MAXIMUM NUMBER OF HUNTERS: call for additional information

GRATUITIES: hunters' discretion

PREFERRED PAYMENT: cash, check

Getting There: charter flight from Sept-Ilses or Mont-Joli, Quebec

NEAREST COMMERCIAL AIRPORT: Mont-Joli, Quebec

Dogs and Facilities: no facilities for hunters' dogs

Guides: one guide with 4x4 ATV and 4x4 crewcab pickup per four hunters

Other Services: bird cleaning, packaging, storage

Other Activities: white-tailed deer hunting; small game hunting for ruffed grouse, spruce grouse

CONTACT:
Gilles Durmaresq
Sépaq-Anticosti, Quebec
Canada
Ph: 800-463-0863 or 418-890-0863
Fax: 418-682-9944
Web: www.sepaq.com

ANTICOSTI Island is a New Jersey-sized island off the southern coast of Quebec, near the mouth of the St. Lawrence River. The name Anticosti comes from the Indian word "Notiskuan," meaning "land where we hunt bear," which was bestowed upon the island some 3,500 years ago by natives. About 1895, a French choclatier named Henri Menier purchased the 4.3 million-acre island as a private hunting and fishing domain. He introduced 220 deer to the island in 1896 and 1897. Over the years, the deer herd grew to become some 120,000 animals, the largest concentration of whitetails in eastern North America.

In 1974, the government of Quebec acquired the island and proceeded to divide up the land and distribute it to private outfitters. Today, Sépaq (*Société des établissements de plein air du Quebec*), a government operated marketing company, manages most of the island and the recreational opportunities offered there.

Known primarily as a paradise for white-tailed deer hunting, Anticosti Island is also a land of great ecological wealth and breathtaking natural beauty where impressive cliffs plunge into the sea. Inland you'll find canyons, waterfalls, lakes, and rivers. Along the coast and in interior marshes, you'll also find ducks. Especially black ducks.

Sépaq-Anticosti, realizing the allure the black duck has for many waterfowlers, has recently begun special waterfowl hunts in the Sainte-Marie sector of the island. The very economical week-long package includes lodging at the St. Marie, a century-old lodge built by—you guessed it— Henri Menier. The lodge is built on the coast and has a spectacular view of the water.

Anticosti is located in the heart of the black duck's principal breeding range, and there's no lack of the birds here. Limits are also generous: four black ducks per hunter per day, as opposed to the more common one-bird limit in most areas of the U.S. A great deal of Anticosti duck hunting takes place along the coastal shoreline, where common eiders and surf scoters share shallow water habitat with black ducks. Where in American waters wary black ducks are often found only in pairs or in small aggregations of a half dozen or so, whole flocks, sometimes up to 50 birds at a time, commonly come to the decoys on Anticosti. Sitting on low, camouflaged recliners at the water's edge, decoys in the surf in front of them, hunters here enjoy black duck shooting unavailable anywhere in the U.S.

Duck hunting also takes place on inland lakes such as 100-acre Canard Lac (Duck Lake, but it sounds much better in French), actually a bulrush marsh surrounded by black spruce. Freshwater areas such as this serve black ducks as evening roosting areas, and a late afternoon hunting on one can produce fantastic shooting when the sun dips to the western horizon.

Duck hunting isn't the only option for wingshooting here. The island's forests are home to ruffed grouse and spruce grouse, which can be hunted at no additional cost to the waterfowl hunting package. As a bonus, the package rate also allows each hunter to take one white-tailed deer (deer license additional). Consider that the $1,899 hunt/lodging/meals package in Candian funds converts to less than $1,400 U.S. and you know what great value an Anticosti duck, deer, or grouse hunt really is.

Roger Gladu Guide Service

St. Ignace de Loyola, Quebec

VITAL STATISTICS:

SPECIES: black duck, mallard, wood duck, teal, lesser and greater scaup, goldeneye

Season: September 25 to early November for marsh; September 25 to mid-December for sink box

Hunting Sites: 700 acres of leased land, including a large Ducks Unlimited project (Commune de l'Ile du Pas); exclusive rights to sink box hunting on Lake St-Pierre (a large widening of the St. Lawrence River)

Accommodations: two cabins accommodating four hunters each; motels nearby

Meals: local restaurants

Rates: $220/day

Maximum Number of Hunters: eight

Gratuities: hunter's discretion

Preferred Payment: cash or Visa

Getting There: on the north shore of the St. Lawrence, 40 miles east of Montreal

Nearest Commercial Airport: Montreal

Dogs and Facilities: hunters are encouraged to bring their dogs; they can be kept in cabin

Guides: two to four hunters per guide; dogs provided

Other Services: bird cleaning

Other Activities: sight seeing

CONTACT:

Roger Gladu
Roger Gladu Guide Service
2435 Rang St- Pierre
St. Ignace de Loyola, Quebec
Canada, J0K2P0
Ph/Fax: 450-836-1317

THE SIGHT of decoys at eye level reminds you that this is not an ordinary duck outing. So too does the fact that when you peer around your position, you see nothing but water. You are, it seems, shooting ducks from a submarine portal. Welcome to the unique and historic world of sink box hunting.

Up on Lake St-Pierre, a 220-square-mile widening of the St. Lawrence River, the art and practice of sink box hunting is still going strong under the tutelage of outfitters such as Roger Gladu. The waters of Quebec remain one of the few places in North America where hunters can still enjoy the legendary pastime of sink box gunning.

Gladu's charges depart very early for a long boat ride into the heart of Lake St-Pierre. There hunters disembark into their sink boxes, often described as water-going pit blinds. Needless to say, the well-prepared hunter is also well insulated with several layers of warm clothing. About 100 decoys are deployed and the tender boat with guides retreats to watch over the hunters but stay out of the line of sight.

Because of the effectiveness of these low-profile blinds, they were first outlawed in 1838 in New York and eventually across the country. But the modern sink box is no longer employed in market hunting and today it is infinitely safer than its counterparts of yesteryear. Most are made with a combination of wood and synthetic materials that keep the boats afloat even if completely filled with water. Sink boxes are towed into position to match the daily flight patterns of local ducks.

Tucked into your submerged blind, you study the horizon for divers moving along close to the water, oblivious to your presence. After you've taken your first ducks of the day, the guides move in to retrieve them, and possibly replenish your supply of coffee, before they retreat to the watery horizon. Puddle ducks pass by, as well, but they fly higher above you and the underwater deception is less likely to fool them. At the end of the morning's gunning, however, you may pause to admire the oldsquaw or canvasback that your guides collected from among the ice-coated decoys, drinking in for a moment the lonely shooting platform and its ties to waterfowling history.

And if the sink box is not your style, Gladu offers early hunts in the marshes along the St. Lawrence. If a limit is not taken in the morning, hunters may go back for an afternoon hunt.

[C A N A D A - E A S T]

Bear Valley Outfitters

S w a n   R i v e r ,   M a n i t o b a

VITAL STATISTICS:

SPECIES: snow goose, Canada goose, ducks

Season: mid-September through October

Hunting Sites: lakes, flooded timber, rivers, agricultural fields

Accommodations: private lodge with rooms for two, four, or six hunters; two additional cabins sleep six; recreation hall, hot tub, dining room

MEALS: home-style cooking

RATES: package rates from $800 for three days of hunting; lodging, meals, guides, bird processing included

MAXIMUM NUMBER OF HUNTERS: 30

GRATUITIES: hunters' discretion

PREFERRED PAYMENT: cash or check

Getting There: on the Manitoba/Saskatchewan border, approximately 320 miles northwest of Winnipeg, Manitoba

NEAREST COMMERCIAL AIRPORT: The Pas, Manitoba

Dogs and Facilities: call for information

Guides: one guide per six hunters

Other Services: self-guided hunts available

Other Activities: big game preserve hunting for elk and bison; upland bird hunting for ruffed grouse, sharptails, Hungarian partridge

CONTACT:

Chris Switzer
Bear Valley Outfitters
Box 2294
Swan River, Manitoba
Canada R0L 1Z0
Ph: 204-734-4658
Email: bvo@escape.ca
Web: www.bearvalleyoutfitters.com

CHRIS SWITZER was a professional fur trapper until the industry crashed some 20 years ago. He took his knowledge of the area he lived and hunted and trapped in, though, and made a different life for himself as a big game and waterfowl outfitter. Since 1983, he's been operating Bear Valley Outfitters, building the operation from a couple of bush camps to today's modern five-star facility with comfortable accommodations for up to 30 hunters. He's particularly proud of the lodge's new recreation hall, which features a slate pool table, big-screen TV, eight-person hot tub, and a new dining hall.

He's well equipped, too, with a bird processing shop, walk-in coolers, 12,000 goose decoys, 500 duck decoys, 75 layout blinds, 200 portable heaters, and plenty of boats. And this is just the gear he keeps on hand for waterfowl hunting clients. There's plenty more for his big game customers, who come here to hunt white-tailed deer, black bear, elk, and bison.

Switzer's government-allocated bird hunting area is approximately 60 miles by 120 miles of farmland with hundreds of lakes, ponds, and marshes inside the perimeter. The barley and wheat fields on those farmlands attract a large variety of ducks and geese.

"We have 16 different varieties of ducks to hunt," says Switzer, "but the majority of our hunters take mallards. We also hunt Canada geese, snows, blues, and even a fair population of specklebellies. A combination of big water, flooded timber, river hunting, and dry land field shooting gives our waterfowl hunters a large variety of hunting techniques to choose from. And," he adds, "our upland bird hunting for ruffed grouse, sharptail, and Huns is second to none."

Switzer accommodates visiting hunters a couple of different ways. He'll provide three- and six-day guided hunt packages that include lodging, meals, bird processing, and guides (usually six hunters per guide). In these hunts, clients are expected to provide their own transportation to and from the hunting sites and to assist the guide with setting out and picking up decoys. Guides scout the hunt sites prior to the hunters arriving the following day.

Another option is self-guided hunting. For a nominal fee, Switzer or his guides will supply fields that they've scouted for geese for morning shoots and areas for evening duck spots, and will escort hunting parties to and from these sites. But you'll need your own vehicles and decoys, and the setting up and calling is all up to you. On these types of hunts, budget-conscious hunters don't need to stay at Switzer's lodge. Switzer will direct you to a local motel or campsite, and nearby restaurants can supply your vittles.

If you're so inclined, Switzer can also guide you to a trophy white-tailed deer, elk, or bison. He maintains 1,000 acres of rolling hay fields, heavy bush, willow runs, swamps, and lakes within a fenced enclosure, where the animals are free to roam. Call ahead to arrange a preserve hunt, though, and be prepared to make a sizable deposit to secure your big game slot.

A pair of hunters hide their boat blind in a stand of bulrush on a Manitoba lake. Despite the clear skies, the duck gods have been favorable to them, as evidenced by the white bellies of bluebills at the feet of the waterfowler in the foreground.

[**C A N A D A - E A S T**]

Carpenter's Clearwater Lake Lodge, Ltd.

The Pas, Manitoba

VITAL STATISTICS:

SPECIES: mallard, pintail, wigeon, other puddlers, canvasback, bluebills, Canada goose, snow goose

Season: September 8 to mid-October

Hunting Sites: public lakes and marshes, agricultural fields

Accommodations: 11 modern light-housekeeping cabins accommodating groups of two to six people

MEALS: catering can be arranged; cabins otherwise equipped with kitchens

RATES: $41 to $46 (Cdn) per person/night; guide fees extra, depending on size of group and species hunted

MAXIMUM NUMBER OF HUNTERS: lodge accommodates 40

GRATUITIES: 10%

PREFERRED PAYMENT: cash, check, credit card (Visa, MasterCard)

Getting There: 23 miles north of The Pas via paved highway

NEAREST COMMERCIAL AIRPORT: The Pas (daily turboprop service from Winnipeg)

Dogs and Facilities: dogs welcome, but must be kenneled in portable kennels in cabins

Guides: must be arranged in advance

Other Services: bird cleaning at extra charge

Other Activities: ruffed grouse hunting; guided black bear hunting; numerous fishing possibilities for walleye, northern pike, lake trout, and more

CONTACT:

Kathy or Doug Sangster
Carpenter's Clearwater Lake Lodge
PO Box 695
The Pas, Manitoba
Canada R9A 1K7
Ph/Fax: 204-624-5467
Web: www.mts.net/~rgallagh/carpenter

ARPENTER'S Lodge is located on the shores of the expansive and appropriately named Clearwater Lake, a true jewel among north country waters. The lodge is also only five miles from the commercial airport at The Pas, one of Manitoba's northernmost communities, so getting there can be relatively easy.

Most waterfowl hunters, though, drive to Carpenter's so that they can trailer their own boats, motors, decoys, and other gear. Many of these "do it yourselfers" have been coming to Carpenter's Lodge for years, and they know their way around the country, so they don't require guides. That's not to say you can't come here without a boat and decoys and other gear. Jim Lorden or Doug Sangster will provide the equipment and guide you to some memorable hunting if you so wish; just be sure to call ahead and make arrangements for those services.

Whether you go with a guide or do it yourself, there is plenty of country for lodge guests to spread out in. There are hundreds of lakes and marshes within driving distance of the lodge. You can stay here a week and never hunt the same water twice. The most notable duck waters include the Root and Reader lakes complex, Saskram Lake (actually a huge marsh), and lesser-known lakes like North Moose, Beverly, Rocky, and Red Earth.

Some of these hotspots are easy to reach on graded gravel or paved roads and have improved access sites for launching boats. Go to some of the out-of-the-way wild rice lakes or other ducky spots, though, and you'll need a four-wheel-drive vehicle, and you may have to launch your boat with the aid of considerable muscle power. This is tough country and easy to get lost in, by the way, so a GPS unit is highly recommended for those choosing to go out on their own.

Still, the back country lakes are idyllic, and in addition to the wilderness setting, you may see a moose or two as well as plenty of ducks. Jim and Doug can point you to the right lake for divers or dabblers, or a combination of both. Want to hunt Canada geese? You may get a shot or two at them on any of the lakes, but hunters who really want to set up for honkers drive over to the Carrot River "triangle," an expansive area devoted to grain farming west of The Pas. Most farmers there are happy to give you permission to set decoys in their fields to hunt ducks or geese.

Fall is a good time for fishing in this area, too. The lake trout in Clearwater Lake come into the shallows to spawn at this time of year, and trolling near shore can be highly productive. The Saskatchewan River, which flows through The Pas, is stacked up with walleyes in September, and other lakes offer huge northern pike for those ready and willing to catch them.

If fishing doesn't interest you, there are hundreds of miles of overgrown logging roads to walk for ruffed grouse, which can be, during highs in their population cycles, as thick as fleas on a hare.

Much of the duck hunting near The Pas, Manitoba, takes place on remote boreal forest lakes.

Crooked Creek Lodge

St. Ambroise, Manitoba

VITAL STATISTICS:

SPECIES: mallard, pintail, teal, canvasback, redhead, other duck species, Canada goose, snow goose

Season: September 25 until early or mid-November (freeze-up)

Hunting Sites: Delta Marsh, Lake Francis Marsh

Accommodations: six-bedroom lodge; double occupancy

MEALS: three meals per day provided with three-day occupancy package

RATES: $250 per hunter/day with three-day minimum stay; group rates available

MAXIMUM NUMBER OF HUNTERS: 12

GRATUITIES: hunters' discretion

PREFERRED PAYMENT: cash or check

Getting There: 50 miles west of Winnipeg in southern Manitoba

NEAREST COMMERCIAL AIRPORT: Winnipeg International Airport

Dogs and Facilities: guests may bring dogs; some kennels provided

Guides: one licensed guide per two hunters; guides do not provide dogs

Other Services: airport pick-up and delivery; bird cleaning

Other Activities: upland bird hunting for ruffed grouse, sharptailed grouse, Hungarian partridge; white-tailed deer hunting; sporting clays

CONTACT:

John Lavallee
Box 23
St. Ambroise, Manitoba
Canada R0H 1G0
Ph: 800-292-3973 or 204-243-2009
Email: 103lavalee@netscape.net

DELTA MARSH lies on the south end of massive Lake Manitoba, separated from that expanse of open water by a narrow wooded sand ridge that skirts the shoreline. The 36,000-acre marsh is a maze of bays, channels, mud flats and meadows interconnected by waterways navigable by rowboat, which is the traditional mode of transportation on the marsh. Bulrush, cattail, flagweed, and marsh grasses provide cover for waterfowl and waterfowl hunters alike in this historic marsh, where statesmen, royalty, and everyday hard-core duck and goose hunters have hunted for more than a century.

The Lavallee family has lived and guided here and on nearby Lake Francis Marsh (30,000 acres) since the early 1900s. Past clients included the legendary outdoor writer Jimmy Robinson and his autumnal cast of celebrity guests at his Sports Afield hunting club, located on the uplands adjacent to Delta Marsh. Brothers Aime and John Lavallee maintain their family tradition today at Crooked Creek Lodge, which is built on 160 acres of private property adjacent to the marsh.

A morning on Delta Marsh with one of the Lavallees or their guides is like a step back in time. You'll board an aged but sturdy wooden marsh boat and be rowed and poled into the marsh until your guide decides where you will set up for the morning. The spot will be determined by his knowledge of how waterfowl are currently frequenting the marsh, based on weather, winds, the timing of migrations, and which species you may be seeking that day. In the boat with you and the guide will be your hunting partner, and maybe a few dozen hand-carved decoys. You may be hunting dabblers that day, but if conditions are right, you may set up to canvasback, birds synonymous with the marsh and which Jimmy Robinson glorified in such popular period stories as "Bull Cans of the Delta." Your guide will handle the rowing, build your blind, call the ducks, and, if you don't have your own favorite retriever with you, pick up your birds.

But expect anything here: mallards, pintail, gadwall, wigeon, blue- and green-winged teal, canvasback, redhead, bluebill, and other divers all frequent the marsh. In the agricultural areas surrounding Delta and Lake Francis marshes, the Lavalees can also set you up on fields they lease to hunt Canada and snow geese, both of which are frequent migrants through the area.

After a morning chasing ducks or geese, you'll enjoy a hot lunch back at the lodge. The afternoon activities are your choice. A sporting clays range is available for those looking for a little practice with the old scattergun. For a small additional fee, though, a guide will take you on a hunt for the real thing. Between the marsh and agricultural fields of the regions are scattered woodlands of poplar, maple, aspen, willow, and oak. Inhabiting these wooded islands are ruffed grouse and sharptails, which, when their populations are on the high side, can provide fast and furious shooting. Otherwise, you can traipse the surrounding grainfields for Hungarian partridge.

By late afternoon, you'll be ready to return to the lodge for dinner, and perhaps to hear some Lavallee stories about Jimmy Robinson, Clark Gable, and Jimmy's other hunter-movie star pals.

Camouflaged boat blinds work well on the many wetlands surrounding Crooked Creek Lodge.

[C A N A D A - E A S T]

Kaskattama Safari Adventures, Ltd.
Kaskattama River Delta, Manitoba

VITAL STATISTICS:

SPECIES: snow goose, blue goose, Ross' goose, Canada (greater and lesser) goose, maxima, brandt, Richardson, Hutchison, mallard, pintail, green-winged teal, black, redhead, canvasback

Season: August 28-31 (snow geese only); September 1-23 (all species)

Hunting Sites: situated on the southeastern side of a 5,000-acre peninsula that borders Hudson Bay to the north and branches of the Kaskattama River to the east and west

Accommodations: main lodge consists of lodge, kitchen, and dining room; two luxury guest cabins each have four bedrooms, four bathrooms, and lounge (each cabin will accommodate eight guests)

Meals: all meals are homemade and included in the package; homestyle comfort foods-breads, appetizers, steaks, ribs, roasts, desserts, and more

Rates: all-inclusive five-day packages (from Winnipeg) $2,295 per person

Maximum Number of Hunters: 16

Gratuities: $15-$20 per day/guest

Preferred Payment: check or Visa

Getting There: guests fly directly from Winnipeg, Manitoba (500 miles south), via the lodge's private charter

Nearest Commercial Airport: Winnipeg, Manitoba

Dogs and Facilities: guests are encouraged to bring their dogs; able to accommodate two portable aircraft kennels per charter from Winnipeg; dogs then stay in portable kennels on the enclosed porches of each guest cabin

Guides: not used

REST ASSURED that any honking you hear at Kaskattama will not be from snarled traffic and angry urban drivers. Most certainly it will be from the incredible numbers of geese around you. After all, Kaskattama Safari Adventures is situated on the 5,000-acre Kaskattama River Delta along the southwest shore of Hudson Bay. It is over 600 miles north of Manitoba's capital city of Winnipeg, and 200 miles from the nearest town. The lodge's dining room and kitchen, in fact, were once the storeroom and warehouse of the original York Factory fur-trading outpost of the Hudson Bay Company. This is quite simply northern wilderness hunting at its finest—home to geese, ducks, ptarmigan, brook trout, polar bears, and stunning beauty.

The geese here come from Hudson Bay, long coveted for its goose hunting, and from James Bay, 200 miles south of Kaska. Due to the increasing numbers of geese on the James Bay breeding grounds, the food sources have become depleted and some of these geese fly north to join locally produced flocks and feed on the tundra grasses and berries of the Kaska Delta. The majority of these geese are young-of-the-year and have never been hunted. And they are here by the thousands, calling day and night. And along with the innumerable geese you'll find mallard, teal, pintail, and wigeon.

On a typical five-day hunting trip to Kaskattama Safari Adventures Ltd. you will depart Winnipeg at 6 a.m. in the charted plane and arrive at Kaska at approximately 10 a.m. Your hosts, Charlie and Christine, will greet you, show you to your assigned cabin, serve you a hearty meal, and give you an orientation session. You'll rise early on your second day in camp, eat a great breakfast (juice, hot and cold cereals, fresh muffins or cinnamon rolls, biscuits and gravy prior to the main course) and then be driven by eight-wheeled ATVs to the blinds. At Kaska Goose Camp there are no guides. The hunters are divided into two groups of eight; the groups hunt alternately on the east and west side of the delta. There are 15 blinds per area for eight hunters, who usually hunt in pairs. If one blind is not productive, hunters may move to another. The blinds are constructed of driftwood to blend with the terrain and some 1,500 decoys are distributed among the blinds. This vast wilderness is yours to walk and hunt in as you like. "We have discovered that our clientele prefer not to have guides, but the hunting expertise is there when and if you need it," Charlie notes.

Other Services: birds are cleaned, packed, and frozen for travel; dry ice is added in Winnipeg; each new guest is given a complimentary helicopter orientation tour on the first day

Other Activities: brook trout fishing; ptarmigan hunting; Bell Jet Ranger helicopter trips to other hunting and fishing locales for wildlife viewing, or day trip to Hudson Bay Company trading post

CONTACT:
Charlie Taylor and Christine Quinlan
Kaskattama Safari Adventures Ltd.
170 Harbison Avenue West
Winnipeg, Manitoba
R2L 0A4 Canada
Ph/Fax: 204-667-1611
Email: kaska@mb.sympatico.ca

When the morning hunt is over, the ATV drivers come out to meet you at a prescribed time and return you to the lodge for a hot lunch and, if you wish, a nap. You can enjoy the afternoon hunting geese or ducks, fishing for brook trout in the Kaskattama River, or walking up ptarmigan. Appetizers and cocktails get the evening started back at the lodge, followed by a home-cooked meal. And for two more days you have nothing further to worry about other than your shooting and whether or not you want to spend the afternoon fishing, hunting, or sightseeing. On Day 5 you'll have breakfast at the lodge and depart Kaska at 10 a.m., arriving in Winnipeg at approximately 2 p.m. with plenty of time to catch your flight home.

The next honking you hear may very well be a car with an upset driver behind the wheel. Pay no mind; just remember your glorious time at the base of Hudson Bay and your blood pressure will return to normal in no time.

The tidal flats of Hudson Bay are breeding grounds for hundreds of thousands of snow geese. In September, additional white geese from all over the Canadian arctic mass here prior to their southern migration.

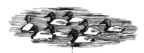

Massey Guides and Outfitters

L o c k p o r t ,   M a n i t o b a

VITAL STATISTICS:

SPECIES: mallard, pintail, teal, gadwall, wigeon, canvasback, redhead, scaup, Canada goose, Ross' goose, snow goose

Season: September 25 to November 28

Hunting Sites: agricultural fields and freshwater marshes

Accommodations: area motel

Meals: restaurant at motel

Rates: begin at $135 per day; call for additional information

Maximum Number of Hunters: 10 over water; 16 in stubble fields

Gratuities: hunters' discretion

Preferred Payment: cash, money order, or traveler's check

Getting There: 25 miles north of Winnipeg, MB

Nearest Commercial Airport: Winnipeg, MB

Dogs and Facilities: motel accepts hunters' dogs

Guides: four hunters per guide in stubble fields; two hunters per guide over water

Other Services: bird cleaning and packaging

Other Activities: upland bird hunting; fishing

CONTACT:

Jim Massey
Massey Guides and Outfitters
20 Ostermann Rd.
Lockport, Manitoba
Canada R1A 3L7
Ph: 800-449-4868

ONLY A HALF-HOUR drive north of the city of Winnipeg lies one of the most expansive wetlands in Manitoba. Oak Hammock Marsh encompasses hundreds of square miles and is a major migration stopover for a wide variety of waterfowl. It's also home to Ducks Unlimited Canada, which is headquartered in a huge wetland ecology interpretive center on the edge of the marsh.

Not far from Oak Hammock lies Netley Marsh, 55,000 acres of public hunting area and also a haven for ducks and geese. Both Netley and Oak Hammock marshes are surrounded by agricultural land—wheat and barley fields—that feed the gathered masses of waterfowl each fall. The grain grazers here include hundreds of thousands of Canada geese, many of which are giant Canadas, and untold numbers of snow geese and Ross' geese. Duck include not only all species of puddle ducks, but also, in the deeper marshes, divers such as redheads, canvasback, and scaup.

Jim Massey has been guiding waterfowl hunters around Oak Hammock and in Netley for the past half-dozen years. His is sort of an a la carte outfitting business: He guides half days for ducks, geese, fishing, or grouse, or full days mixing any two of those activities, one in the morning and one in the afternoon. His rates, too, can include guiding services (and required decoys, and other gear) only, or he can quote a rate that includes lodging and meals at a local motel and restaurant. And, for do-it-yourselfers who bring all their own equipment and waterfowling expertise, he can provide leased goose hunting fields or show them the best ways to traverse the marsh areas for ducks.

Massey's duck hunts take place in Netley Marsh. He or one of his guides provides everything you'll need in the way of gear, including boats, motors, decoys, and most necessary of all, the knowledge of how to get into and back out of the 86-square-mile wetland. Although a public hunting area, this huge marsh actually sees little hunting pressure. Eighteen different species of ducks are found in the marsh as well as four species of geese.

Most of Massey's goose hunts take place over land, in and around Oak Hammock and the stubble fields on its perimeter. With peak populations of 650,000 Canada geese in the region in the fall, successful hunting for the big birds is almost a given. In recent years, bag limits on Canadas here have been five birds a day, with a possession limit of 15. Snow goose limits are 10 a day and 40 in possession.

If you would like to mix up your hunting with a little fishing, Massey can take you out for the trophy walleye and humongous channel catfish that swim in the nearby Red River. He'll also put together a custom fishing trip for northern pike, smallmouth bass, and brook, brown, rainbow, or lake trout.

Most duck hunting on Netley Marsh is from boat blinds hidden in vegetation on the expansive wetlands.

Nanuk Lodge

H u d s o n   B a y ,   M a n i t o b a

VITAL STATISTICS:

SPECIES: snow goose (white and blue color phases), Ross' goose, Canada goose, puddle ducks

Season: September 1 through September 20

Hunting Sites: Hudson Bay coastal waters, beaches, freshwater ponds

Accommodations: bunkroom cabins, main lodge for dining; lounge, showers, sauna

MEALS: three hot, homemade meals daily

RATES: four-, five-, and seven-day hunt packages at $2,300, $2,500, and $2,700 (US) respectively

MAXIMUM NUMBER OF HUNTERS: 16

GRATUITIES: $15-$25 per hunter/day

PREFERRED PAYMENT: check or cash

Getting There: camp location is Cape Tatum on Hudson Bay, Manitoba

NEAREST COMMERCIAL AIRPORT: Gilliam, MB

Dogs and Facilities: can accommodate hunters' dogs

Guides: Cree Indian guides; number per party varies

Other Services: bird cleaning, packaging, freezing

Other Activities: coastal brook trout fishing; polar bear sightseeing safari

CONTACT:
Stewart and Barb Webber
Box 242
Frontier, Saskatchewan
Canada S0N 0W0
Ph: 306-296-4403
Fax: 306-296-4405
Email: nanuk1@sk.sympatico
Web: www.nanuk1.com

RUGGEDLY BEAUTIFUL. The coast of Hudson Bay is all that and more. It is a major staging area for migratory geese in September, a bailiwick of pintail, mallard, wigeon and other ducks, and a thoroughfare for polar bears. The polar bears, of course, you really don't want to see, at least not up close.

Nanuk Lodge is one of only a few places that accommodate waterfowl hunters on Hudson Bay. There aren't many outfitters or lodges here because the hunting season is short (winter comes as soon as early October), and the good hunting areas—and lodges—are as remote as any you'll find on the continent. Everything from kitchen supplies to gas for the generators has to come here by air, and so do you. But the fly-in is only part of the adventure that awaits you here in the land of *nanuk*, the Cree Indian word for polar bear.

Upon your arrival, you'll know what I mean. After your gear is stored in your sleeping cabin, head over to the main lodge building, grab a drink, sit down, and gaze out the picture window at the sight before you: a Hudson Bay beach is the front yard. Snow and Canada geese will be flying over the water and, overhead, it can be clear or unimaginably beautiful cloud formations may sweep the sky. (At night, the aerial displays of northern lights are frighteningly awesome.)

Morning starts at 4:30 at Nanuk, because that's when they turn on the generator and the lights go on. Breakfast at the lodge is at 5:30, then grab your gun and hip boots and head out. Your guide will take you by ATV or tundra buggy to where you'll hunt that day, which could be a salt grass marsh, a beach near a river outlet, or a freshwater pond. A couple dozen decoys will be put out, all that's really necessary here, and the hunt begins. Your Cree guide may soon advise that a flock of 747s—giant Canadas, not the aircraft—is approaching, or it could be a flock of lesser Canadas, or snows, blues, or tiny Ross' geese. Maybe ducks. You never know here, nor do you know if the birds will be flying on the deck, only feet above the ground, or 30 yards up. But you'll see so many in a day it won't matter how high they are, you'll always get good shooting. The geese certainly won't be decoy-shy, and the guides will call the traditional Indian way—by mouth.

If you're not done hunting by noon, you can ride back to the lodge for a hot lunch, or one can even be delivered to you if you're not too far away.

Otherwise, your guide will pack sandwiches and other goodies to ward off thirst and hunger. You can stay out all day if you wish, even if just to see the country. The next day you'll see more of it, too, because you'll be taken to a different hunting spot each day.

Before the cocktail hour, at least, though, you may want to grab rod and reel and head for a nearby stream. Coastal brook trout head out of the bay and upstream to spawn at this time of year, trout that grow up to seven pounds. Seven pounds! Just remember: Dinner's at 7 sharp.

The tundra lowlands of Hudson Bay near Nanuk Lodge are the breeding grounds of hundreds of thousands of Canada geese and snow geese.

CANADA WEST

NORTHWEST TERRITORIES, ALBERTA, SASKATCHEWAN

W ESTERN CANADA: THE ROCKIES, the plains, the remote vastness of Great Slave Lake. Here, as in eastern Canada, you can experience an eclectic variety of waterfowl hunting. From the Northwest Territories, which, although it is the size of several collective U.S. states, has only one waterfowl hunting outfitter, to Alberta, which has more outfitters than all the other Canadian provinces combined, to Saskatchewan, which has wonderful hunting opportunities and a handful of outfitters, you'll have plenty to choose from.

On Great Slave Lake, you can hunt bluebills and mallards, and finish your day with a grouse hunt or fish for giant pike. The beauty of this remote country is breathtaking; fishing and hunting here is a wilderness experience not to be forgotten by those who venture to this magic land.

Alberta's Peace River country is magic, too. Canada geese and mallards concentrate here in almost unimaginable numbers. The local farmers are aware of this, and they sometimes have to plead with outfitters to come and shoot their fields. Central and southern Alberta see untold congregations of waterfowl, too, and there are plenty of guides who can take you and your hunting buddies on memorable excursions in the stubble fields and potholes that cover the landscape.

In Saskatchewan, it's much the same as Alberta, but throw in more snow geese, specklebellies, and sandhill cranes. The rolling prairies here are dotted with lakes, potholes, and marshes, and agricultural landowners here have the same problems as the farmers in Alberta—too many ducks, a surfeit of geese. Won't you please help? Come hunt some of these bothersome waterfowl. It would be a neighborly thing to do.

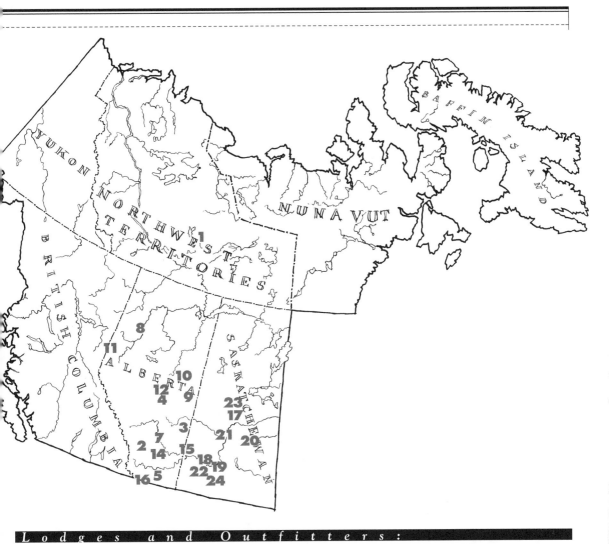

Lodges and Outfitters:

NW Territories

1 TROUT ROCK WILDERNESS LODGE, YELLOWKNIFE

Alberta

2 ALBERTA FLYWAY WATERFOWL OUTFITTERS, CALGARY

3 BATTLE RIVER LODGE, CORONATION

4 BUCK MOUNTAIN OUTFITTERS, SHERWOOD PARK

5 CHINOOK COUNTRY OUTFITTERS, LETHBRIDGE

6 DARREL WISE GUIDE SERVICE, EAST-CENTRAL ALBERTA (LOCATION NOT SHOWN)

7 FALL FEATHERS OUTFITTING, DRUMHELLER

8 GOOSE MASTER, PEACE RIVER

9 GREATER CANADIANS, INNISFREE

10 GREEN HEAD ADVENTURES, ST. PAUL

11 MAVERICK WATERFOWLERS, BEAVERLODGE

12 ONGARO OUTDOORS, EDMONTON

13 SEAN MANN'S OUTDOOR ADVENTURES, CENTRAL ALBERTA (LOC. NOT SHOWN)

14 TARGET GUIDE SERVICES, BASSANO

15 WESTERN GUIDING SERVICE, EMPRESS

16 WILDLIFE WEST ADVENTURES, CARDSTON

Saskatchewan

17 HIGH BRASS, QUILL LAKES

18 K & P OUTFITTERS, KYLE

19 MONTGOMERY OUTFITTING SERVICE, MORSE

20 RATHMORE OUTFITTING, CLAIR

21 SAFARI RIVER OUTDOORS, SASKATOON

22 THISTLETHWAITE OUTFITTERS, STEWART VALLEY

23 TOBY'S TROPHY TREKS, CHRISTOPHER LAKE

24 WILD WINGS OUTFITTERS, SWIFT CURRENT

[C A N A D A - W E S T]

Trout Rock Wilderness Lodge

Y e l l o w k n i f e ,   N o r t h w e s t   T e r r i t o r i e s

VITAL STATISTICS:

SPECIES: bluebill, scoter, bufflehead, goldeneye, canvasback, ring-necked duck, spoonbill, mallard, wigeon, pintail, green-winged and blue-winged teal

Season: September 1 through first week in October

Hunting Sites: thousands of acres of pristine wilderness in the north arm of Great Slave Lake

Accommodations: three separate cabins that can house up to four people

Meals: home-cooked, hearty meals for breakfast and dinner; lunch is often a shore lunch

Rates: $1,125 plus 3.5% tax per hunter/three days, nights-includes pick up from airport, float plane from Yellowknife to lodge, accommodations, meals, guides

Maximum Number of Hunters: 12

Gratuities: $25-$75

Preferred Payment: check, money order, or traveler checks

Getting There: float plane from Yellowknife, Northwest Territories

Nearest Commercial Airport: Yellowknife, NWT

Dogs and Facilities: dogs welcome; will provide dog house and chain

Guides: two to three hunters per guide/boat

Other Services: bird cleaning and shipping

Other Activities: trophy pike fishing; grouse hunting; nature watching

CONTACT:
Ragnar Wesstrom
Box 2382
Yellowknife, NWT
Canada, X1A 2P8
Ph: 867-873-4334
Email: ducks@enodah.com
Web: www.enodah.com

FOR A TRUE backcountry experience there are few places on the planet that can rival the rugged and pristine wilderness of Canada's Northwest Territories. Picture yourself along the edge of the Canadian Shield, on the North Arm of Great Slave Lake, a traditional staging ground for thousands of waterfowl from all four of the continent's flyways. Now imagine having myriad acres of prime hunting grounds to yourself, a generous daily bag limit of eight ducks with no species restrictions, plus the opportunity to chase spruce, sharp-tailed, and ruffed grouse through the surrounding forests, as well as trophy pike in the waters of the continent's fifth largest lake.

If any of this sounds appealing, then Trout Rock Wilderness Lodge is your kind of place. Fly into the Northwest Territories' capitol of Yellowknife and leave the rest to outfitter Ragnar Wesstrom, who will arrange to have you delivered via float plane to Trout Rock Island, a one-square-mile island with a spacious lodge built on a rocky outcropping overlooking Great Slave Lake. It's the only commercial lodge in the area, so you'll have plenty of elbow room as you hunt and fish till your heart's content.

You'll head out in the morning by boat with one or two other hunters and a guide to any of the numerous remote coves, inlets, and bays that attract ducks by the thousands. Hunting divers is the main game, and the bluebill action can be phenomenal, with flocks not accustomed to heavy hunting pressure. Scoter, bufflehead, goldeneye, ringneck, mallard, wigeon, pintail, and teal are also in abundance and provide plenty of waterfowling action.

In the afternoon you'll take a break for a scrumptious shore lunch of fresh pike, duck, moose, caribou, or muskox. Then, with your batteries recharged, you can choose to stay on the water and hunt trophy-size pike, many of which range well over 30 pounds, or you can opt to exercise your legs a little in search of the area's three grouse species.

The pike fishing in Great Slave Lake is legendary, and people come from all over the world to wrestle trophy pike in the heart of the Canadian wilderness. Anglers arrive with great expectations and rarely leave disappointed. Whether you battle them with a traditional spincasting rig or a fly-fishing outfit, these freshwater barracuda aren't likely to be forgotten. The taste of a freshly prepared pike filet is out of this world, say most guests—and many say they even prefer it hands down over walleye!

If you're into nature watching, keep your eyes peeled for eagles, otters, beavers, mink, black bears, and maybe even a moose. Whether you choose to focus your sights or take the broader view, this pristine archipelago looks pretty much the same as it did a thousand years ago. A spectacular view of the northern lights is a bonus many visitors never forget.

Top it all off with a delicious home-cooked meal and a relaxing soak in the wood-stove operated hot tub in the main lodge.

[C ̧ A N A D A - W E S T]

Alberta Flyway Waterfowl Outfitters, Ltd.

Calgary, Alberta

VITAL STATISTICS:

SPECIES: Canada goose, snow goose, white-fronted goose, mallards, pintails, many other duck species

Season: September 1 to October 30

Hunting Sites: North Saskatchewan and Birch Lake river systems; 5 million acres of public land

Accommodations: private 3,000-square-foot lodge with semi-private rooms, family rooms, satellite TV, pool table

Meals: three home-cooked meals per day at lodge

Rates: $400 (US) per hunter/day; $125 per nonhunter/day; includes guided hunting, accommodations, meals, transportation to and from Edmonton airport

Maximum Number of Hunters: 12 hunters; maximum of six per field

Gratuities: suggest 10% daily

Preferred Payment: check or cash

Getting There: 120 miles east of Edmonton, Alberta

Nearest Commercial Airport: Edmonton, AB

Dogs and Facilities: well-trained dogs welcome; outdoor kennels provided

Guides: trained guides available; maximum of six hunters per guide

Other Services: bird cleaning, packaging available at extra charge

Other Activities: skeet shooting; released pheasants, turkeys, partridge at additional cost

CONTACT:

Jeff Klotz
Alberta Flyway Waterfowl Outfitters Ltd.
856 Scimitar Bay NW
Calgary, Alberta
Canada T3L 2B3
Ph: 877-208-2884
Fax: 403-208-7043
Email: jdklotz@telusplanet.net
Web: www.albertaflyway.net

CENTRAL ALBERTA is a waterfowl hunter's paradise. There are plenty of birds here and generous bag limits of, as of this writing, eight ducks and eight dark geese (Canada geese and white-fronted geese), and 10 snow geese per day. This far north, too, the birds see little hunting pressure, and if you're staying with Alberta Flyway Waterfowl Outfitters, you may not see hunters outside of your own party the whole time you are there.

Outfitter Jeff Klutz goes out of his way to make your stay at his lodge an enjoyable one. If you fly to Edmonton, he'll pick you up and take you and your hunting partners to the lodge as part of his three-day hunt rate (he'll return you to the airport at the end of your stay as part of the deal, too). The first afternoon in camp is devoted to getting settled in the comfortable lodge, practicing some warm-up shooting on the skeet range, then sitting down to an evening meal that could lead to a sleepy stupor. That's good. You'll be getting up early in the morning and you'll need a good night's rest.

Before sunrise, you'll down a quick breakfast and head for a field that Jeff's scouts have reconned the prior evening. The decoys are spread—you can help if you want or sit back and have a cup of coffee from the Thermos and listen to the coyotes wail in the distance—and everything will be in order before the first flock of geese has taken wing. Be sure to bring plenty of ammo, because over the next few hours you'll have plenty of opportunities to burn it up. The morning hunt is usually devoted to geese, but that doesn't mean flocks of mallards and pintails won't be buzzing the blocks, too. But if the geese are working, and no doubt they will be, you might want to hold off on the ducks until later in the day.

Guides will do the calling, unless you'd prefer to join in or even do all the calling yourself. You'll be in a blind with up to but not more than five other hunters in addition to the guide. When the birds come, though, they'll usually be in flocks instead of singles and doubles, so you won't have to worry about picking out your own target. Usually, you'll have a limit well before noon.

After a hot lunch and a nap, it's back to work. By mid-afternoon, you'll be set up for ducks, and what a variety you'll find here—mallards, pintail, green- and blue-winged teal, gadwall, canvasback, bluebill, and redhead are all available on sloughs and potholes a short drive from the lodge. Come sundown, or earlier if the duck gods smile upon you and you shoot straight, you'll ride back to a sumptuous hot dinner and a relaxing hour before the fireplace before cashing in your chips for the evening.

Of course, if all this waterfowling gets to be too boring for you, Jeff can arrange for an afternoon hunt for released pheasants. Somehow, though, hunting roosters in a waterfowl paradise seems to be a waste of otherwise valuable time.

Swathed barley is all these hunters need to provide a "hide" to conceal them from incoming Canadas. The big birds seek out these types of fields for the surfeit of grain they provide.

[C A N A D A - W E S T]

Battle River Lodge

C o r o n a t i o n ,   A l b e r t a

VITAL STATISTICS:

SPECIES: Canada goose, white-fronted goose, snow goose, mallard, pintail

Season: September 10 through October 20

Hunting Sites: thousands of acres of private grainfields

Accommodations: 3,600-square-foot lodge; seven semi-private guest bedrooms with private baths; kitchen/dining room; lounge

MEALS: hearty, home-cooked meals

RATES: $1,350 for three-day package including guided hunt, lodging, all meals, Edmonton airport pickup and return (licenses extra)

MAXIMUM NUMBER OF HUNTERS: eight hunters plus nonhunters

GRATUITIES: $100 (US) per hunter/day (suggested)

PREFERRED PAYMENT: cash or check

Getting There: in southeast Alberta, three-hour drive from Edmonton

NEAREST COMMERCIAL AIRPORT: Edmonton, AB

Dogs and Facilities: kennels provided for guests' dogs

Guides: five guides per eight hunters

Other Services: bird cleaning, packaging (extra fee)

Other Activities: released pheasant hunting

CONTACT:
Dan or Nick Frederick
Battle River Lodge
c/o Ameri-Cana Expeditions
4707 - 106A Avenue
Edmonton, Alberta
Canada T6A 1J3
Ph: 780-469-0579
Fax: 780-465-5040
Email: americana@sport4u.com
Web: www.ameri-cana.com

BATTLE RIVER LODGE is located near Coronation, a small farm town in southeast Alberta. The area comprises farmland and ranches, which provide plenty of grains to feed hungry, migrating birds. And the birds do come. This is a large staging area for geese winging southward from northern Canada, Alaska, and even Russia. With the region's abundance of good grazing and numerous sanctuary roosting lakes, it's no wonder that Ross' geese, snow geese, specklebellies, and greater and lesser Canada geese often linger here until freeze-up in early November. Huge flocks of mallards and pintails are just icing on the waterfowler's cake.

Battle River Lodge is operated by Ameri-Cana Expeditions, a family-owned business operating since 1985. Pat Frederick and his sons, Nick and Dan, operate the lodge and also offer hunting and fishing expeditions all around the world. Looking for polar bear in the Canadian arctic? Trophy whitetails in Alberta? An African safari? A Marco Polo sheep? They can fill the bill.

In fall, when not off in some far-flung corner of the world, though, the Fredericks are home on the range, at their waterfowl lodge, that is. And why not? Exotic travel can be adventuresome, but September and October is the nicest time of year on the Canadian prairie. It's harvest time and Indian summer. The skies and fields are thick with birds. No need to be questing for any other game anywhere else.

You'll see the logic behind this when you arrive at the lodge after the drive from Edmonton (or fly your own plane or arrive by charter at the 3,000-foot paved airstrip 10 miles from the lodge). Check into your room and relax for a while. You may go out that first afternoon in camp to help the guides scout the next morning's field shoot. Or, if there's an afternoon shoot available right off the bat, you may have an opportunity to break the ice early. You really don't have to worry about not getting your birds here. If anything, you may not want to shoot limits, just to keep the weight of your cooler down for the return trip home. (Alberta currently allows eight dark geese per day, of which five can be whitefronts, and an additional 10 snow geese daily. For ducks, limits are also generous—eight ducks per day, of which four can be pintails. Possession limits are 16 dark geese and 16 ducks. That's a lot of cooler space.)

By evening, it's head to the lodge for cocktails and dinner. Lights out early, though, because you'll be up and out before sunrise to help set up blinds and decoys. After the morning shoot, which lasts until 10 or can run as late as 11, it's back to the lodge again for a big, hearty breakfast. After a nap, perhaps an afternoon shoot for ducks and geese, or maybe released pheasants will be in order. By evening you'll head to the lodge again for cocktails and dinner. Your daily cycle at Battle River Lodge has begun.

An afternoon pothole hunt for ducks is a great way to wind down a day after a morning prairie goose hunt in Alberta.

[**C A N A D A - W E S T**]

Buck Mountain Outfitters

Sherwood Park, Alberta

VITAL STATISTICS:

SPECIES: mallard, pintail, gadwall, Canada goose, white-fronted goose

Season: September 1 to October 15

Hunting Sites: agricultural land, potholes

Accommodations: South Camp: large mobile home; North Camp: three log cabins

MEALS: home-style; three meals daily

RATES: North Camp: geese and grouse-$500 per hunter/day; South Camp: geese and ducks-$400 per hunter/day

MAXIMUM NUMBER OF HUNTERS: 10 (prefer six)

GRATUITIES: hunters' discretion

PREFERRED PAYMENT: cash or check

Getting There: South Camp: one hour southeast of Edmonton, AB; North Camp: five hours north of Edmonton near Peace River, AB

NEAREST COMMERCIAL AIRPORT: Edmonton, AB, and Peace River, AB

Dogs and Facilities: outside kennels available

Guides: three hunters per guide; guides provide dogs

Other Services: airport transportation; bird cleaning available

Other Activities: upland bird hunting; big game hunting

CONTACT:

Merv Purschke
Buck Mountain Outfitters
20 Canterbury Lane
Sherwood Park, Alberta
Canada T8H 1E7
Ph: 1-888-313-2825 or
780-467-1788
Fax: 780-467-8296
Email: buckmountain@yahoo.com

MERV PURSCHKE has been guiding in Alberta since 1987, mostly for big game—bear, deer, and moose. A couple of years ago, he decided to get into the bird hunting side of things, and he's done such a good job of it that he now runs two camps, one about an hour southeast of Edmonton (South Camp), the other up near Peace River country (North Camp).

South Camp is in an area that sees little hunting pressure but lots of ducks and geese. Shooting here is over sloughs and harvested pea fields for Canada geese, mallards, and pintails. This hunt area is in the heart of Alberta's pothole country, which has one of the largest breeding populations of mallards on the continent. Duck populations here are approximately 80 percent mallards, while the remaining 20 percent are pintails, gadwalls, spoonbill, teal, and other dabbling ducks. At the right time of the migration, hunters will also have the opportunity to bag specklebellies in the same fields they hunt Canada geese.

According to Purschke, "The goose hunting in this area has literally exploded over the last few years, so we have options to hunt either ducks or geese each day. Ninety percent of the geese here are Canadas, with a few specks mixed in. All of our hunts take place on privately owned agricultural land, and the majority of the action is over decoys, with hunters placed in coffin blinds or goose chairs in grain fields. The rest of our hunting is over potholes with pop-up blinds, or we use natural cover."

Hunters in South Camp are lodged in a comfortable mobile home with a large built-on addition; meals are prepared and served in an adjacent house that also serves as housing for guides. At South Camp, too, hunters will have the opportunity to hunt upland birds—sharptails and Hungarian partridge—in the afternoon if they prefer to do so.

North Camp is the newest operation for Purschke, at least for waterfowl and ruffed grouse. In the past, he's used this camp later in the fall for a big game outfitting quarters. Having discovered the exceptional goose and grouse hunting available in the area, though, he has now opened it for scattergunners from mid-September to mid-October.

"North camp is four and a half hours north of Edmonton and consists of three log cabins," Purshke says. "The two smaller cabins are new and equipped with two sets of bunks each. A fourth building contains a commode, shower, and sink. The bar is located in an outfitter-style tent and is our central meeting area. The camp is remote and outdoorsy—a generator supplies electricity, and a campfire is a nightly scenario."

Goose hunting at North Camp is exceptional, as is most hunting for Canadas in the Peace River Valley of Alberta. A bonus here is the ruffed grouse, which in years when the bird's population cycle is high, can also provide excellent hunting in aspen woods throughout the valley.

A party of hunters poses with a morning's mixed bag of mallards and geese outside their lodging at Buck Mountain Outfitters.

[C A N A D A - W E S T]

Chinook Country Outfitters

L e t h b r i d g e ,   A l b e r t a

VITAL STATISTICS:

SPECIES: Canada goose, snow goose, white-fronted goose, mallard, pintail, gadwall, wigeon, teal, canvasback, redhead, scaup, goldeneye

Season: September 7 until late December

Hunting Sites: agricultural fields, lakes, marshes

Accommodations: private lodge available with inclusive package; local restaurants and motels for guiding-only package

Meals: home-cooked meals at lodge

Rates: $250 per hunter/day for guiding-only package; $350 per day for lodge package

Maximum Number of Hunters: eight (prefer four to six)

Gratuities: 10%-15%

Preferred Payment: cash or check

Getting There: near Lethbridge, Alberta, 120 miles southeast of Calgary

Nearest Commercial Airport: Lethbridge, AB

Dogs and Facilities: hunters welcome to bring own dogs; limited kennel space available

Guides: two to four hunters per guide; guides have trained retrievers

Other Services: airport transportation

Other Activities: upland bird hunting

CONTACT:
Wayne Lamb
Chinook Country Outfitters
823 9th St.
Lethbridge, Alberta
Canada T1J 2L8
Ph/Fax: 403-380-3949
Email: guideus@telusplanet.net
Web: www.chinookoutfitters.com

LOOK WEST from Lethbridge and you'll see the rugged spine of the Rocky Mountains heading north and south as far as the eye can see. The mountains influence the weather here a good deal—it's usually windy. This is chinook country, named for the warm winter winds that often roar over the mountains and through the plains to melt the snowpack, even in January.

This part of southern Alberta is also a way station for migrating ducks and geese. Besides the migrants, thousands of local Canada geese and ducks are hatched in this pothole country, making it a waterfowl hunter's paradise. The grass prairies and wheat and barley fields are also home to nonmigratory birds: ring-necked pheasants, Hungarian partridge, and sharp-tailed grouse.

Wayne Lamb, a local resident who has hunted this country for more than 30 years, saw the potential for running an outfitter's service here five years ago. A dog trainer and field-trialer who owns three Labs of his own, he now gives his dogs a marathon workout from September to Christmas each year. But he says he won't necessarily work his clients as hard as his Labs.

"I have clients who want to hunt from dawn to dusk, and others who want to be home sipping on a martini by four in the afternoon," says Lamb. "I can accommodate pretty much any style of hunter, from the fanatic to the more inexperienced and laid-back types.

"A typical hunt with me generally involves a waterfowl hunt in the morning and upland bird hunting in the afternoon. Goose hunting is very good for the first week or so for the local birds that breed in this area. After the opening week, goose hunting gets pretty tough until the big migration of waterfowl begins, usually about the third week of October. From that time on, the goose hunting is second to none. We host literally hundreds of thousands of Canada geese, including giant Canadas as well as snows and specklebellies. If you like to shoot geese, late October and November is the time to be here.

"The duck hunting is excellent earlier in the season," Lamb says. "We have world-class open water duck shooting. If you enjoy shooting ducks when the weather is nice, I highly recommend a September hunt. October, when the birds start to gather in larger flocks in preparation for the migration, is also excellent for ducks. Usually by the end of October the water areas begin to freeze up, and hunting is mostly restricted to field shoots."

Lamb's hunters quarter themselves in area motels and hotels in nearby Lethbridge, a modern city of 60,000. Meals are available in the city in a variety of restaurants. As part of his lodging package, he has a "not fancy, but clean and comfortable cabin" that will accommodate six hunters in two double rooms and two single rooms. Home-cooked meals are available with the lodging package at the cabin. For either the hunt-only package or the lodging/meals/hunt package, Lamb provides all other equipment, including decoys, field blinds, boats, and a Suburban to transport hunters to and from the field.

Field layout blinds render a pair of waterfowl hunters almost invisible to ducks and geese approaching the decoys in this stubble field.

[C A N A D A - W E S T]

Darrel Wise Guide Service

E a s t - C e n t r a l   A l b e r t a

VITAL STATISTICS:

SPECIES: Canada goose, white-fronted goose, snow goose, Ross' goose, mallard, pintail

Season: September 1 through November

Hunting Sites: several hundred square miles of agricultural fields, potholes, sloughs

Accommodations: private log lodge with eight bedrooms, three showers; private bar

MEALS: home-style

RATES: $1,500 three-day package

MAXIMUM NUMBER OF HUNTERS: nine

GRATUITIES: (daily) cook: $10 to $15 per guest; guide: $25 to $50 per guest

PREFERRED PAYMENT: cash, check, credit card

Getting There: east-central Alberta, about a three-hour drive from Edmonton

NEAREST COMMERCIAL AIRPORT: Edmonton, AB

Dogs and Facilities: call to make arrangements

Guides: all guiding by Darrel Wise; guide provides trained retriever

Other Services: bird cleaning and packaging (additional charge)

Other Activities: 10-station sporting clays; upland hunting for ruffed grouse and Hungarian partridge

CONTACT:

Darrel Wise
Darrel Wise Guide Service
506 Ashton Dr.
Corvallis, MT 59828
Ph: 406-961-5234
Fax: 406-961-5413
Web: www.thewiseman.com

HOW PICKY can you be about your decoys and decoy layouts? Do they look right to incoming geese? Well, during the off-season, just to find out, Darrel Wise sets out spreads of the Real-Geese Canada goose and snow goose decoys he manufactures to find out just that. Then he flies over them in an ultra-light aircraft to get a bird's-eye view of what a flying goose sees of its counterfeit brethren on the ground. This, and studying groups of actual, living geese, helps him design a top-notch decoy and gives him insights to the dynamics of a feeding flock.

These insights have also helped Wise become highly successful at guiding goose hunters, which, in addition to designing decoys, he's been doing for more than 35 years. He's become legendary among clients for his ability to call and decoy birds so close—"in your face" close—that you can shoot them with a .28-gauge (although he still doesn't recommend that unless you are a proficient shooter).

Wise's custom-made cylindrical hay bale goose blinds are part of his secret to bringing geese within such close range. He uses these exclusively at his outfitting operation in Alberta. The two-man blinds were designed by Wise to provide his hunters with a clear view of decoying geese while keeping them off the ground and protected from the wind. Sitting inside the camouflaged blinds on folding chairs, the hunters need only to slide back the bale blind's moveable top and shoot when "The Wise Man" (as he's become known in the industry) calls the shot.

Not only are Wise's blinds comfortable, but so is his lodge, located in one of the best goose hunting areas in the province. The modern log lodge accommodates up to nine hunters, has eight bedrooms and three bathrooms equipped with showers. The great room features digital television and surround sound, and a bar. On the grounds is a 10-station sporting clays range, where you can wile away the afternoon hours if you decide not to hump the surrounding prairie hills and woodlots for ruffed grouse and Hungarian partridge. (Otherwise, Wise will drop you off at a local pothole to hunt ducks while he scouts fields for the next morning's goose hunt.)

All the goose hunting here is field shooting. A typical morning begins with a light breakfast and a drive to a selected grainfield or harvested pea field (lentil peas) where geese were observed feeding the afternoon before your hunt. The horse trailers behind the two Suburbans that transport you to the hunt site carry the goose blinds and decoys. Before sunup, these will be strategically deployed, and you'll be sipping a cup of coffee from a Thermos before the first goose arrives.

The geese will arrive, in flocks large and small. Your hand may be trembling as you grip the blind cover, ready to slide it back and pick a target. Don't get too antsy. Wise may land half the flock before he yells "Take 'em." He likes 'em close, you know.

Darrel Wise hunts over his own silhouette decoys and from hay bale blinds he custom built for shooting in stubble fields. Both work extremely well in duping geese well within shotgun range.

[C A N A D A - W E S T]

Fall Feathers Outfitting

D r u m h e l l e r ,   A l b e r t a

VITAL STATISTICS:

SPECIES: snow goose, Canada goose, white-fronted goose, mallards
Season: September to October
Hunting Sites: more than 200 square miles of agricultural fields; duck sloughs and potholes
Accommodations: four 800-square-foot units with individual bedrooms, living area, refrigerator, stove, washer and dryer
MEALS: home-style, traditional beef and chicken entrees and wild game
RATES: two-and-a-half and five-day package rates from $1,350 to $1,700 (US)
MAXIMUM NUMBER OF HUNTERS: eight
GRATUITIES: $100 per hunter per trip
PREFERRED PAYMENT: check
Getting There: south-central Alberta, east of Calgary and near the Saskatchewan border
NEAREST COMMERCIAL AIRPORT: Calgary, AB
Dogs and Facilities: can accommodate dogs upon request
Guides: one guide per two or three hunters
Other Services: airport transportation; bird cleaning and packaging
Other Activities: upland game hunting (released birds, additional charge)

CONTACT:

Greg Molloy
Fall Feathers Outfitting
1004 2nd St, SE
Drumheller, Alberta
Canada T0J 0Y6
Ph: 403-823-7172
Email: ffo2telusplanet.net
Web: www.fallfeathers.com/info.html

PIECE OF CAKE. Get off the plane, clear customs, and outfitter Greg Molloy will meet you at the international arrivals gate at Calgary International Airport. Then it's a couple-hour drive east to Drumheller, near the Saskatchewan border where the goose hunting is out of this world. Of course, you can drive there yourself and enjoy the quiet, rolling prairie, google-eye at the roadside potholes filled with ducks, and wonder why you haven't discovered this waterfowl hunting nirvana years earlier.

But don't waste time on the road. Greg's wife, Linda, will have dinner on the stove, and you don't want to miss the traditional wild goose Louisiana gumbo served on the eve of your first hunting day. During your stay, she'll prepare beef and chicken dishes, too, but count on eating some goose marmalade, pineapple goose, marinated goose breast wrapped in bacon and barbecued, and some partridge and pheasant dishes. It's the only way to prevent going over your possession limit, and besides, as they say, a man has got to eat.

About the time you are sitting down for the evening victuals, Greg's guides will be returning home from scouting the surrounding agricultural fields. They'll have pinpointed the next day's hunt, having located a hot field and obtained landowner permission to set up there the next morning. The geese will be there, the only question you'll have before you book your hunt is when to come.

"The hunting in September is very good as the birds are fresh and tend to decoy unheeded," Greg says. "They are, however, limited to good numbers of mostly whitefronts, some Ross' geese, and some local greater Canadas. Ducks are pretty abundant at this time and hunters usually enjoy some good late afternoon shoots over ponds, as well as getting some ducks over the morning goose set-ups.

"Near the end of September," he says, "we get major pushes of migrating birds, usually accompanying weather fronts. These migrants include lesser and greater Canadas, scads of snow geese, and lots of ducks. The whitefronts will stay as long as the weather stays favorable, often long enough to be joined by the peak of the migration, but weather plays a crucial role in this. Generally, by the middle of October, the peak of the migration will be over."

The daily ritual begins with a quick breakfast and a drive to the selected field for the day. Depending on the terrain, time of season and natural cover, the guides will set up either brush blinds, straw bale blinds, or Final Approach blinds. Around these they'll spread a couple of dozen magnum Big Foot decoys and a couple of hundred white rag decoys. You're all set. The guides will do the calling, and if you haven't brought good old Rex with you, will do the retrieving, too.

On a good morning, you'll be done shooting geese well before noon. After lunch, you can go hunting for upland birds or set up on a pothole and irritate the local duck population. If it's not a good morning, or if you have one of those can't-seem-to-get-my-lead-right days, Greg will take you on an afternoon goose hunt to try and fill your limit. After all, the geese feed twice a day, like clockwork—so go for it.

Specklebellies and Canadas plague farmers' fields near Drumheller, Alberta. Outfitter Greg Molloy and his clients are welcome guests on these properties, although the geese might think otherwise.

[C A N A D A · W E S T]

Goose Master

Peace River, Alberta

VITAL STATISTICS:

SPECIES: Canada goose, white-fronted goose, mallard, pintail, teal
Season: September 1 through November 1
Hunting Sites: more than 300,000 acres of grain fields, plus lakes, marshes and public land
Accommodations: Tailfeathers private lodge sleeps eight; includes bar, dining room; additional accommodations at local motel with restaurant, bar, hot tub
Meals: full-course meals, desserts included in package price
Rates: $1,750 package, includes three full days of goose and duck hunting, lodging, meals, licenses
Maximum Number of Hunters: 12
Gratuities: hunters' discretion, $25/day average
Preferred Payment: check or money order
Getting There: Alberta's Peace River Valley, 250 miles north of Edmonton
Nearest Commercial Airport: Peace River, AB
Dogs and Facilities: hunters' dogs welcome; outside, enclosed kennels provided, but dogs can sleep in the lodge with their owners
Guides: guides have retrievers; four hunters per guide for goose hunts; one or two hunters per guide for duck hunting
Other Services: bird cleaning, packaging, freezing (fee)
Other Activities: clay trap shooting; released pheasant hunting; upland hunting for wild ruffed and sharp-tailed grouse
CONTACT:
Garry Checknita
Goose Master
8422-100 Ave.
Peace River, Alberta
Canada T8S 1N4
Ph: 780-624-1839
Fax: 780-624-8488

ALBERTA'S PEACE RIVER Valley is some of the prettiest country in the northern part of the province. This is parkland habitat, where aspen groves and shrub meadows are interspersed with prairie, potholes, sloughs, and marshes. This is also a prime agricultural area and an initial stop for migrating ducks and geese. The valley extends for hundreds of miles and is a staging area where hungry waterfowl can dine on thousands of acres of peas, barley, and wheat before continuing their southward journey each fall.

And the hunting pressure is almost nonexistent. So, when flocks of hungry geese descend on their crops, farmers are more than happy to call Garry Checknita and have him and his hunter clients on their property to rectify the situation.

Checknita has been operating his Tailfeathers Lodge in Peace River for 15 years. He has developed working arrangements with local farmers who welcome hunters to alleviate the tremendous crop damage caused by migrating ducks and geese. Almost all of Checknita's hunting is conducted within an hour drive of Peace River. This includes goose hunting from blinds over decoys in fields, duck hunting in and around sloughs, and grouse hunting in the nearby aspen parkland and prairie.

Stan Warren of Bethel Springs, Tennessee (901-934-9659), is a seasoned waterfowl hunter who guides for Goose Master in the fall. He describes a day of hunting in the game-rich valley: "Wake-up call is based on the location of the field to be hunted in the morning, and it varies, too, as the length of the days gets shorter. We rise and have breakfast at either the lodge kitchen or our reserved breakfast room at the motel, then ride to the field. There, the guide and spotter will assemble a portable blind and set the decoys."

The field to be hunted is usually a hot one where a farmer is having trouble with birds on swathed wheat or barley, or a heavily grazed harvested field that one of the spotters has located. "A goose hunt on a field like this can be over in half an hour or continue over a four-hour period," says Warren, "depending on how the birds arrive and on gunner success. Usually it's somewhere in between. You can have a nice flock of geese descending on the decoys one minute, a hundred or more mallards decoying the next. You never know."

"After the morning hunt is over, we pick up the decoys and blind, have lunch and a siesta, then go to another field or to marsh blinds for ducks. There are also lots of grouse here, and some guests opt to hunt for those in the afternoon, too. It's whatever the hunter wants to do."

For all the excellent hunting available in Peace River country, you'd think it would be difficult to get there. It's not. Most visiting hunters fly to Edmonton or Calgary, clear customs, and take a short flight on to Peace River on the same day. For more information on travel arrangements, quotes, and schedules, call Thomas Cook Miller Travel in Peace River at 780-624-2437.

[C A N A D A - W E S T]

Greater Canadians

I n n i s f r e e ,   A l b e r t a

VITAL STATISTICS:

SPECIES: Canada goose, white-fronted goose, snow goose, mallard, pintail

Season: September 1 through October 15

Hunting Sites: 1,500 square miles of agricultural land and marshes, lakes, and rivers

Accommodations: 4,000-square-foot home designed as hunting lodge, semi-private rooms, trophy room with satellite TV

MEALS: three home-cooked meals daily

RATES: three days of hunting, including lodging and meals $1,495 US

MAXIMUM NUMBER OF HUNTERS: eight

GRATUITIES: hunters' discretion

PREFERRED PAYMENT: cash, check, or money order

Getting There: 110 miles east of Edmonton, AB

NEAREST COMMERCIAL AIRPORT: Edmonton, AB

Dogs and Facilities: dogs welcome; outdoor kennel runs available

Guides: two guides per six hunters

Other Services: airport transportation; bird cleaning and packaging (extra charge)

Other Activities: upland bird hunting

CONTACT:

Kirk Sharp or Barry Lundy
Greater Canadians
PO Box 239
Innisfree, Alberta
Canada T0B 2G0
Ph: 780-592-2224 (Sharp) or
403-285-9163 (Lundy)
Email: ksharp@telusplanet.net
Web: www.greatercanadians.com

FRIENDS and hunting buddies since childhood, Kirk Sharp and Barry Lundy were raised in the Innisfree area, about an hour and a half drive from the city of Edmonton. This is a parkland region, a transition zone between the mixed-wood forests to the north and west and the drier prairies to the south and east. It's also great country for waterfowl and waterfowl hunting. With its rolling pea (lentil) and cereal grain fields, and an abundance of water—be it large ponds, lakes, or the Vermilion River and its tributaries—the area is home to one of Alberta's largest local populations of greater Canada geese.

Greater Canadians offers a three-day hunt at $1,495 (US) that includes airport transportation, guiding services, meals, accommodations, and all applicable taxes. Waterfowl hunting licenses are extra and cost approximately $100 for both federal and provincial permits. Bird care—cleaned, plucked, waxed, and totally prepared for export—costs are extra, and steel shot cartridges are also available at an extra charge. An all-inclusive package including licenses, bird care, and ammunition is available for $1,850.

Sharp and Lundy employ the finest tools of the trade. "We use all the newest and most innovative decoys and blinds, from goose chairs to bale blinds," says Sharp. "Also, we still use natural willow blinds as the need arises. Our decoys are the newest in full-body and shell design. We also utilize some of today's new silhouettes."

Describing a day's hunt, Sharp says, "We start early, rising about 4 a.m. We have a small breakfast and then head for the fields. On most mornings, we are loading decoys and on our way back to camp with our morning limit by 10:30." (And bag limits in Alberta are traditionally generous. Recently, they've included eight geese and eight ducks per day. This includes a daily bag limit of five white-fronted geese within the daily bag of eight geese. Four pintail are allowed in the daily bag limit of eight ducks. Possession limits are twice the daily bag limit.)

"Upon arriving back at camp, our cook will have a large and hearty breakfast ready to serve. We all tend to eat too much, then exchange a few stories. While some hunters will then relax and have a nap, others prefer to go out for a little grouse or duck hunting.

"At about 2 p.m." says Sharp, "we'll have lunch and then prepare for the evening hunt. Most evenings are spent duck hunting either in a grain field, on a pond, or along the Vermilion River. After the evening hunt, we return to camp for supper. Our cook prepares a variety of different foods, including wild game. After we've eaten, most hunters relax in our trophy room, where we exchange more stories, watch a little TV or some hunting videos.

Sounds like a pretty grueling schedule, doesn't it?

In addition to outstanding goose hunting, Peace River country offers good opportunities to bag ruffed grouse and sharptails in wooded habitat throughout the valley.

[C A N A D A - W E S T]

Green Head Adventures

St. Paul, Alberta

VITAL STATISTICS:

SPECIES: all major species of geese and ducks

Season: September 1 to December 15; prime time September 1 to October 20

Hunting Sites: agricultural fields surrounding hundreds of large lakes and medium-sized basins in northeast Alberta's Lakeland District

Accommodations: private 4,000-square-foot log home with three rooms that hold two to three hunters each, plus shower, whirlpool tub, trophy room, bar area.

MEALS: homemade meals featuring roasts, chicken, pies, and other good food

RATES: $1,200 for 3-day hunt, all-inclusive except bird cleaning

MAXIMUM NUMBER OF HUNTERS: six

GRATUITIES: hunters' discretion

PREFERRED PAYMENT: cash or check

Getting There: fly to Edmonton, Alberta, where hunters are picked up and transported to the lodge, a two-hour drive

NEAREST COMMERCIAL AIRPORT: Edmonton, Alberta

Dogs and Facilities: dogs welcome; outside kennel or run provided

Guides: one guide per three to four hunters

Other Services: birds cleaned, breasted, washed, and frozen; $1.75 per bird

Other Activities: upland hunting, golf, fishing

CONTACT:
Denis Gauvreau
Green Head Adventures
Box 1751
St. Paul, Alberta
Canada T0A 3A0
Ph: 780-724-4609
Cell Ph: 780-645-8001
Email: greenhed@telusplanet.net

SEEN FROM a goose-eye perspective, it is easy to understand why the Lakeland District of northeastern Alberta is such a magnet for the huge numbers of ducks and geese that have nested in the Canadian subarctic. Here is a vast mosaic of hundreds of lakes and wetlands, interspersed with agricultural fields planted to cereal grains and field peas. These are the first agricultural fields seen by ducks and geese flying south from their nesting grounds, and the attraction is powerful and undeniable.

For the last 10 years or so, Denis and Clare Gauvreau have operated a quality duck and goose hunting operation in the heart of this bird mecca. Designed to take just six hunters at a time in three-day blocks, Green Head specializes in providing a quality hunting experience on an intimate scale. Small-scale is not the way you'd describe the decoy spreads Denis and his guides put out for the visiting hunter, however. These massive spreads of full-bodied decoys are among the largest in all of Alberta, and all the equipment used is top-notch. Nearly every species of geese and ducks that nest north of here passes through this area and is available to the hunters. It is not uncommon to shoot large Canadas, whitefronts, snow geese, mallards, and pintails on the same outing. And because the area has low resident hunting pressure, the birds decoy well.

Hunts are usually done from large, round-bale field blinds, but willow blinds, coffin blinds, and decoy chairs are also employed as conditions dictate. Hunters begin the day with a hearty home-cooked breakfast before being transported to the fields for the morning's shooting. Most of the birds decoy to within 30 to 40 yards of the blinds, providing ideal shooting. The morning shoot is followed by a light lunch around 2 p.m. and, for many, a nap; there is also grouse hunting on private land for those with the stamina for it. Around 4 p.m. hunters are taken out for the evening shoot, unless they have filled their limits in the morning. The day is capped off with a large supper at the lodge. Alberta has liberal limits, with eight dark geese, eight ducks, and 10 white geese allowed per day.

The lodge provides all the comfort you could ask for after a busy day of shooting ducks and geese. The 4,000-square-foot log home features three rooms for hunters, a whirlpool tub, a trophy room, and a bar. There is satellite television and a well-stocked library if you can keep your eyes open after a full day of hunting.

Maverick Waterfowlers

Beaverlodge, Alberta

VITAL STATISTICS:

SPECIES: Canada goose, mallard, pintail

Season: September 1 through November 1

Hunting Sites: thousands of acres of fields, lakes, sloughs, and potholes in northwestern Alberta

Accommodations: log lodge with four rooms on Lake Valhalla

MEALS: home-cooked meals, including goose and duck dishes

RATES: $2,500 (US) per hunter plus tax, five days/six nights (Monday through Friday), includes all accommodations and meals

MAXIMUM NUMBER OF HUNTERS: four hunters/week

GRATUITIES: hunters' discretion

PREFERRED PAYMENT: cash or check

Getting There: commercial flight to Grand Prairie, AB

NEAREST COMMERCIAL AIRPORT: Grand Prairie, AB

Dogs and Facilities: outside dog kennel and runs available

Guides: one guide with dog for up to four hunters

Other Services: bird cleaning and shipping

Other Activities: planning for your next hunt

CONTACT:
Mick Scott
Maverick Waterfowlers
Box 946
Beaverlodge, Alberta
TOH 0C0
Ph: 780-356-2515

THE NEAREST BURG and lake are appropriately named Valhalla, and it won't take you long to realize you've discovered a duck and goose hunter's paradise here in northwestern Alberta, where the prairies are endless, the potholes are plentiful, and the waterfowl are legion.

Mick Scott's Maverick Waterfowlers is also aptly named. It's a one-man, one-woman operation that can accommodate up to four hunters on week-long hunts that will make you think you're at the center of the universe—and as far as waterfowling is concerned, perhaps you are. Mick and his wife, Andi, are host and hostess and the service is always first-rate, from the delicious home-cooked meals to the expert guidance afield. It's hands-on, personalized service that you can't get from bigger outfitters, and it adds tremendously to the quality of the whole experience.

Your day will begin about an hour before sunup with a drive to one of the area's many grain or pea fields, potholes, sloughs, or lakes in the company of Mick and his two Chessies. After setup, it's time for a field breakfast in the blind as you wait for the multitudes of ducks and geese to roll in for their early-morning feeding. That may be the last pause you get, because once the sun comes up the action can be fast and furious as flocks of pintails, mallards, and Canada geese answer Mick's expert calling and pitch in among the decoys.

If you've never hunted this region before, you're in for a real treat. The sheer numbers of birds will leave you awestruck. And little wonder. Alberta produces about 20 percent of the continent's waterfowl population. In other words, a hell of a lot of birds.

At 11 a.m., it's back to the lodge for a delicious home-cooked lunch and a rest or nap before the afternoon hunt. The afternoon is more of the same: the ducks and geese swarm in and your gun grows hot and heavy. With an eight-duck, eight-goose limit, you'll swear you've died and gone to heaven.

At night, in the rustic two-story cabin on Valhalla Lake, you'll be serenaded by the many ducks, geese, and swans that gather on the lake before their great migrations south. You'll understand why Mick and Andi emigrated all the way from England to be here among the ducks and geese. In spite of the prairie's vastness, it's an intimate setting that will put you back in touch with a few of the things that matter most. Good friends, good food, and great hunting.

[**C A N A D A - W E S T**]

Ongaro Outdoors, Ltd.

E d m o n t o n ,   A l b e r t a

CLAUDIO ONGARO does what you always wanted to do as a kid: he skips school every day of the waterfowl season to go hunting. And he's a schoolteacher. Well, he does that full-time, but not in the fall, which is when he turns all of his attention to his outfitting business in east-central Alberta. He knows his ABCs, in the classroom as well as in the goose fields and duck sloughs.

Ongaro operates out of his modern lodge, which is located in some of the best duck and goose hunting country in Canada. There are hundreds of potholes and many staging waters for migratory waterfowl within a 20-minute drive of his facility. The staging waters include Buffalo Lake, Dried Meat Lake, Forestburg Reservoir, Battle River, Gough Lake, Marion Lake, Shooting Lake, Lone Pine Lake, and Sullivan Lake. All these waters provide night roosts for ducks and geese that prowl the surrounding wheat, barley, or pea fields by day.

The bulk of the birds Ongaro's clients harvest are Canada geese and mallards, many of which breed in this part of Alberta. Which means that plenty of local birds—especially greater Canada geese—are available to hunters as soon as the season starts in September. Throughout the fall, birds that breed in other parts of Canada migrate into the area. These include tens of thousands of snow geese and white-fronted geese, which are usually abundant through early October. Other ducks that frequent the area's ponds and sloughs include wigeon, gadwall, teal, and diving ducks.

In addition to himself, Ongaro employs four guides. This allows him to keep two groups of up to five hunters (he prefers four) each hunting in the mornings and afternoons, each with a guide and a trained retriever, while the other guides act as spotters for the next day's hunts. "We hunt two parties of four in separate fields miles apart," says Ongaro. "When you roll in on your first evening, we have been spotting the fields and potholes, putting duck and goose hunts together for you—patterning birds and setting up access. While you hunt with one of the two guides in the morning, the other guides not hunting are out spotting hunts for the evening and next morning. Your afternoon hunt, then, presents a new guide and a new hunting situation. This system involves a great deal of teamwork and communication. There is no competition among the guides as we are all aware that the spotting program is the key to delivering a quality hunt."

Morning goose hunts begin early, at least an hour before the first birds are expected to arrive. This gives Ongaro's guides plenty of time to set up decoys (you can help here) and blinds. Don't worry about laying on the cold, cold ground, either. You'll be off the turf, propped up in a reclining position in an adjustable Goose Chair Decoy Blind (where you hide beneath a giant, hinged-back shell decoy) or hidden in a Stealth Layout Field Blind (which also suspends you off the ground).

Sounds like great equipment, doesn't it? That's because when Claudio Ongaro isn't outfitting or teaching school, he designs, develops, and tests hunting items, including decoys and blinds, for an outdoor-products manufacturer.

[C A N A D A - W E S T]

Sean Mann's Outdoor Adventures

C e n t r a l   A l b e r t a

VITAL STATISTICS:

SPECIES: several subspecies of Canada goose, lesser snow goose, Ross' goose, white-fronted goose, mallard, pintail

Season: September 1 through October 31

Hunting Sites: 6,000 acres of private croplands

Accommodations: motel; semi-private rooms, pool room, lounge

Meals: motel restaurant serves lunch and dinner; breakfast served in goose blind

Rates: $1,500 package includes guide fees, lodging, and meals

Maximum Number of Hunters: eight (prefer four to six)

Gratuities: hunters' discretion

Preferred Payment: check (in advance) or cash

Getting There: central Alberta, about a two-hour drive from Edmonton

Nearest Commercial Airport: Edmonton, AB

Dogs and Facilities: dogs welcome; stay in motel room with owner

Guides: one guide for up to eight hunters

Other Services: bird cleaning, packaging

Other Activities: sporting clays (additional cost)

CONTACT:

Sean or Susan Mann
Sean Mann's Outdoor Adventures
901 Radcliffe Rd.
Towson, MD 21204
Ph: 800-345-4539
Fax: 410-828-0606
Email: worldchamp@duck-goose-calls.com
Web: www.duck-goosecalls.com

ALBERTA IS a waterfowler's paradise. Practically every variety of Canada goose is found here, from the diminutive cackler to the majestic giant Canada. White-fronted geese (specklebellies) and two varieties of white geese, the lesser snow goose and the tiny Ross' goose, stage here in fantastic numbers. Thousands of mallards and pintails also breed in this region and concentrate each fall on prairie potholes, sloughs, and lakes.

Sign up for a package hunt in the central part of the province with Sean Mann and you'll truly be in for an outdoor adventure. If Sean's name sounds familiar, the answer is: Yes, that Sean Mann—former World Goose Calling Champion, World Goose Calling Champion of Champions, Mason-Dixon Duck Calling Champion. He also manufactures The Eastern Shoreman goose call and the Sean Mann Championship duck call. (Just a suggestion, but while you're hunting with him, don't insist on doing your own duck and goose calling.)

Mann is a seasoned guide, not only in Alberta but also in his home country on Maryland's Eastern Shore. His operation in Alberta keeps him there during the months of September and October, then it's back home to guide duck and goose hunters in the Chesapeake Bay area.

In central Alberta, Mann houses his clients in a motel with an attached restaurant and cocktail lounge. Lunch and dinner are served in the restaurant and are included in his three-day package rate. Breakfast, due to the early hour of daily hunting departures, is served in the field—coffee, juice, rolls, muffins, and fruit served in the blind while the morning sun begins arcing over the Alberta prairie.

But don't get caught with a cup of coffee in your hand when the birds are coming. Mann calls them in often and calls them in close. He says his clients are often shooting at landing ducks and geese that are within a few feet of the ground when the shot is called. "Typically," Mann relates, "our shots are from five feet to 15 yards away and two to five feet from the ground. This is why I suggest my hunters use open chokes—skeet or improved cylinder. Most people bring 12-gauge 3-inch guns, but they shouldn't be afraid to bring a 20-gauge with skeet tubes."

Mann's expert calling isn't the only thing bringing ducks and geese close to the decoys. "I use safe, comfortable, portable blinds that shield you from the elements and hide you from the birds," says Mann. "These blinds are constructed so that you can comfortably watch the birds work and, when the time comes, get to them quickly, accurately, and safely. No lying on the cold ground, trying to make impossible shots, or kneeling behind a willow switch in freezing temperatures until you can't move. Instead, you sit in a nice blind, in a chair with a back, and sip hot coffee until I say 'Take 'em.'"

Sounds easy enough. The best part, though, is listening to the sound 100 Ross' geese make when they're only 10 feet off the ground, or feeling the air move under the wings of 60 giant Canadas only a broomstick's height above your head.

Hay bale blinds camouflaged with barley stubble will fool even the wariest geese on the prairies.

[C A N A D A - W E S T]

Target Guide Services

Bassano, Alberta

BRING HIP BOOTS or waders, upland boots, and your golf shoes. Next to Norris Iverson's two-story cedar cabin, headquarters for his Bassano- and Brooks Range-area waterfowl hunts, is a nine-hole golf course. He even has clubs and carts right at the cabin, but warns that few of his guests have the energy to play golf after a morning hunt for ducks and geese.

If you're not a duffer and prefer to stay in a motel, Iverson can arrange that as part of your hunt package. He can put you up in either nearby Bassano or, 30 to 40 minutes away from his hunting area, in Brooks, a somewhat larger town with a wider range of restaurants and a few nightclubs. Whether you choose to stay at the cabin or a motel, though, his package rates include lodging and meals.

Iverson usually hunts geese in the mornings and ducks in the afternoon, but he will vary his target species according to his clients' wishes. "Early in the morning," he says, "we set out about 100 super magnum shell decoys for geese and silhouette decoys for ducks in a wheat or barley field. We use low profile Final Approach Eliminator blinds for the clients and guides. Guides will do the calling, but our hunters are welcome to join in if they want to. Calling is a crucial part of the hunt and we encourage our clients to get involved. Loud hail calls followed by in-close clucking and double clucking will usually do the trick on geese.

"Ducks will usually be in the decoys at first light," Iverson says, "well before the geese arrive. We often have limits of ducks down before we fire a single shot at a goose. But if you'd rather wait to shoot ducks in the afternoon, over water, you can hold off and wait for geese. In fact, we prefer to hunt geese in the mornings and ducks in the evenings."

Depending on the time of the season, goose hunting may be for Canadas, specklebellies, or snow geese. "Unlike in Saskatchewan," Iverson explains, "where specklebellies feed with snow geese, here they often mingle with Canadas. Our spreads of 100 super magnum Canada shells for both Canadas and specks increase to 10 to 12 dozen decoys, including windsocks and flyers, as the season progresses. For snow geese, we set out spreads of several hundred wind socks and rags.

Most of Iverson's morning goose hunts are over by 11 a.m. After the decoys are picked up, he or one of his guides will take you back to the cabin or a local restaurant for lunch. Then it's a nap or golf while your birds are being cleaned and frozen. Unless you've already shot a limit of ducks in the morning, afternoon hunts resume at 3. These hunts are usually focused on local potholes, where the hunters are positioned in natural cover and hunt over floater decoys.

If you are limited out on both ducks and geese, you can still play golf, hunt upland birds during the open season for them, or help spot ducks and geese to determine which fields they're using and where you'll set up the following morning.

Western Guiding Service

Empress, Alberta

VITAL STATISTICS:

SPECIES: mallard, pintail, Canada goose, white-fronted goose, Ross' goose, snow goose, sandhill crane
Season: September 15 to October 15
Hunting Sites: agricultural fields, potholes and sloughs
Accommodations: lodge with six private bedrooms, showers, bath, billiard table, hosted bar
Meals: home-style, hearty and wholesome
Rates: three-day package rates from $1,225 to $2,150 (US); call for details
Maximum Number of Hunters: six
Gratuities: voluntary
Preferred Payment: cash or check
Getting There: three-hour drive from Calgary, AB
Nearest Commercial Airport: Calgary, AB
Dogs and Facilities: outside kennels provided for clients' dogs
Guides: three guides per six hunters
Other Services: bird cleaning and packaging
Other Activities: upland bird hunting: sharp-tailed grouse, Hungarian partridge, pheasant
CONTACT:
Dave Molloy
Western Guiding Services
Box 191
Empress, Alberta
Canada T0J 1E0
Ph: 403-565-3775 or 403-676-3300
Email: gorfsss9@telusplanet.net
Web: www.usa10.com/western

WANT A DOUBLE whammy, as in hunting two Canadian provinces on the same trip? Call Dave Molloy of Western Guiding Service. He operates from Empress, Alberta, with a lodge near Alask, Saskatchewan. Molloy normally hunts geese in the mornings in Saskatchewan, then shifts to Alberta in the afternoon. This is a bit different from the way most Canadian outfitters operate, but after 20 years in business, Molloy isn't going to argue with his own success.

Molloy does something else different than most other outfitters, too. He hunts over stuffers. Not exclusively, of course, because his taxidermy investment in full-body goose mounts would otherwise be astronomical. He mixes the stuffers with plastic full-body goose decoys and rag spreads. "Which decoys we use," he says, "is dictated by the species most available at the time and how decoy-shy the birds may be. Usually, we don't need the stuffers until later in the season, when the hunting gets tougher and birds get wiser to the game."

Molloy houses his clients in his six-bedroom private lodge near Alask. The facilities include a dining area, kitchen, three bathrooms, and a "tall tales" room with a hosted bar and pool table. The lodge caters to wingshooters from mid-September to mid-October, and to deer hunters in late October. His goose and duck hunts take place on wheat stubble and harvested pea (lentil) fields within a 30-mile radius of the lodge. Normally, three hunters are taken to a field by two non-shooting guides, which helps keep group shooting within comfortable levels.

"We arise about 4:30," Molloy says of a typical day of hunting, "and partake of a light breakfast of coffee and toast. Then we proceed to selected fields in Saskatchewan and place the decoys. In most cases, we don't call the birds, because we've scouted the fields and know that the geese are feeding there, so calling isn't always necessary. Our guides will put out commercial ground blinds or bale blinds and monitor the hunt. They and their dogs will mark and retrieve the downed birds.

"We shoot until about 9:30," Molloy says, "or until our hunters reach a limit. Then we return to the lodge for a real breakfast. After that, we hunt sharptails, Hungarian partridge, and pheasants until early afternoon, then take an hour off to rest. By mid-afternoon, we're in Alberta for afternoon duck hunts, usually in a pothole or slough on private property where we have permission to hunt, or we'll hunt for more geese if some guests didn't fill their limit in the morning."

Sounds like a full day, eh? It will feel like that, too, when you return to the lodge, usually by 7:30, for a hearty supper. Then, perhaps, a game of billiards and a sundowner as you swap stories in the aptly named "tall tales" room. According to Molloy, more ducks and geese are often shot in that room in one night than anywhere else in Canada all season long.

Wildlife West Adventures, Inc.

C a r d s t o n ,   A l b e r t a

VITAL STATISTICS:

SPECIES: Canada goose, snow goose, mallard, pintail
Season: September through December
Hunting Sites: agricultural fields, potholes, reservoirs
Accommodations: modern motel with pool, hot tub
MEALS: home-cooked meals at outfitter's home
RATES: four nights lodging, meals, and three full days hunting for $1,400 US
MAXIMUM NUMBER OF HUNTERS: six
GRATUITIES: $25-$50 per hunter
PREFERRED PAYMENT: cash or check
Getting There: approximately 120 miles from Calgary, AB
NEAREST COMMERCIAL AIRPORT: Lethbridge, AB
Dogs and Facilities: limited kennel space available for hunters' dogs
Guides: one guide for four to six hunters
Other Services: airport transportation; bird cleaning (extra charge) and packaging
Other Activities: sporting clays; upland bird hunting; fly-fishing for trout

CONTACT:
Don Jensen
Wildlife West Adventures Inc.
Box 1373
Cardston, Alberta
Canada T0K 0K0
Ph/Fax: 403-653-1737
Email: wildlife@telusplanet.net

IF YOU ARE a waterfowl hunter and trout fisherman, Don Jensen, owner of Wildlife West Adventures, can offer you some of the best of both worlds. Jensen is headquartered in Cardston, Alberta, only a stone's throw from the rugged east slope of the Northern Rockies and minutes away from Waterton National Park, the Canadian extension of Montana's Glacier National Park. The prairie foothills of the region are ribboned and dotted with rivers, lakes, and wheat fields that offer world-class trout fishing as well as spectacular waterfowl hunting opportunities.

This prairie country of southern Alberta is a prime breeding area for mallard, pintail, and giant Canada geese. Hunting for these local birds is best in mid-September. Later in the season, from early October on, hundreds of thousands of geese and ducks migrate through the area, stopping to feed on the abundant waste grains left in farmers' fields after the fall harvest. Local reservoirs and the many potholes and marshes that are scattered over the countryside offer the birds freshwater to drink and roost on at night.

Jensen's normal waterfowl hunts begin with a morning goose shoot. That doesn't mean you won't have opportunities to bag ducks, which will work the same stubble fields and decoys where you set up for Canadas. The goose hunts last until 10:30 or 11. After that it's time for lunch and a quick snooze (time permitting). Afternoons are given to staking out a pothole or slough for mallards, pintail, and wigeon. The best duck hunting usually occurs in the last half hour of legal shooting time, when thousands of ducks come looking for a piece of marsh to roost on for the evening.

If you are a trout fisherman and want to customize your hunt into a "cast and blast," Jensen will be happy to accommodate you. Some widely known trout rivers—including the Crowsnest, Castle, and Old Man—are a short drive from the waterfowl hunting areas. Drift boat trips are available through late September. Otherwise, you can walk and wade the same rivers, streams, or spring creeks to catch browns, cutthroats, brook trout, grayling, or trophy northern pike.

The foothills and plains around Cardston are also home to sharp-tailed grouse and Hungarian partridge. So if fishing isn't your game, Jensen can guide you to upland birds as well. Be prepared to walk some for these wild birds, though, as they have plenty of room to roam over the hundreds of thousands of square miles of rolling hills in this part of Alberta. Jensen can also arrange for a day or half day of hunting released pheasants, too, which don't require quite the same amount of hiking to bag a few birds.

After a day of challenging hill and dale or thrashing in rivers and streams, soaking in a hot tub will be a welcome experience. The proprietors of the modern motel where Jensen lodges his clients will have it heated up and ready for you when you return from your day afield. Dinner, before or after you soak, will be home-cooked and served at Jensen's home. Roast turkey with all the fix'ns and German chocolate cake are house specialties.

The Northern Rocky Mountains provide a spectacular backdrop for waterfowlers seeking geese in the wheat fields of southeastern Alberta.

High Brass

Quill Lakes, Saskatchewan

VITAL STATISTICS:

SPECIES: Canada goose, snow goose, blues, mallards, gadwall, wigeon, canvasback, bufflehead, bluebill, blue-winged and green-winged teal, and sandhill crane

Season: white geese and sandhill crane seasons open September 1; ducks and Canada geese open second Monday in September

Hunting Sites: thousands of acres of grain fields, sloughs, and puddles in Saskatchewan

Accommodations: three remodeled farm houses that include ten bedrooms and six baths

MEALS: dinners feature duck, goose, and sandhill crane–"a big favorite among our hunters"

RATES: $1,600 for a three-day package

MAXIMUM NUMBER OF HUNTERS: up to 10 hunters

GRATUITIES: hunters' discretion

PREFERRED PAYMENT: check

Getting There: fly into Regina, Saskatchewan, rent a car and drive two hours to camp

NEAREST COMMERCIAL AIRPORT: Regina, Saskatchewan

Dogs and Facilities: dogs allowed

Guides: one guide for up to five hunters

Other Services: bird cleaning

Other Activities: pheasant, sharp-tailed and prairie grouse hunting in South Dakota; quail hunting in Texas and Mexico

CONTACT:
Tom or Kelly Koehn
R.R. 1, Box 4X
Chamberlain, SD 57325
Ph: 605-734-6047
Fax: 605-734-5033
Email: tkbrass@highbrass.com
Web: wwwhighbrass.com

"IF THE HUNT'S worth doing, it's worth doing right." That's the motto of High Brass outfitters, owned and operated by brothers Tom and Kelly Koehn of Chamberlain, South Dakota. The credo comes from their father, who instilled in them the desire to get the most out of every hunt, to do everything first class, without cutting corners. Thus the name High Brass, and the first-rate service that lives up to the billing.

Born and bred to it, Tom and Kelly have more than 60 years of hunting experience between them. Both are hands-on guides, and when you're out in the field, one of them will be there with you, setting out the decoys, calling in the ducks and geese, giving you last-minute instruction, and doing little things that make a big difference in terms of your success and enjoyment.

High Brass' waterfowl hunts take place in the western Canada province of Saskatchewan, where the birds are plenty and the limits are liberal. A wide variety of duck hunting is available, including mallards, gadwall, pintails, wigeon, green-winged teal, blue-winged teal, and shovelers in a number of sloughs and potholes. There's also some challenging diver hunting—canvasbacks, redheads, buffleheads, and bluebills—on a few big lakes. Limits on ducks are eight per day per person.

For goose hunting, you'll set up in a stubble field, placing out about 100 decoys if you're after Canada geese, and up to 1,000 dekes if you're preparing for snow and blue goose action. The limit on Canada geese is 8 and the limit on snows and blues is 28.

No matter what success you've had, by late morning you're in for a special treat, as your hosts get you set up in the marshlands for some pass-shooting at big sandhill cranes as they fly over on their way to roost. "Generally, a hunter's first reaction is, 'Cranes? No, thanks. I'll pass,'" says Tom. "That is, until they see the cranes. You won't believe the thrill of this hunt. We've seen more 'buck fever' in crane hunting than in any type of hunting we do." Limits on cranes are five per person per day.

In the afternoon you'll hunt ducks or snows or cranes (you can't shoot Canadas in the afternoon). Then back to the lodge for a little rest and relaxation before dinner. Expect delicious home-cooked meals featuring ducks, geese, and, yes, even sandhill cranes. "The sandhill crane is one of the best meals you'll ever eat," explains Tom. "It's a favorite of our hunting groups."

*Sam and Craig Buskirk operate out of Kyle, Saskatchewan,
in the heart of the province's best goose hunting country.
For the past dozen years, this pair of guides has been enticing
parties of hunters to return annually for productive
hunts in this rolling coteau prairieland.*

[C A N A D A - W E S T]

K & P Outfitters

K y l e ,   S a s k a t c h e w a n

VITAL STATISTICS:

SPECIES: white-fronted goose, sandhill cranes, snow goose, Ross' goose, mallard, pintail, wigeon, teal

Season: mid-September through October

Hunting Sites: agricultural fields, potholes near the South Saskatchewan River

Accommodations: 13-room motel, one or two hunters per room

MEALS: home-cooked

RATES: three-, five-, and six-day packages available at $1,000, $1,400, and $1,600, respectively; includes license, lodging, meals, guide fees, and bird cleaning/packaging/freezing

MAXIMUM NUMBER OF HUNTERS: 12

GRATUITIES: $10 per hunter/day

PREFERRED PAYMENT: cash or check

Getting There: Kyle is in southern Saskatchewan, 45 miles north of Swift Current and 125 miles southwest of Saskatoon

NEAREST COMMERCIAL AIRPORT: Saskatoon, SK

Dogs and Facilities: hunters may bring own dogs; dogs stay in motel rooms with owners

Guides: four hunters per guide

Other Services: bird cleaning, packaging, freezing

Other Activities: sharp-tailed grouse, Hungarian partridge hunting; walleye and northern pike fishing

CONTACT:
Sam Van Buskirk
K & P Outfitters
Box 212
Kyle, Saskatchewan
Canada S0L 1T0
Ph: 306-375-2270
Fax: 306-375-2601

THE SMALL TOWN of Kyle is situated on the rolling prairies of southern Saskatchewan, near the South Saskatchewan River. This is the heart of the Central Flyway. In fall, thousands upon thousands of ducks and geese concentrate here to fatten up on farmers' grain before continuing their inexorable southern migration. When they're not flying or eating, many of these birds concentrate on the countless pothole sloughs and small lakes that dot the countryside. But the biggest concentrations of ducks and geese roost on the river, especially its lake-sized widening known as Galloway Bay.

Stand on a prairie hill that overlooks the bay and you'll witness an impressive sight. Huge groups of Canadas, snow geese, and Ross' geese may cover the water. But, most of all, you'll be seeing white-fronted geese, or specklebellies. This part of Saskatchewan is a main staging area for southbound specklebellies, and Galloway Bay holds some of the largest numbers of this species you'll ever see in one place in North America—an eyeful. Sometimes hundreds of thousands of them. Whitefront nirvana.

Sam and Craig Van Buskirk know this country well. They are local farmers, and they grew up here. For the last 12 years, they've also been guiding waterfowl hunters. Being born and raised in the community, they know the country as well as anyone could, and they also know all the other farmers in it. Getting permission to hunt is not a problem.

Arrive at Kyle in the afternoon and check into your motel. Or, *the* motel. There's only one in town. Get settled in. Then Sam and Craig may pick you up for a tour of the area. A view of Galloway Bay is a must. It's not really a tour. Sam and Craig are actually scouting for your first morning's hunt. It won't take long to determine one or two fields that plenty of specks are using. Then it's back to the Van Buskirk's place for a home-made dinner while calls are made for permission to hunt.

In the morning, after breakfast at the motel, it's back to the fields, where you'll be hunting from pits or portable blinds. When the first flocks start to take off from the bay for the morning feeding flight it will be shortly after dawn. Eyes up—ducks may buzz the decoys first. What's that strange, raucous sound coming from behind you? A flock of sandhill cranes. Saskatchewan has a nonresident season for the huge, gangly birds, so if you're there at the right time, you can shoot. As another writer once aptly phrased it, a wingshot sand-hill falls from the sky like a broken lawn chair. Lead 'em far enough, though, that long neck is deceiving.

When the geese start buzzing the decoys, you might expect Canadas or snows, but most likely they will be specks. At a distance, the specks will look like Canadas, but their high-pitched three-note yodel will give them away immediately. Watch closely. The young-of-the-year birds have grey bellies and will readily come to the decoys. Hold your fire. Wait for the oldsters, the ones with the irregular black bars on their chests and bellies. These are the trophy birds, and you may want to have one mounted for your den. All of them, young and old alike, are great on the table, probably the best eating of all geese.

[C A N A D A - W E S T]

Montgomery Outfitting Service, Ltd.

M o r s e ,   S a s k a t c h e w a n

VITAL STATISTICS:

SPECIES: mallard, pintail, snow goose, white-fronted goose, Canada goose

Season: mid-September into November

Hunting Sites: hundreds of thousands of acres of stubble fields, lakes, ponds, and grasslands

Accommodations: private lodge with 13 rooms with baths

Meals: full-menu dining room

Rates: $1,600/3-day hunt (1999)

Maximum Number of Hunters: 12

Gratuities: $50 to $70 per day

Preferred Payment: cash or traveler's checks

Getting There: fly to Regina where guide service will pick you up

Nearest Commercial Airport: Regina, Saskatchewan

Dogs and Facilities: well-trained dogs welcome; may be kept in room

Guides: guide for each party of three

Other Services: bird cleaning and packing

Other Activities: Hungarian partridge and sharp-tailed grouse hunting; clay target shooting with instructor on staff

CONTACT:

Doug Montgomery
Montgomery Outfitting Service Ltd.
P.O. Box 92
Morse, Saskatchewan
Canada, S0H 3C0
Ph/Fax: 306-629-3752
Email: hunterland@sk.sympatico.ca
Web: www.di.com/montgomery

THE 17,000-SQUARE-MILE expanse of prairie known as the Missouri Coteau forms one of the great wonders of the waterfowl world. Stretching from South and North Dakota into southern Saskatchewan, no place on the planet rivals this region's capacity to grow waterfowl. And with its innumerable ponds and sloughs brimming with water after the decade-long drought of the 1980s, it is once again one of the world's leading nurseries for ducks and other waterfowl.

For Doug Montgomery, a native of the Saskatchewan prairie, this is just the right place to nurture his passion for decoying ducks and geese, and for walking up sharptails and Huns in the seemingly endless landscape. Happily, this farmer-turned-outfitter shares his nearly 30 years of experience hunting the prairies with guests of the Montgomery Outfitting Service, Ltd. You can fly into Regina, where you'll be picked up and driven to a comfortable lodge that provides excellent personal service and serves superb game-bird meals. The area's hundreds of potholes and lakes, including the huge Ducks Unlimited Thunder Creek project, provide substantial opportunities for calling in mallards. Grainfield blinds also produce their share of ducks intent on a healthy meal.

And if it's geese you crave, you'll find them here by the tens of thousands—lesser snows, Ross', whitefronts, and Canadas. The guides' scouting expeditions will reveal where the birds have been feeding, and the next morning before dawn the guides spatter the harvested wheat field with a mixture of silhouettes, shells, and wind socks. At first light you see the inaugural flights lift off a nearby lake that served as the evening roost. Soon you hear the din of thousands of white geese lifting from the water en masse and you watch as they spiral into the sky like a great white waterspout heading for you and your field of deception.

When the morning hunt is over, it is easy to remind yourself that you are also in the heart of some of North America's best Hungarian partridge and sharp-tailed grouse habitat. If you enjoy walking for upland birds, you'll find nothing to hold you back here. Montgomery says that well-trained dogs are welcome, but he notes that pointing dogs don't work well on the birds in these parts since they don't hold tight for most dogs.

Early morning ducks and long afternoon walks can work up a thirst for a cocktail and a hearty appetite for a fine meal. You'll find both at the deluxe lodge. And speaking of pampering yourself, how about one day marking your calendar for the ultimate prairie hunting experience—12 solid days of hunting. Each fall Doug offers this special treat to a party of four. Two guides are dedicated to your party. Each day is devoted to chasing the best shooting opportunity, whatever it may be. For instance, on overcast days, you will head to the duck blinds, or if the guides have scouted an excellent goose field, you'll go for it. Bluebird day? Just right for walking up Huns and sharpies. You'll have a simple mission for these two weeks: enjoy the hunt and soak in the true splendor of this gift of nature.

A smaller, juvenile white-fronted goose and a mature member of its species bagged on the same hunt. The dark markings on the bellies of mature whitefronts give rise to their common name of specklebellies.

Rathmore Outfitting

C l a i r ,   S a s k a t c h e w a n

VITAL STATISTICS:

SPECIES: mallard, pintail, teal, canvasback, scaup, gadwall, Canada goose, snow goose, Ross' goose

Season: ducks: September through October; geese mid-September through October

Hunting Sites: potholes, freshwater marshes, private farmlands

Accommodations: private lodge with four semi-private bedrooms

Meals: home-style cooking; light breakfast, lunch, dinner

Rates: three- and five-day package rates available on request

Maximum Number of Hunters: eight

Gratuities: hunters' discretion

Preferred Payment: cash or check

Getting There: in east-central Saskatchewan, 120 miles north of Regina, SK

Nearest Commercial Airport: Regina or Saskatoon, SK

Dogs and Facilities: dogs welcome; "house rules" apply

Guides: four or five hunters per guide; guides do not have dogs

Other Services: none

Other Activities: none

CONTACT:
Michael Quinn
Rathmore Outfitting
Box 17
Clair, Saskatchewan
Canada S0A 0N0
Ph: 306-545-9589 or 306-383-2218
Fax: 306-721-2330
Email: mquinn@cableregina.com
Web: www.cableregina.com/business/mquinn/

THE QUILL LAKES area of Saskatchewan is well known among waterfowlers. It's sort of a mecca for both American and Canadian wingshooters looking for the ultimate duck and goose destination. That's because Quill Lakes is a major migratory staging area for both types of waterfowl. It has grainfields on which the birds establish grazing rights in fall. It also has plenty of marshes, sloughs, and lakes where the birds can roost at night and drink their fill. It has plenty of room for hunters to spread out and not be tripping over one another.

What it doesn't have is a lot of motel rooms for visiting hunters, nor does it have enough guide services to supply the demand. Sure, you can freelance here and maybe find a room someplace—if you're lucky. But you may end up tenting it or sleeping in your car. You can also drive endless miles around the country to try and find a farmer or two who will give you permission to hunt his fields and wetlands—unless he's already given permission to someone else. Or you can give up those hassles and call Michael Quinn.

Quinn is an area native. He knows the local farmers. He knows the local wetlands. He knows ducks and geese and which farm fields and wetlands they're using. And he has accommodations: warm, dry lodging and three meals a day for his clients. He'll even arrange to have your birds processed and packaged for travel, though he encourages you to do that yourself. He can even supply a cooler for you to take your game home with you.

Like most other prairie outfitters, Quinn starts his and your day with an early call to breakfast. This will be a light breakfast, because you'll have work to do soon. You've got a drive to a field ahead of you and a big spread of decoys to help assemble in the wheat stubble. Bring a Thermos of coffee. You may need a cup before the action begins. It's always coldest just before dawn, which is when you'll be climbing into your blind to get ready for the first flight of the day.

There's no telling what that first flight may be. Ducks. Canada geese. Snow geese. They're all here in fantastic numbers. If it's ducks, you can only shoot if there are no geese heading for the spread. The morning shoot is primarily devoted to hunting the big birds. Duck hunting will come later, in the afternoon. If it's geese, you'll hear them coming from a distance, the Canadas honking but generally less vocal than snow geese. When snows do come, they come in huge flocks, their yodeling calls audible from a great distance. Milling over your decoys, they are almost deafening. There will be times, too, when both species of geese are within shotgun range at the same time. This is fast, exciting shooting at a multitude of flying targets. It's what has earned the Quill Lakes region its reputation among waterfowlers.

After the morning goose hunt and lunch, Quinn and his guides will be scouting out the next day's goose hunt. On their way, they'll take you to a duck-rich pothole to wile away the afternoon.

Snow geese in both their white phase and blue phase are common fall migrants in Saskatchewan. Most hunting for these bountiful but wary geese occurs in barley or wheat stubble.

[C A N A D A - W E S T]

Safari River Outdoors, Ltd.

S a s k a t o o n ,   S a s k a t c h e w a n

VITAL STATISTICS:

SPECIES: Canada goose, mallard, wigeon, bluebill, canvasback, ring-necked duck

Season: September 1 to October 20

Hunting Sites: private agricultural land; private and public marshes, ponds and wild rice lakes

Accommodations: refurbished three-bedroom log ranch house

MEALS: traditional American fare, steaks, wildfowl

RATES: $1,495 five-day package rate includes lodging, meals, guided hunting

MAXIMUM NUMBER OF HUNTERS: six

GRATUITIES: $25 per day (optional)

PREFERRED PAYMENT: cash or check

Getting There: camp is located in west-central Saskatchewan, 18 miles northeast of Meadow Lake (3¹/₂-hour drive north of Saskatoon)

NEAREST COMMERCIAL AIRPORT: Saskatoon, SK

Dogs and Facilities: hunters' dogs welcome only outside sleeping and dining area; no kennels provided

Guides: one guide per three hunters; some guides use dogs, other do not

Other Services: bird cleaning (but not plucking) and freezing included in rate package

Other Activities: northern pike or walleye fishing; released pheasant hunting; black bear hunting (arrange in advance); upland bird hunting for ruffed, spruce, and sharp-tailed grouse

CONTACT:

Barry Samson
Safari River Outdoors Ltd.
203 B Dunlop St.
Saskatoon, Saskatchewan
Canada S7N 2B8
Ph: 888-244-1461 or 306-239-3905
(August to November)
Fax: 306-244-6366
Email: info@huntcanada.com
Web: www.huntcanada.com

THE MAILING ADDRESS may be Saskatoon, but Safari River Outoors' camp is a bit farther north, eh? As in, on the northern border of the last agricultural areas in the province, and where the woods beyond stretch out to the tundra of the Northwest Territories. But these are also the first grainfields migrating geese see on their way south in fall, and big Canada geese begin flocking here as early as September. The hunting stays hot from then until the middle of October.

Geese aren't the only attraction for waterfowlers in these parts, though. The country around Safari Outfitters' lodge also includes marshes, ponds, and wild rice lakes that attract hordes of ducks, as well as geese. Depending on the timing of the migration, you may be shooting at anything from mallard, wigeon, teal, pintail, and gadwall, for dabblers, to, in the diver category, canvasback, bluebill, ringneck, redhead, and goldeneye.

Usually, in September the giant Canadas cruise the stubble fields in small flocks. Still, some flocks may number up to 1,000 birds, and hunting pressure is light to nonexistent. Safari guides will set you up to hunt geese in the fields, or, as a bit of departure from normal operations, have you shooting them over open water. (Your choice, of course, but if you've never hunted Canadas over water, you're missing quite an experience.)

Duck hunting here starts with a large variety of species early in the season, but October is the best time for mallards. Canvasback numbers are up, and the daily bag limit for the species here is, at present, liberal.

A waterfowling day at Safari Outfitters begins with a light breakfast, and then a trip by truck, ATV, or boat, depending on the hunt location. Field goose hunts are usually over by midmorning, when you'll be returned to the lodge for a large breakfast and a nap. (On a typical five-day booking, there will usually be two to three days of goose hunting.) An afternoon shoot for ducks will start at mid-afternoon and last until dusk. If you choose to hunt a remote wild rice lake in the morning, you'll not only enjoy a wilderness adventure, you'll also experience a traditional Canadian shore lunch after the morning shoot. On the menu will be fresh marinated duck strips, fresh pike, stewed onions, fried potatoes, corn, and beans. The hot lunch is served out of the wind so that you can sit back and enjoy the feast while watching the last of the morning flight over the lake.

The fresh pike in your shore lunch, by the way, comes from the same rice lake. Don't forget to bring a rod, reel, and a few pike spoons, because northern pike as well as walleyes are plentiful here.

If you don't care for fishing, a guide can take you to some unforgettable hotspots for ruffed grouse and sharptails. Or, through prior arrangement with Safari, you can mix your waterfowling mornings with afternoon black bear hunting. Fishing, upland birds, black bears—however you spend your afternoon, you'll have plenty to talk about at the evening campfire after dinner.

Mallards often buzz goose decoy setups in the early morning hours, providing fast shooting for hunters before geese leave their evening roosts to feed.

[C A N A D A - W E S T]

Thistlethwaite Outfitters

S t e w a r t   V a l l e y ,   S a s k a t c h e w a n

VITAL STATISTICS:

SPECIES: Canada goose, snow goose, Ross' goose, white-fronted goose, mallard, pintail, wigeon, blue- and green-winged teal, canvasback, gadwall, shovelers

Season: mid-September to first week in November

Hunting Sites: 10,000 square miles in southwest Saskatchewan

Accommodations: local motel with pool, bar, restaurant

MEALS: home-cooked meals at farm

RATES: $995 for three-day package

MAXIMUM NUMBER OF HUNTERS: 15

GRATUITIES: $25 per day suggested

PREFERRED PAYMENT: cash or check

Getting There: fly into Regina, Saskatchewan, and rent a car for two-hour drive west

NEAREST COMMERCIAL AIRPORT: Regina, Saskatchewan

Dogs and Facilities: dogs welcome; modern kennels and runs or welcome in your motel room

Guides: guide/hunter ratio varies

Other Services: bird cleaning and packaging

Other Activities: upland bird hunting for Huns and sharptails; fishing for walleye, pike, trout, and whitefish

CONTACT:

Thistlethwaite Outfitters
Box 123
Stewart Valley, SK
Canada SON 2PO
Ph: 306-778-348
Email: thlsr@sk.sympatico.ca

"LOVE LIKES a gander, and adores a goose," wrote the American poet Theodore Roethke. And so will you, when you get a gander at the thousands of excited honkers descending on your spread in the middle of a southwest Saskatchewan grain field. Let's just say that you'll be goosed so bad you'll want to jump right up . . . and shoot.

And so it is at Thistlethwaite Outfitters and Guiding Service in Swift Current, Saskatchewan, a staging area where three major flyways converge, bringing together untold numbers of geese of various species—Canadas, snows, Ross'—a veritable goose hunter's paradise. This is the heart of goose country, and goose hunting is the heart of Thistlethwaite's business, though the outfitter also offers duck hunting packages, sharptail and Hungarian partridge hunting, and even lake fishing for walleyes, pike, rainbow trout, and whitefish.

Thistlethwaite will supply almost everything you need for a successful goose hunt, including pits, blinds, decoys, land, and guides. Activities are tailored to your wishes. You can go out the afternoon before the morning hunt and join your guide in scouting and planning where and how you'll set up. Finding a field with thousands of geese feeding in it is a great way to increase your anticipation, and appreciation, of the approaching hunt. The guide will be happy to include your suggestions, and if you have a special goose call or favorite decoys—bring them along, too. If, however, you'd prefer a simple, relaxing hunt, all you have to do is step out of the truck into the shooting blind. Again, the choice is yours.

A three-day goose hunting package, cost $995, includes accommodations at the Imperial 400 Motel, one of the best motels in Saskatchewan, featuring rooms with two double beds, color TV, and a private bathroom. The motel also comes with a heated indoor pool, coffee shop, dining room, and cocktail lounge. Included also are a light breakfast, a hearty, home-cooked midday meal at the farm, morning hunt with guide on all three days, two afternoon hunts, and free bird cleaning, packaging, and freezer storage.

Hunters traveling by motor home or camper are welcome to set up in Thistlethwaite's farm yard, which has electrical and water hook-ups. Dogs are welcome at the motel, and the farm provides free kennel service, if you prefer to go that route.

Waterfowlers traveling to Regina can also take advantage of a special airfare package offered by Northwest Airlines and Uniglobe Travel. Advantages include discounted fares with Northwest (no Saturday night stay required), no goods and service tax for American fliers, rental car and motel reservations, and assistance with firearm registration forms for American hunters. For more information, call Uniglobe at 800-565-6562, ext. 2, or e-mail <wc.preferred@uniglobe.com>, and tell them you are hunting this fall with Thistlethwaite Outfitters.

Galloway Bay on the Saskatchewan River is a major fall staging area for waterfowl and contains the largest fall concentration of white-fronted geese anywhere on the continent.

[C A N A D A - W E S T]

Toby's Trophy Treks

C h r i s t o p h e r   L a k e ,   S a s k a t c h e w a n

VITAL STATISTICS:

SPECIES: Canada goose, mallard, occasional snow goose and white-fronted goose early in the season

Season: September 1 until birds leave, usually mid-November

Hunting Sites: thousands of acres of private land in Saskatchewan, 25 miles north of Prince Albert

Accommodations: two-bedroom guesthouse attached to year-round home at Emma Lake

MEALS: home-cooked meals served in home; stocked bar in trophy room

RATES: $1,750 for five-day package with all meals, accommodations, and transportation to and from Saskatoon; $500 deposit

MAXIMUM NUMBER OF HUNTERS: six

GRATUITIES: $100 to $200 per day

PREFERRED PAYMENT: cash or check

Getting There: fly to Saskatoon, Saskatchewan, where lodge guests are picked up and transported to lodge

NEAREST COMMERCIAL AIRPORT: Saskatoon, Saskatchewan

Dogs and Facilities: dogs welcome and are accommodated in guesthouse with master

Guides: guides employed to locate birds and assist in setting up and tearing down decoys; guides do not use dogs.

Other Services: bird cleaning, freezing, packing, and shipping

Other Activities: fishing and beautiful golf course nearby

CONTACT:
A.C. "Toby" Coleman
Toby's Trophy Treks
P.O. Box 204
Christopher Lake, Saskatchewan
Canada S0J 0N0
Ph: 306-982-2020
Fax: 306-982-2500
Email: toby@trophytreks.com
Web: www.trophytreks.com

WHEN YOU COME THIS FAR north to hunt ducks and geese—25 miles north of Prince Albert, Saskatchewan—it will seem appropriate and comforting to know that you've put yourself in the hands of a retired member of the Royal Canadian Mounted Police. A.C. "Toby" Coleman spent a career serving people through the Mounted Police, and when it came time to retire, he devoted himself to serving hunters through his outfitting business.

The emphasis on Toby's Trophy Treks is on personal service and customer satisfaction. Toby hunts no more than six persons at a time and they stay in the comfortable two-bedroom guesthouse attached to his own home near Emma Lake. In addition to duck and goose hunters, he guides deer and bear hunters in season. Perhaps the greatest testament to the quality of his service is that Toby is now taking reservations nearly two years out, and to get a spot you'd better hurry.

It also helps that mallards are at a 10-year high in these latitudes and the goose hunting has never been better. Hunters at the camp head out for the goose blinds in the morning in half-ton trucks and four wheelers. After several hours of shooting honkers, guests return to camp and have the big meal between 1:30-2 p.m. After a short rest, they are then taken to another field or a pond where they are left to shoot ducks. While the guests are busy gunning mallards, Toby and the guides scout geese for the next morning's shoot. After a hot bowl of soup, and perhaps a beer, cocktail, or soda, hunters retire for the evening so they can be at it early the next day. Life for your five-day stay in Saskatchewan is reduced to basics that will delight any waterfowler—nature at its finest, ducks and geese in abundance, good shooting, and home-cooked food. And in case your memories of the hunt start to fade a bit after you've been back in the grip of civilization, Toby's Trophy Treks provides a video of your group's morning goose hunts. Turn out the lights, flick on the VCR, and you're back in the blissful world of northern Saskatchewan once again.

A goose hunter scans the horizon for incomers.
A Ross' goose and a pair of whitefronts already adorn his
game strap, but there's always room for more.

[**C A N A D A - W E S T**]

Wild Wings Outfitters

S w i f t   C u r r e n t ,   S a s k a t c h e w a n

VITAL STATISTICS:

SPECIES: mallard, pintail, wigeon, gadwall, teal, redhead, canvasback, white-fronted goose, Canada goose, snow goose

Season: mid-September through October

Hunting Sites: freshwater marshes and agricultural fields

Accommodations: motel in Swift Current with restaurant, cocktail lounge

MEALS: family dining in motel steakhouse

RATES: $1,300 per person for three-day hunt; includes lodging, meals, licenses, bird processing, guide fees, airport transportation; custom packages upon request

MAXIMUM NUMBER OF HUNTERS: 12

GRATUITIES: $25 to $100 daily

PREFERRED PAYMENT: cash or check

Getting There: southwest Saskatchewan

NEAREST COMMERCIAL AIRPORT: Swift Current, SK

Dogs and Facilities: outside kennel run or dogs permitted in motel rooms

Guides: guides have trained dogs; four hunters per guide

Other Services: airport transportation; bird cleaning and packaging

Other Activities: fishing for walleye and northern pike; upland hunting for sharp-tailed grouse and Hungarian partridge

CONTACT:

Ron Button
Wild Wings Outfitters
Box 692
Swift Current, Saskatchewan
Canada S9H 3W7
Ph/Fax: 306-773-5940
Email: rbutton@t2.net
Web: www.t2.net/wildwings

SWIFT CURRENT, Saskatchewan, is located in the heart of the Central Flyway and has populations of waterfowl and upland birds as large as you'll find anywhere on the continent. This is true native prairie country. The land is flat and the horizon stretches forever. Stubble fields, native grasslands, small lakes, and potholes provide habitat for breeding and migrating ducks and geese, as well as for resident populations of upland birds, especially sharptails and Huns.

Abandoned farms and old windrows dot the countryside, landmarks attesting to the severity of prairie droughts and winters. It takes persistence and tenacity to make a living farming here, and, despite the failures of some pioneers, successful farmers have planted wheat, barley, and other crops here for generations.

Ron Button has been guiding waterfowl and upland hunters in this country for a decade, and he brings his clients to the properties of many of those farmers. Their grain fields are often plundered by ducks and geese, you see, and the farmers like nothing more than seeing an armed posse running those feathered outlaws off their land. Geese, especially, are a bane to grain raisers.

The goose population is growing in this country every year. These migrant birds breed farther north, in the Canadian tundra, but when they migrate through southern Saskatchewan, they stay as long as they can for the free lunch the farmers provide. Most common here is the greater, or giant, Canada goose, which often weighs in at more than 12 pounds. The closely related but smaller lesser Canada goose is the next most abundant goose here, followed by the white-fronted, or specklebelly, goose. Snow geese are also abundant during certain parts of the season.

Button houses his hunter clients in style at the "K" Motel in Swift Current. This is a modern motel that offers five-star meals in its restaurant, where clients also dine and can order whatever their hearts desire from the menu as part of a hunt package rate. For lunch and dinner, that is. Due to early morning starts for the hunting fields, figure on coffee and donuts for breakfast.

But lunch won't be too far off. Every morning Button and his guides will have a new field scouted and staked out where they know that geese will be

ming for their own sunrise meal. The morning hunt, ergo, may be a short
e, depending more on the hunters' shooting abilities than the abundance
honking targets. Button's guides are skilled, knowledgeable, and hard work-
g, but it will be up to you and your party to shoot the game as the opportu-
ties present themselves.

The opportunities will mostly be shots at geese in the grain fields, but
cks are not out of the question, either. The duck population is largely com-
sed of mallards, also known for their appetite for farmers' grain.

After a morning hunt for geese, the daily agenda will find you back at
e "K" for brunch. Depending on your wishes, the afternoon can be spent
ishing your duck limit on a local pothole, or you can opt to walk up sharp-
ls or Huns behind one of the guides' dogs, or your own if you have chosen
bring 'ol Rex.

Hunting from pit blinds is a standard operating procedure on
the rolling prairies of Saskatchewan, and one of the best tactics
for avoiding the prying eyes of specklebellies and snow geese.

INDEX

[I N D E X]